BIEN CUIT

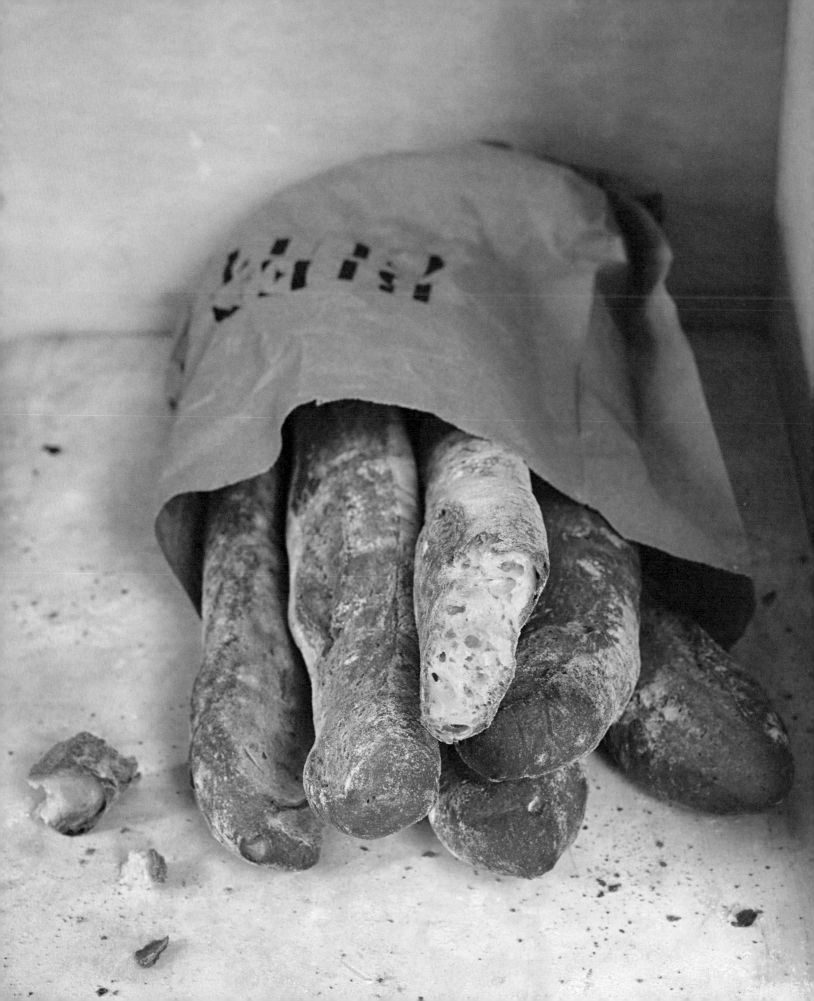

BIEN CUIT

THE ART OF BREAD

ZACHARY GOLPER

AND PETER KAMINSKY

PHOTOGRAPHS BY THOMAS SCHAUER

Regan
Arts.

Regan Arts.

65 Bleecker Street
New York, NY 10012

First Regan Arts hardcover edition, November 2015

Library of Congress Control Number: 2015938343

ISBN 978-1-941393-41-3

Interior design by Steve Attardo / Ninetynorth Design
Jacket design by Richard Ljoenes
Jacket art by Thomas Schauer

Printed in China

10 9 8 7 6 5 4 3 2 1

TO MAMA TAZ (K. CLARK OF THE MILFORD TRACK, LITTLE ROCK, AR). YOU SET THE BENCHMARK FOR A BALANCED TEMPERAMENT IN THE PROFESSIONAL KITCHEN. I'M SO GLAD YOU GAVE A KID A CHANCE. THANK YOU, K.

CONTENTS

INTRODUCTION
NEW GUY IN TOWN

As you cut into the first Bien Cuit bread you bake, you will know this is a different kind of loaf. The crust is dark as old mahogany. Next comes a rasping sound as the knife slices into the crust, like a woodsman's handsaw on a piece of oak. The inside—bakers call it the crumb—will be airy, slightly moist, and dense at the same time. Inhale the aroma; it will be yeasty as a mug of dark brown ale and maybe a little nutty, like a pecan pie cooling by an open window. Take a bite. Chances are you will get more of that nuttiness, the tang of fermented grain, the scent of an orchard in late September, and a hard-to-pin-down aroma that might be rye, might be wheat, walnuts, or raisins or, equally likely, all of the above. Zachary Golper's bread combines ingredients in a way that brings out seductive flavors, some pronounced, some nuanced, and as complex, in their way, as the flavors and aromas of another fermented food: fine wine.

I first discovered Zachary Golper's bread three years ago as I was biking home from Brooklyn's Prospect Park on a fine spring day. I noticed a new bakery two blocks from my house. "Bien Cuit," the sign read, a phrase the French use to describe the darkest, crunchiest loaves, baked to the point of perfection. To create bread that achieves this elusive status, Zachary walks a gustatory high wire between burnt ruination and delicious elegance.

As soon as I'd taken a few steps into Bien Cuit's spare, brick-walled storefront, I was gobsmacked by the almost inebriating aroma of yeast and toasted grain wafting from the oven. It looked and felt like something *bien* was definitely happening here.

A display case held stacks of gnarly loaves in various shades of brown: deeply golden baguettes, chestnut tones for the country bread and darker, earthen hues for the Raisin Walnut Bread. Self-effacingly tucked off to one side, as if to say, "I don't need to strut my stuff," was Zachary's *miche*: three pounds of dense, crusty, dark bread that would win the heart of the neighborhood and later the business of many of New York's most demanding chefs. It is killer.

Zachary's journey is the story of a pilgrimage alongside some of the world's most accomplished bakers, who took this hardworking prodigy under their wings to share the secrets of their craft. Many of the breads that follow are inspired by the lessons learned in his travels and apprenticeships. A gifted artisan, Zachary has stood on the shoulders of these giants of baking to invent his own signature techniques and new breads.

For many, the hardest part of becoming a home baker is getting over the initial hump of starting out—dough that's too sticky, too much flour all over the kitchen, too many hard-to-clean bowls. If you have felt this way, you'll be pleasantly surprised by Zachary's recipes. Almost all of the following doughs were made on the limited counter space of a New York apartment kitchen. As for the fear of flour flying everywhere, put that worry aside. It won't happen. Most of the mixing is done in a large bowl, and the kneading and shaping on a lightly floured counter—no expensive stand mixer required.

All of the breads in this book are mixed the way a thousand generations of people have done it: by hand. The process is efficient, surprisingly quick, and cleanup afterward is a lot easier than if you use a mixer.

Likewise, kneading and shaping by hand are both relatively quick operations. And perhaps more importantly, they give you an intimate experience of how a dough develops, allowing you to learn to feel when a dough has reached the right point for baking.

In watching Zachary work, I have come to realize that the actual baking part of the bread-making process is just the last step—and, all things considered, probably not the most important one. Putting a loaf in the oven and taking it out later requires no great skill. Rather, it is in the art of fermentation—the interaction of yeast, grain, and water—that Zachary's mastery of his craft never ceases to impress me. If there is one distinguishing element in his baking, it is his commitment to long, cold fermentation. He says it was the single most important discovery in his career. Letting yeast do its work for a long time is the only way to develop full flavor.

Wheat ferments at one rate, rye ferments at another, and buckwheat at yet another. The amount of water, milk, or cream can accelerate or slow the process. When Zachary combines any of these elements to create a new bread, he's like an orchestra conductor pulling out different themes over the course of a performance. Yet his goal is always the same: to control the process that's responsible for the deep, complex flavor of great bread. All of the fermenting ingredients have to reach their peak of flavor at the same time, just before the dough goes into the oven. You need to have baked legions of loaves to gauge when things are going well; then you can just feel it. The recipes in this book will allow you to benefit from Zachary's experience. Following instinct—and a lot of trial and error—he has determined what goes into each dough and at what stage of fermentation.

Figuring out the right combination at the right time demands the kind of exacting skill that only comes with native talent and endless practice. There is a dizzying amount of theory and "breadspeak" that Zachary could, at the drop of a hat, use to explain a loaf, but you don't need a PhD in breadology to bake these

> ## "IN THIS BOOK, YOU WILL EXPLORE BOTH AN HOMAGE TO TRADITION AND THE EXCITEMENT OF INVENTION."

breads. Just follow the recipes, and you'll find that Zachary has blazed the trail for you and marked every step along the way.

In this book, you will explore both an homage to tradition and the excitement of invention. For example, not satisfied with the contemporary state of the New York bagel (supersized and tasteless) or the meal-in-a-loaf known as Sicilian prosciutto bread, Zachary and I have searched high and low through the ethnic enclaves and old-time neighborhoods of New York as part of a research effort that ended with what he imagines these classics want to be. His bagels are the best I have tasted in decades. These Bread Quests will appear from time to time in the book and will enable you to become a full-fledged bagel bender, lard bread laborer, or Kaiser roll king.

Equally exciting for me, right alongside Zachary's reinvention of classics, he conjures up his new "gastronomic" breads, which are much more than just something to stick in bread baskets to fill people up between courses. As much as he is a baker, Zachary thinks like a chef, challenging himself to create and reinforce flavors the way a fine-dining demigod accents nuances of tastes, textures, aromas to create a meal that's a memorable experience. Whole grains, nuts, fruits, port wine, oatmeal, pears, apricots, bourbon, carrots, parsnips, honey, grapes, figs—all have their place in Zachary's breads. In a recent creative burst, he invented a dozen breads—all of them in this book—by fermenting and combining ingredients in ways that no one has ever tried before.

So how should you use this book? By all means read through the introductory pages. They truly set forth Zachary's approach to bread, present key techniques that are repeated throughout the book, and specify equipment that will make you more efficient and tidy. If you want to bake with sourdough—the most ancient and often the most flavorful form of leavening—you might get going on his Sourdough Starter on page 122 (which takes twenty-four days *minimum*), then go back and work your way through other recipes that don't require as much fermentation. Some experts may tell you that you can create a good sourdough starter in seven days. Don't believe them. Give your starter time to develop, and you'll assuredly notice the satisfying difference immediately.

In this time when the term "artisan" is tossed about wantonly, you might skip over it as meaningless marketing jargon. But Zachary Golper is a devoted artisan and creative spirit who has spent years—and thousands of hours of trial, error, and triumph—developing the breads in this book, which are shared with home bakers for the first time in these pages.

Fire up your oven!

—*Peter Kaminsky, Cobble Hill, Brooklyn, New York*

BORN TO BAKE

My mother never tires of telling the story of how, when I was five, she gave me a paper plate and asked me to draw a picture of what I wanted to be when I grew up. I went to work on a portrait of my grown-up self wearing a chef's coat, maybe in tribute to the Swedish Chef on *The Muppet Show*. Or perhaps the smell of bread at the Wonder Bread factory that I visited on a class trip had burrowed into my subconscious. (Or, in the way that dreams work, maybe it was a mash-up of the two.) In addition to the white coat, on my head I wore a tall chef's toque, and in my hand I held a wad of dough. "Zach Dog," I wrote by way of a caption. In later years, I wondered what that scene had to do with a dog, until one day my mother cleared up the mystery. "You were just learning to write, and D-O-G was your first-grader's way of spelling 'dough,'" she told me. "You wanted to be a baker!" If only I had listened to my inner child, I might have saved years of trying to find myself and been a baker from the get-go.

But that primal event was buried somewhere in my memory bank when I found myself in Oregon at age twenty, working on a three-hundred-acre organic farm. It was the turn of the millennium, and many of the people I was hanging out with before that move were certain that the world was going to end, or at least get shaken up pretty well. They were all stocking up on flashlights, bottled water, and food rations. For damn sure, they weren't going to be caught napping when the trouble started. So I went to Oregon, not so much fleeing the apocalypse as trying to get away from the people who were readying for the Rapture.

I didn't believe any of that end-of-the-world stuff. I just wanted to move on—to connect with the land and to connect with myself in a way that I hadn't yet.

The farm fit the bill. By night it was a meditation center and by day a certified and diversified organic farm. We grew grapes for local wineries, a half dozen varieties of Asian pears, and lots of apples, maybe thirty different kinds. The farm was the right place for me. I got pretty good at driving the tractor, although I preferred to work by hand, as did most of my farm mates. I mastered the rhythmic art of swinging a sickle. I learned how to store and pack fruits and vegetables so they would keep longer, and that onions and garlic have to stay dry or they'll rot in the damp, bone-chilling fog that rises off the Umpqua River every day and descended on us every night, quite literally like a wet blanket. In time, I could judge how mature a fruit was by the color and texture of its skin. I could read how bountiful the yield from a certain tree might be, based on the strength of its branches.

Our goal at the farm was to work hard all day, then meditate a good part of the night, saving a few hours for sleep. I was good at the work part and fair at the sleep part, but I won no prizes as a meditator. That's why, at 1 a.m. one morning when I should have been meditating, I was deep into a dream about bread that was so sensual it was borderline erotic. It felt real. As it turned out, that was because it was real. No question about it: I was awake and I smelled bread. Not dream bread—real bread. And with that sweet scent as a lullaby, I slipped back into slumber.

This went on for days. But instead of growing

4

accustomed to the smell of bread in the oven, I became more and more entranced by it. Nothing had ever haunted me so. Or, now that I think back, maybe fascination with bread had always been there in my soul, ready to be awakened.

So there I was in Oregon, living the meditation/organic farming lifestyle having given very little thought to where this was taking me. All I knew was that the sweet aroma of bread in the oven kept waking me, making it harder and harder to sleep. I wanted to be part of whatever middle-of-the-night ritual was being conducted just upwind from my room. Finally, I could no longer contain myself. I threw off my blanket and followed my nose. The aroma grew stronger, wrapped around me, and bore me uphill to where I came upon an ancient bread oven. It was situated in a "room" that consisted of a roof and no walls, yet the heat from the oven easily overcame the cold night air. Standing by the oven was a muscular guy with the strong back and hands of a bread baker and the lean muscularity that comes from lifelong manual labor. He reminded me of someone out of Walker Evans's Dust Bowl photos. (I'll call him Andres because he is a private man and will be pleased to remain undisturbed.)

Andres looked up. "What are you doing here?" he asked by way of faint welcome.

"Your baking has woken me every night for the past week," I replied. "It's amazing!"

Andres stood there without saying anything. Telling him that his bread smelled amazing was like telling him it was winter or that we were in Oregon. He knew that already. I took his silence as an invitation to explain myself.

"I guess I'd like to watch you work."

"I'm not really interested in having anyone watch," he said. "If you want to *work*, well that's another story. You can do that, but you need to be here on my schedule, and if that means starting at 1 a.m. or 3 a.m. or whenever, remember: The bread is the boss. We make it when it's ready to be made and the fire is right."

"Deal," I said, and I meant it. But true to form, I often slept well past the appointed hour.

Thankfully, Andres cut me some slack. Working at his side was like entering into a bread-making time machine. We made the dough in an unheated sheep barn by candlelight. "Electricity creates negative vibrations," he said. He explained that bread dough is a living thing and that he wanted everything we did to come from a living thing. Philosophically, it made sense, but as I continued to spend chilly evenings with him, Andres's New Age common sense seemed punishing. Even though we had a big Hobart mixer (the same model used in many commercial bakeries), Andres insisted that we mix the dough by hand. It was an arduous process. Picture yourself riding a bicycle through a patch of thick mud. That's the same motion we made with our hands as we mixed flour, sourdough starter, and water. It was downright aerobic…and entrancing. After a few minutes, I would break a sweat and warm up, ready to shed my jacket. Cold? What cold?

After mixing, we would fold the dough and let it rest for half an hour. We repeated this three times, then left the dough to rest for many hours as the starter worked its sorcery, digesting starch and releasing carbon dioxide into the dough, causing it to rise.

Making dough turned out to be more time-consuming than I imagined. After three hours I was eager to bake and create that irresistible aroma that had first summoned me to Andres's oven. "Not so fast," he said. Andres was a proponent of long, cold fermentation.

As I would later learn when I worked with some of the top bakers in the world, fermentation is the heart of bread making. Making great bread is less about what happens in the oven than how you get the dough ready to bake. Sure, you start by mixing up a batch of dough with some fast-rising commercial yeast, pop it in the oven and, a few hours later, have some bread. But, the longer you allow things to ferment, the more complex and delicious the flavors will be. In order for that to happen, you have to slow down the process. An unheated sheep barn in the chilly Umpqua Valley fit the bill. So will your home refrigerator.

After mixing the dough and letting it ferment until it tripled in size, we were ready to shape it into loaves. The way Andres accomplished this deceptively simple-looking task was like a well-choreographed ballet starring two hands and a ball of dough. He was precise and elegant in his economy of motion and, like many great artists, he made his craft look easy. It wasn't. It would be years before I could truly shape dough with confidence and precision.

We often worked from one in the morning until one in the afternoon, mixing, fermenting, and shaping loaves, then leaving them in a cold room to develop more flavor for another two and a half days. On the third day, the loaves were ready to bake. Andres would light the wood fire at 9 p.m., and typically about four hours later, the heat was just right. Finally, we began to bake, and soon I was swaddled in a cloud of bready perfume.

That experience changed my life. But I still hadn't connected the dots from my first-grade drawing to my nights at Andres's side to the vocation I would later take up. As I look back on my time on the farm, I can now see that there was something literally tapping at my soul. Bread making was calling to me, inviting me to become part of something that's been around for generations and generations. But at that time, I had too much youthful wanderlust in me to listen to the inner voice that was urging me to bake.

An inner voice was telling me I had to go to Chile. I really didn't know why, but something compelled me to make that journey—the same way Richard Dreyfuss had to get to Devils Tower in *Close Encounters of the Third Kind*. I spent the next two years on a South American odyssey. In Mexico, I learned to speak Spanish while I watched a friend's dad drink himself into the grave. His downward spiral sent me a message that we are all here for a finite time, so you need to follow your heart. In Nicaragua I struck up a conversation with a grandmother who told me that, through all the years of war and terror, the thing she wanted most was to wake up and smell fresh mint in her garden. It took some time, but I made that garden for her. Then I breezed my way through Panama, Colombia, and Ecuador as a ranch hand, bartender, short-order cook—whatever it took to get me through the next day and eventually to the next step in my journey.

I finally made it to Chile, crossing the Atacama Desert on a rickety train that struggled up the mountains to Potosí, Bolivia (a legendary city that Cervantes singled out for its extraordinary riches). Much of the silver that Spain took from the New World came from these mountains whose ore—what little is left of it—is still mined by locals. It's a dangerous profession. The miners start as young as eight years old, and not many make it into their thirties.

And then it happened—*it* being the same thing that drew me to Andres's wood-fired oven. At 3 a.m. one morning there was that same siren smell of bread. I followed the aroma and came to a little shop. Inside, through the barred window, I saw a tiny, ancient, pale-skinned Native American woman covered from head to toe in traditional garb, leaving only her face and hands exposed. She was pulling perfectly shaped loaves from her oven, and they were very *bien cuit*.

Bear in mind that I hadn't eaten any really good bread since I left the United States. It was all soft and kind of pasty, sort of like wannabe English muffins. From the Rio Grande to Tierra del Fuego, good bread is almost impossible to find. But somehow, in this city that claims to be the highest in the world, this woman, whose name I never learned, had mastered the bread baker's art. She sold me a loaf. It cost less than a dime, but it was the real thing. The crust crackled like the bread from the best French boulangeries, and it tasted like it, too. Quite astonishing, all in all.

I realized then how much I missed good bread. And with that, I knew my travels were over. I returned to the United States and listened to that inner voice, the same one that guided my hand as a first-grader when I drew Zach and his "dog." It had drawn me to Andres's ovens and to that small bakeshop in Potosí.

And so I became a baker.

LEARNING A CRAFT

As I look back on it, the way I make bread today owes much—I can't overstate how much—to the teachers I had along the way. Each contributed to the breads we sell at Bien Cuit and to the recipes in this book.

ANDRES

First, of course, was Andres on the farm in Oregon. The only grain his breads contained was wheat, and they were marvelous. I have since begun using a mix of grains—mostly wheat, rye, and buckwheat—but I'm glad I started out with wheat and wheat alone. Bread, as we've come to know it, is primarily a wheat product. Learn the many facets of this grain and you will have learned much about what goes into the making of the best bread. Because of its uniquely strong capacity for developing gluten, nothing else can give bread such an airy crumb. The flavor is deep and nutty. Andres provided my first introduction to long, cold fermentation. I don't know if he gave much thought to long versus rapid fermentation or to the virtues of cold temperatures. He made his bread in a cold room in a cold place because that's the hand he was dealt. If he wanted it to ferment properly, he had no choice but to ferment it for a long time. This turned out to be just the right combination for what was—at that point—the very best bread I had ever tasted.

WILLIAM

A few years (and jobs) later, I found myself in Seattle working under William Leaman, a brilliant baker who would shortly bring great honor to American baking as captain of the winning team at the Coupe du Monde de la Boulangerie—the Super Bowl of bread making. His training, technique, and precision bear the hallmarks of his teachers, all of whom were *classique* French bakers and pastry chefs. Like a true French chef, the only way William wanted things done was his way, yet he didn't so much explain what he wanted as tell you his goal and leave you to figure out how to get there. His recipes were the roughest of sketches, and from them he expected me to execute finished paintings. I knew that he wanted his bread to have a particular open crumb structure and a certain flavor, which he felt could only be achieved if the loaf was at least 70 percent white flour. He left the remaining mix of flours up to me.

By spending what seemed like a life sentence at the mixing bench and the oven, I began to understand the finer points of blending flours, mix times, dough temperatures, grades of flour, and managing oven temperatures. It was really hard work for which the reward was often a sarcastic remark. Happily, I was finally able to master his recipes and, tough as the whole process was, it made me a better baker. Or perhaps I should say it made me a baker. I left William with the confidence that I understood the complex process of combining simple ingredients to create a nuanced and satisfying result. I will always be grateful to him for leading me to that jumping-off point in my career.

JEAN CLAUDE

My next stop was Las Vegas, where I went to work for Jean Claude Canestrier at the M Resort.

Jean Claude was an MOF, which is short for Meilleur Ouvrier de France, a highly coveted award given to the greatest artisans in France, and the object of heated competition. If you ever see a pastry chef with a collar on his coat that has the red, white, and blue stripes of the French flag, it means he's an MOF (and it is usually a "he" in the male-centric world of French cuisine). His standards will be very high. Count on it.

If I thought William was tough on me, it was because I hadn't yet met Jean Claude. He wasn't averse to getting right in my face and letting me know exactly how he felt. Typically, his reaction was spirit-crushing disappointment at anything less than perfect. He pushed me like no one had ever done before. What he wanted was a beautifully crusted loaf with great flavor and a soft and creamy crumb. Right alongside that, he demanded pastry that was as French as any Parisian baker's. Jean Claude told me that we were going to compete with each other and that he wouldn't be happy until I could create a bread that was equal to his. I'm sure he thought I could never surpass him. Every day I went to his house with a dough I had prepared. He would have shaped a loaf as well. Both were baked in his home oven. *Le chef* acted as judge and jury, and not surprisingly, his bread would emerge victorious, despite the fact that Jean Claude had a lot on his plate, whereas I had only one thing: attempting to make an exemplary bread. It was only long after I moved on from Las Vegas that I received a phone call from Jean Claude conceding that my bread had, in fact, been the winner. I really appreciated it. Although Jean Claude was miserly with his encouragement, he and the top brass in Vegas were quite generous with the equipment they afforded me so that I could experiment to my heart's content to come up with breads that were served in all of the facilities at the sprawling M Resort. My expectation is that the lessons I learned during this intense period of experimentation will save you, the reader, from much of the guesswork and many of the common missteps in bread making so you don't have to build your own research facility!

> "HE PUSHED ME LIKE NO ONE HAD EVER DONE BEFORE. WHAT HE WANTED WAS A BEAUTIFULLY CRUSTED LOAF WITH GREAT FLAVOR AND A SOFT AND CREAMY CRUMB."

My breakthrough during my time with Jean Claude was in understanding the limits of fermentation. While it's true that long, cold fermentation is the key to the fullest flavor, there is a limit. At low temperatures, that limit—depending on the proportions in your mix—is somewhere between 64 and 72 hours. After that, you begin to lose good flavor and start to develop less-pleasant ones. However, for my breads—and yours—I am not interested in hitting that red line. I just want to create the fullest flavor, a crackling and chewy crust, and a smooth, airy crumb.

GEORGES

From the pristine state-of-the-art facilities at the M Resort, my next stop was in Philadelphia, as baker-in-chief for the great Georges Perrier. His restaurant, Le Bec-Fin, was one of the very top dining destinations in the country, but true to French form, the facilities were cramped, crowded, noisy, and hot. Perrier didn't turn out great food because of his kitchen, but in spite of it. My workroom was almost too hot for making bread, and I was forced to chill my water in the refrigerator. The water was chlorinated to boot, so I had to leave it standing overnight to allow the chlorine gas to escape. (Chlorine interferes with the ability of the dough to ferment—a tip worth remembering if your water is chlorinated.) Because of the heat in the bread kitchen, I had no choice but

"SO THAT FINAL PIECE OF THE PUZZLE IN BROOKLYN WAS ALSO THE FIRST PIECE..."

to ferment my dough (a process commonly known as proofing) in the refrigerator.

Yet all of the inconveniences of that time proved invaluable for developing my craft. In that cramped urban environment, I was forced to learn how to store ingredients to keep them safe from the various critters that would infiltrate any open container. Then there was the question of finding the right ratios for the flours that were available and how those flours would interact with the local wild yeasts in my starter.

Way over on the plus side of my Philadelphia balance sheet, there was Georges. He was so enthusiastic about food. "Flavor, flavor, flavor!" he would exclaim. That was both his philosophy and a command. With his wavy salt-and-pepper hair and his tinted glasses like Bono, he cut quite a figure.

Although a succession of good bakers had worked for him in Philadelphia, I could tell that Georges had never tasted an American bread that he would deem awesome. I was determined to change that. Armed with the knowledge of the classic technique that I brought from Seattle and the secret of long fermentation that I had finally unlocked in Las Vegas, I set about creating a levain, or sourdough starter, for Georges. By my third try, I nailed it.

Georges was absolutely wild about the texture and depth of flavor that I achieved by baking my sourdough bread with a really dark crust. This bread was truly *bien cuit*—mahogany dark, and way darker than I'd thought I could get away with. He truly loved it. And every time I increased the baking time to further darken the crust, Georges would scrunch his face until it reminded me of a French-speaking raisin with a

large nose, then shout, "I love it!" For me, those three words made all the effort worthwhile. From there on out, it was *bien cuit* for me, with no looking back.

AND BEYOND

I had arrived at a point where I understood fermentation, knew how to control it. Equally important: I now had mastered the *bien cuit* style that people would come to know me by. After nearly fifteen years of learning from some of the best in the business, I was ready to strike out on my own, which is how, in 2011, I ended up on Smith Street in Brooklyn's Cobble Hill neighborhood, a hotbed of new restaurants. In all my travels, though, I had yet to find perfect grains. Or if I found good grains, they weren't from the region where I was baking, which meant the flour in my starter was unacquainted with the wild yeasts in my workrooms. I wanted to remedy this because I've always subscribed to the idea that "if it grows together, it goes together."

When I got to Brooklyn, I found some regional farmers who grew grains that have been cultivated in the Northeast for centuries: heritage strains such as Danko rye, Warthog winter wheat, and Glenn spring wheat. Just like the customers who crowded the farm-to-table restaurants all over Brooklyn, my sourdough starter could now eat local. I was especially happy with the results I got baking with hard red winter wheat milled in Watertown, New York.

It's funny how things come around to their beginnings. When I made those first loaves on the farm in Oregon, we used wheat that was grown, harvested, and milled nearby. So that final piece of the puzzle in Brooklyn was also the first piece many years ago, in that cold room with Andres. After all the years, all the travels, and all the trial and error, I was finally able to make the kind of bread that had been my holy grail for so long.

WHAT DOES BIEN CUIT MEAN AND WHY IS IT IMPORTANT?

When bread is *bien cuit*, it is baked to a dark, often mahogany-colored crust. On first seeing a loaf that is *bien cuit*, you might think it's burnt. Most people do. But I believe there is a bliss point when foods are almost, but not quite, burnt. This is equally true of meat cookery, as any great grillmaster knows. It is exactly that moment at which bread or meat (or anything cooked that contains a fair amount of protein) develops maximum flavor. In addition to bread and steak, the beautiful color and flavor of beer is also a product of this wonderful alchemy. The chemistry behind this is complicated, and you need a deep scientific background in order to truly understand the process, which is known as the Maillard reaction. For the purposes of this book, it's sufficient to say that the Maillard reaction is a transformation that protein undergoes when combined with a sugar and heat. The result is hundreds—maybe thousands—of flavor and aroma components that are complex and pleasurable. This is the reason why my breads are *bien cuit, pas trop cuit*, which is the French way of saying "well baked, but not overdone."

FERMENTATION + TIME + HEAT = THE ALCHEMY OF BREAD

Basic bread is nothing more than flour, yeast, salt, and water. Yet these four simple ingredients produce immense variety in breads, and the pleasure we derive from them. A fitting metaphor is a string quartet: It has only four instruments, but by varying the tempo, volume, and tones, a violin, viola, cello, and bass can produce an almost infinite number of musical pieces. And although Bach, Beethoven, and Mozart each worked with the same instruments and the same notes, each piece they wrote was different, offering new and surprising pleasures every time. Bread is a melody written with a few simple ingredients, yet by varying how it is fermented, how the dough is developed and handled, and how loaves are shaped and, ultimately, baked, we can create a world of variety in breads.

If there is magic in bread—and I believe there is—you will first encounter it when yeast, flour, and water meet. The interaction of yeast with grains creates heavenly and complex flavors. When yeast works its sorcery, it consumes flour and creates the gases that makes bread rise, producing hundreds of subtle and exquisite flavors in the process. And every variety of grain produces its own signature flavors thanks to this transformation. My goal, always, is to maximize those flavors and lock them up inside the crackling crust of a loaf.

Since the time I realized that fermentation was the key to creating flavor, I've never stopped trying to coax the maximum amount out of ingredients as they ferment. Like every bread baker, I ferment wheat flour, and I also use rye, barley, corn, and oats, and each brings a different array of flavors to a bread. But I haven't stopped there. I've fermented almonds, walnuts,

> ## "IF THERE IS MAGIC IN BREAD...YOU WILL FIRST ENCOUNTER IT WHEN YEAST, FLOUR, AND WATER MEET."

and hazelnuts. Buckwheat, apricots, cherries, fresh corn, too. Each ingredient is different, with a unique way of fermenting and creating flavor, and each offers its own special gifts.

Yeast occurs naturally on all fruits, vegetables, and grains. Bakers often add extra yeast (the "instant yeast" sold in packets) in order to develop dough in a desired way. However, if you simply combine flour and water and leave the mixture for a few days, the bubbling creation that results is due to the action of wild yeast. This is undoubtedly how the original baker created her first dough.

When yeast grows at cold temperature, it will slow down and develop over a long period of time, producing a bounty of the by-products that make for flavor. The longer the yeast can work, the greater the quantity and variety of flavorful compounds it will contribute to a fully baked loaf. So much of what I do is based on this principle. Creaminess, nuttiness, a hint of pear or butter, or any of the hundreds of other flavors and aromas that are the hallmarks of great bread—all take time. Vintage wine and pungent cheese require time as well; there's no way around it. Time is the artful baker's best friend.

THE BUILDING BLOCKS: GRAINS AND FLOURS

At its heart, bread baking is the art of turning dry, relatively flavorless ground grain—flour—into a delicious food with great complexity and variety. There are many tricks to the bread baker's art but no escaping the fact that it all begins with flour.

WHEAT

For most of us, wheat is bread and bread is wheat. Without wheat there would be no bread, or at least no bread as we know it. Even when a bread is made with other flours, the aroma that spreads through the house when a loaf is in the oven is first and foremost wheat, comforting as a favorite flannel shirt on a chilly day. It entices like the whiff of steak on the grill, onions caramelizing in a pan, or coffee beans fresh from the roaster. Its flavor is both sweet and savory in a way that few other foods are. But good bread is more than the allure of wheat. Equally important is texture, and only wheat can produce both the beautiful crust and light airy interior (crumb, in baker's terms) of a loaf that both nourishes and delights. It's true that all grains contain protein, but only wheat has the right amount of two key proteins, glutenin and gliadin, that combine to form gluten—the strands that create a network of air chambers, which form the crumb structure of bread. Water is all that's required for glutenin and gliadin to come together and rearrange themselves in this way, enabling the baker to stretch dough as it's prepared. When it's baked, the gas released by fermentation inflates the gluten and—presto!—you have the architecture of the classic loaf of bread.

Not all wheat is ideal for the bread baker. To achieve an effective gluten structure, you need white flour that is relatively high in protein, about 11.3 to 12.7 percent. You can make bread with flours with a lower or higher percentage of protein, but I've found that this range is the "Goldilocks zone" for my breads. It allows me to gauge my fermentation quite accurately, and the result is a better developed dough and a more full-flavored bread. Some flours don't list the amount of protein on the bag, but that information is usually available at the website of the flour company. Even better, farmers or millers at your local farmers' market may have flour with this midrange of protein. Ask them. Even if the percentage is a little lower, the added flavor provided by a locally grown and milled flour is worth the trade-off. All of that said, you can certainly use all-purpose flour for many of the breads in this book.

It's quite possible that some local farmers and millers are producing great bread-making flour in your region. I urge you to check this out and, if it's available, to try it. Local grains will have an affinity for local yeasts. If it's a little lower in protein, try mixing it with a good-quality bread flour, such as King Arthur or Bob's Red Mill (see Resources, page 313). That way you'll get the benefit of high protein from the commercial flour combined with the unique qualities of local flour. Farmer's markets and health food stores (or the health food aisle in many supermarkets) are a good place to look for specialty flours

Some of my recipes also call for medium whole wheat flour. This simply means the flour has a higher bran content, rather than most of it being sifted out; as a result, this flour will have, much of the nutritional

value of whole kernels of wheat. Without getting into a microscopic explanation, the little bits of bran in whole wheat, though nutritious, inhibit gluten development. The result is a moister crumb without any extra chewiness. Whole wheat bread is never as airy as bread made with pure white flour.

Finally, you may see flours labeled "stone-ground." This refers to the way in which the grain is milled and means it is passed through a series of metal rollers or stone grinders. Stone grinding generates less heat, so I believe it is less damaging to delicate starches, but this is just my opinion. You can certainly make good bread with conventionally milled grains. When given a choice, though, I go for old-fashioned stone-ground.

Rye

After wheat, rye is the second most important grain for the bread baker. In much the same way that wheat flour comes in varieties ranging from white to medium to dark (100 percent whole wheat), rye does as well. These gradations are a function of how much of the original kernel remains in the final flour, with paler flours having more of the outer layers of bran and endosperm removed. Darker, more whole grain flour absorbs liquid more readily.

You may have noticed that rye bread is often denser than wheat. This is because although rye has the same gluten-forming proteins as wheat (glutenin and gliadin), it doesn't have them in the same ratio as wheat; when compared to wheat, rye has only 10 percent the amount of glutenin. Still, rye has its own signature flavors and aromas, expanding the baker's arsenal, and I find it indispensable to sourdough starter and as a supplement to many of my commercial yeast starters. It adds a note of aromatic sweetness that reminds me of premium vodka, and the accelerated way it interacts with yeast jump-starts and amplifies fermentation. In a final dough mixture, white rye adds a distinctive sweetness. Dark rye also contributes a deep brown color that makes for an appealing appearance: one that says "put some cold cuts or hard smoked cheese on me." I find rye to be an ingredient

that plays well with others; it's great in a supporting role but challenging as a solo act. When it's the primary flour, it makes for a super-dense bread—something I want to make only occasionally and only for specific reasons, like to serve with smoked wild salmon. Because rye adds such distinct flavors, depending on whether it's white rye, medium rye, or dark rye, I recommend that you stay with what I call for in the recipes. I've done many experiments to arrive at the flavor profile of each bread, and I've learned from my mistakes so you don't have to.

Oats

Oats can grow and prosper under conditions that won't produce thriving wheat. I think that's part of the reason oats were traditionally used for animal feed in many places where wheat wasn't cultivated. They don't contain gluten-producing proteins, however, and for that reason they're daunting for bread makers because they don't contribute to the crumb of a loaf. I think you may already have a good idea about where I stand on the gluten issue. For most people they provide good, high-quality nutrition. The bottom line is that I rarely use oats in flour form (the exception is Toasted Oat Bread, page 75).

Corn

I wish we had a tradition of using cornmeal more often in bread. It's high in natural sugars, so it turbocharges fermentation and adds sweetness. As a baker who likes to work with local grains, it's hard to find anything more genuinely local or American than this amazing grain, which was first hybridized more than ten thousand years ago by Native Americans. Although they lacked the wheel and other technological advances, the fact that they created corn from its genetic forebears out of the combination of three wild grasses points to a very sophisticated grasp of agriculture. Corn does have a small amount of gluten; however, it's chemically and structurally different from wheat-based gluten, so it doesn't create the same sort of air pockets and crumb. That said, the sweet butteriness

it brings to a loaf is attractive. Plus, when cornmeal is fermented, it basically creates a mixture similar to a bourbon mash. This gets my vote right away. On the downside, breads made with cornmeal tend to stale quickly, so they should be eaten within a day or so.

Buckwheat

Buckwheat isn't a grain in the conventional sense of the term. Rather, it's the seeds from a plant related to rhubarb and sorrel. Historically, buckwheat flour was used to fortify dough when wheat was at a premium. Today, buckwheat is mostly used as a cover crop that helps replenish nutrients in the soils of fields where wheat and other grains are grown. I particularly like the idea of using a plant that helps soil stay fertile. Happily, buckwheat also imparts some wonderful and unique flavor characteristics to bread. When fermented, it contributes deep, nutty aromas and light alcohol notes without increasing acidity. As with wheat and rye flours, there are lighter and darker forms of buckwheat flour, but in this case the color has little effect on nutritional value. I've also found that it doesn't affect how buckwheat flour interacts with other ingredients.

MEASURING

Like most people in the United States, I grew up seeing recipes written in terms of ounces, pounds, cups, and so on. This doesn't work as well for breads, so I list metric measurements first before the conventional cups, spoons, and ounces. I find that weights, whether metric or conventional, are more accurate. The fact is, 1 cup of flour will vary in weight depending on many factors: how aerated the flour is, how you scoop it, whether and how you level it, and more. On the other hand, 100 grams of flour is always 100 grams of flour, so using a scale is much more reliable.

You may wonder why I prefer metric measurements even for smaller amounts, like teaspoons and tablespoons. In the case of salt, the variations in density are even greater than for different types of flour. For example, 1 teaspoon of coarse salt weighs less than 1 teaspoon of finely ground table salt and more than 1 teaspoon of flaky sea salt. To ensure accuracy for even these smaller quantities, I recommend a kitchen scale that measures at least to the gram level and preferably down to tenths of grams.

In this book, I've worked hard to make the recipes as foolproof as possible. Measuring ingredients by weight is an important part of that. In fact, the recipes were tested with metric measurements. These considerations give some insight into why baking is often referred to as a science. However, there is a lot of art and chance involved as well, and I hope to convey some of that art to you in these pages, while also helping you avoid the pitfalls of chance.

Then, to make the book as reader-friendly as possible, for other units of measure in the book, such as temperature and lengths, I've used standard US measures, but I've also provided metric equivalencies. In addition, I've provided ounce equivalents for produce, since this will make it easier to purchase the amount needed for the recipe.

WORKING WITH WATER AND SALT

Tap water is hard, soft, or somewhere in between. And at different times of the year it runs at different temperatures. When I recommend a water temperature, it is an approximation. Water is said to be hard or soft according to its mineral content. Very hard water can produce a tougher dough, while very soft water can produce a slack dough. My general rule of thumb is this: If the tap water is drinkable, you can make bread with it. Still, if you follow the instructions and your bread has the characteristics of dough made with soft or hard water and you aren't not satisfied with the results, bottled water may be the way to go. Finally, chlorine is the enemy of yeast and fermentation. If your water is chlorinated, let it stand overnight before using to allow the chlorine gas to dissipate. I use fine, high-quality, non-iodized sea salt such as Bealeine for seasoning my dough. If you use a coarser grind make sure you weigh the salt since coarser salt will take up more space than a fine grind. It is the amount (weight) of salt not the volume that is critical.

GET TO KNOW YOUR OVEN

Every oven is different, from how long it takes to preheat to where the hot spots are. Here are some tips that will help you get optimal results, whatever the vagaries of your oven may be.

Let your oven preheat for 1 hour. This seems like a long time, but most ovens cycle off and on after they preheat, and the temperature may fluctuate by as much as 50°F (10°C) when they do. Preheating for an hour usually allows the oven to go through three cycles, building up more even heat within before the dough goes in the oven.

Use the temperatures given in the recipes as a starting point. As you'll see, the recipes call for some temperatures that aren't standard, like 480°F (250°C) or 460°F (240°C); that's because I've found that these temperatures work best for specific breads. Most ovens with a digital display will allow you to select these temperatures. If you have an oven with dials, try to approximate as best you can—for example, putting the dial a bit higher than 475°F (245°C) if you're aiming for 480°F (250°C). All of these recipes were tested multiple times in calibrated gas and electric ovens, but every oven is different. Take notes on your results and adjust the temperature up or down as needed, perhaps by 25°F (14°C), if the baking times don't seem to match up. If you don't have an oven thermometer, get one. This is a good time to see how accurate your oven settings are.

To ensure more even baking, I always rotate loaves (including those in Dutch ovens) and sheet pans of baked goods. With time, you'll discover where the hot spots are in your oven. As a general rule, I rotate about two-thirds of the way through the baking time. At that point, the dough has reached a good internal temperature and is set and shouldn't be disrupted by moving it.

One final consideration: It's always best to bake multiple sheet pans of bread or rolls in batches for even heating and best results. However, this is particularly important if your oven has heating elements on both the top and the bottom. In this case, if you don't bake in batches your bread may come too close to the top of the oven and go beyond *bien cuit* to burnt!

EQUIPMENT

If you're going to take up bread baking for more than the occasional loaf, the right equipment makes the job much easier. Although you can find many of the following items in cookware stores, the Kerekes website (bakedeco.com) is hard to beat for one-stop shopping. The San Francisco Baking Institute (sfbi.com/baking-supplies) is also a good source. As you go through the recipes, if you come to a piece of equipment that isn't familiar, refer back to this section for full details.

Digital Scale with Metric Measurements

There are so many variables in baking, but weighing ingredients accurately takes a big one out of the equation. Professionals prefer metric weights, because the round numbers are easy to scale up or down depending on how many loaves are being made. Because my recipes even use weights for yeast—sometimes as little as 0.1 gram—it would be best to have a kitchen scale accurate down to a tenth of a gram. Several companies make inexpensive kitchen scales with at least this degree of accuracy, including My Weigh, Smart Weigh, and American Weigh. However, if you have a scale that measures only down to the nearest gram, that will also work, because the recipes include a conversion in US measures that you can use for very small amounts of ingredients.

High-Powered Blender

For chopping and grinding nuts, spices, and grains, I find that a high-powered blender makes the job so much easier. Vitamix is my preferred blender, but they are pricey. Any quality high-powered blender will get the job done with nuts, while a coffee grinder works fine with spices and whole grains.

Lidded 1-Quart Plastic Storage Container

For mixing starters and storing them while they ferment, a 1-quart (1 L) Tupperware container or something similar works well.

Large Mixing Bowls

You'll want to have two large bowls: one for the roll and tuck step, and one for the stretch and fold step (I'll describe both of these steps shortly). The roll and tuck method for developing gluten is much less messy and much more physically accessible with a big mixing bowl. The bowl I use is 23 inches (58 cm) in diameter at the top. If your kitchen is small and you don't have much shelf space, an 18-inch (46 cm) bowl will work almost as well. Then, after rolling and tucking, and between stretch and fold sequences, you'll need a container in which to let the dough rest. I recommend a bowl that's at least 12 inches (30 cm) in diameter at its widest. I prefer stainless steel because it's light; however, plastic or Pyrex is also fine.

Plastic Bowl Scraper

If you hate sticky fingers, you're going to find bread baking very challenging. Still, you can avoid a lot of stickiness if you work with a plastic bowl scraper. It's a very useful tool in rolling and tucking any dough. Plus, its shape fits the curve of a bowl, so as its name suggests, you can scrape up every last bit of usable dough. Waste not, want not.

BENCH SCRAPER

A metal bench scraper is the best tool for dividing doughs. It is also great, as its name suggests, for cleaning up your workbench (or other work surface) between steps.

CAST-IRON DUTCH OVEN

The easiest and most foolproof way to get a good crust and a predictable rise with a round loaf is to bake it in the closed environment of a Dutch oven, with its even heat. A smaller Dutch oven may work acceptably, but I find that a 6-quart (5.7 L) Dutch oven, measuring 10 inches (25 cm) in diameter at the bottom, is ideal. Lodge is the most common brand, and a very good one. Some home bakers use enameled Dutch Ovens, but if you do, be prepared for scorch marks on your pretty pot.

BAKING STONE

The right amount of heat is critical to turning out a well-baked loaf with a nice crust. Unless you have a professional baker's oven, your home oven probably can't maintain optimum bread-baking temperatures without a little help. A baking stone, also called a pizza stone, is the solution for most of the oval or tube-shaped breads in this book. Baking stones are made of thick, ovenproof materials that hold a lot of heat. For oval loaves or tubes, buy the largest stone that will fit easily into your oven. There will be times when you want to make multiple loaves, and then you'll appreciate having the extra space.

CAST-IRON SKILLET

When using a baking stone, you also need a cast-iron skillet. You'll place it in the oven below the baking stone and add ice cubes to it to generate steam, which is necessary to create a proper crust (see Baking Stones and Steam, page 296). A skillet 8 inches (20 cm) in diameter is ideal.

SHEET PANS

I use restaurant-style rimmed sheet pans for breads that don't require a baking stone or Dutch oven, and also for rolls, scones, and biscuits. Either 13 by 18-inch (33 by 46 cm) half sheet pans or 9½ by 13-inch (24 by 33 cm) quarter sheet pans are fine for the recipes in this book.

HEAVY-DUTY OVEN GLOVES WITH FOREARM PROTECTION

Moving loaves in and out of the oven and handling superhot Dutch ovens and cast-iron skillets make heavy-duty oven gloves or barbecue mitts a must for safe baking. Heavy-duty potholders will also work, but mitts or gloves give maximum protection.

KITCHEN TOWELS

Linen or cotton kitchen towels (dish towels) are perfect for covering dough while fermenting. Synthetic materials don't let doughs breathe enough while fermenting, so stick to natural fibers.

WICKER OR PLASTIC PROOFING BASKETS OR BOWLS

Whether they are traditional willow baskets or plastic replicas, proofing baskets, or *bannetons* in French, help support a loaf so that it keeps its shape during fermentation. However, they aren't an absolute necessity. A mixing bowl lined with a floured kitchen towel will also work just fine. The optimum size for recipes in this book is 9 inches (23 cm) in diameter.

LINEN LINER

When making an oval or tube-shaped loaf, it's most practical to ferment the shaped loaf nestled within folds or pleats in a stiffer linen liner (aka *couche*) measuring approximately 24 by 26 inches (61 by 66 cm). In addition to protecting the surface of the loaf so it doesn't form a skin, the stiff fabric helps maintain the shape of the loaf.

Transfer Peel

Before baking a loaf that is fermented on a linen liner, you need to move it from the linen liner to the baking peel (described below). The best way to do this is to use something rigid to turn the dough upside down and then gently place it on the baking peel, seam-side down. You don't need to buy a specialty piece of equipment for this: A thin, rigid material—wood, plastic, or cardboard—bigger than the loaf will do the trick.

Wooden Baking Peel

If baking on a stone, you need a safe way to transfer shaped loaves on and off the baking stone without burning yourself or messing up the shape of the loaf. I recommend using a baking peel, which is like a long, oversized spatula. Baking peels are also used by pizza makers to slide pizzas into and out of the oven.

Lame or Single-Edge Razor Blade

To score loaves without tearing them (see Scoring, page 290), you need a very thin, sharp blade. Scoring allows the skin of the dough to expand without tearing. Aesthetically, scoring gives bread a very artisanal look. A *lame* is the traditional tool that bakers use, but you can forego the *lame* and just use a single-edge razor blade or, in a pinch, a very sharp paring knife.

MAKING A DOUGH

Mixing dough and shaping a loaf are fundamental processes in every type of bread making. There are many ways to go about this. I've developed a hand mixing method that is quite practical and not that hard to master. Besides being one less piece of equipment to clean, mixing by hand also yields a somewhat denser loaf with a cakey texture that's really nice. Most importantly, using your hands connects you to the dough in a more intimate and tactile way as it develops. The more you mix and manipulate dough by hand, the better you'll become at telling when it's ready by feel and shaping it. The basic steps are as follows:

1. MIXING

All of the dry ingredients and liquids are incorporated to create a mass with uniformly distributed ingredients.

2. ROLLING AND TUCKING

The wet dough is folded over on itself a number of times. In the process, the gluten starts to develop and the dough becomes firmer and easier to work with.

3. STRETCHING AND FOLDING

The dough is stretched out somewhat and then folded over like a letter, developing the gluten structure even further as gas pockets form in the dough due to fermentation. This is often repeated three or four times at intervals of 45 minutes to 1 hour.

4. SHAPING

The dough is shaped into a loaf, rolls, or other forms.

5. FINAL FERMENTATION

Now the baker takes a rest and the yeast really goes to work, expanding the dough and developing flavor. For the recipes in this book, the dough generally rests in the refrigerator to promote long, cold fermentation. This stage is often called "proofing."

6. SCORING

Making shallow incisions in the surface of the loaf allows gases to expand the dough without rupturing the crust as it bakes in the oven.

7. BAKING

Finally, the loaf goes into the oven and undergoes oven spring, meaning it expands rapidly as the dough heats up and the yeast becomes more active. Then the yeast dies and the bread takes its final form. The crust browns and the crumb is set.

8. COOLING

This is an important but often overlooked step. Most of my breads develop full flavor if they rest for a day. My 60-Hour Sourdough Loaf (page 125) reaches its maximum flavor two days after baking.

There is, however, an all-important step that precedes the process outlined above: making a starter.

STARTERS: THE KEY TO THE FULLEST FLAVOR

I jump-start fermentation (which boosts flavor) before I begin to mix dough by making a starter. This is a technique used by all artisan bakers. These starters are also known as pre-ferments, and they're absolutely essential. Basically, they're just a mixture of small amounts of flour, water, and yeast. When I make starters, sometimes I add nuts, whole grains, or malted or sprouted grains. Every bread calls for its own particular approach, but what all starters have in common is they put yeast to work creating flavor well in advance of mixing the dough.

If you've baked your way through other bread books, you may know these different starters by the terms professional bakers use: Poolish is a starter that is 50 percent water and 50 percent flour; a biga has less water in relation to flour and, in my baking, often includes other flours or whole grains; and a levain is a sourdough made with flour and wild yeasts. For this book, I've just lumped them together and called them starters. After all, the bread doesn't care what you call a starter. I've found that every starter has a window of time when it's at its peak, so when I say "ferment for 12 to 14 hours," at any point in that interval it will produce peak or near-peak flavor. I've done a lot of experiments with every bread in this book to establish that sweet spot in time. You'll get the best results if you follow the suggested times.

GETTING PAST THE STICKY PART

During the first few roll and tuck sequences, while the dough is at its stickiest, dust it with the reserved flour mixture from time to time to keep it dry and manageable. You may also need to add as much as 30 to 50 grams (3 to 5 tablespoons) of additional white flour during the rolling and tucking process. However, the goal is to use only enough flour to keep the dough from sticking. All of my recipes are calculated to use a certain ratio of dry ingredients to liquid. When you add flour to aid in managing the dough, you are changing that ratio, which can affect the final bread. So here, as elsewhere in life, less is often more.

Once the dough is less sticky, you may prefer to roll and tuck by hand, rather than with the scraper. And as your technique and familiarity with working with dough increase, you may wish to forgo the scraper altogether. Rolling and tucking by hand has advantages, including allowing you to be more intimate with the ingredients. When working by hand, lightly dust your hands with flour to keep the dough from sticking. If at any point the dough seems too uncooperative, or if you start feeling frustrated, cover it with a clean kitchen towel, let it rest for a few minutes, then start again.

BREADS

The heart of my craft is a loaf of bread. And by "loaf," I generally mean something that ferments for a good long time and weighs from 1 to 3 pounds (0.45 to 1.4 kg); though there are some breads better suited to a slightly smaller loaf. In most cases, only doughs of that size will give you the dose of pure flavor and texture that satisfies. While it's true that rolls, which are smaller, are fun to pass around the dinner table, a standard loaf provides the ideal environment for yeast and fermentation to reach their full potential. Although bread doughs usually consist of very few ingredients, the variations are nearly endless. Do you use refined flour or whole grains? Do you add kernels to the dough? Do you ferment in stages? Do you mix salt in at the beginning or the end of the process?

How long do you ferment? Sometimes I think of bread making the way others have explained the art of pitching in baseball. For most pitchers, there are just four pitches to choose from. Just as with bread, there aren't a lot of elements, but there are many variations. Where do you place your pitches, in what order you throw them, and at what speed? There are hundreds of choices for the artful pitcher. So, too, for the artful baker. I have worked for years, and in some cases decades, to perfect most of the recipes in this section. To keep things interesting, I've thrown in a few new ones that excite me. No doubt you will come up with your own personal refinements. More power to you! But for now, try these. That should keep you busy for a while.

A SIMPLE LOAF

This bread, as with many of my favorite recipes, happened by accident. In testing the Pan Pugliese recipe (page 37), both Peter and our tireless recipe tester, Amy Vogler, thought the dough—minus the potato chunks that go into the Pugliese—was so nice that it warranted its own place in the book. They also convinced me that this is among the easiest of my breads to make. It looks completely rustic—which is always important with artisan breads—and has a crackling crust and a nutty interior. I am never one to argue against a good recipe. For most of the breads in this book, developing the recipes involved a great deal of trial and error, so it was a pleasure to have a recipe fall into my lap this way. It's great for sandwiches, too, and also toasted and served with butter, jam, or a pungent Taleggio cheese.

STARTER

75 grams (½ c + 2 tbsp) white rye flour

50 grams (¼ c + 2½ tbsp) dark rye flour

1 gram (generous ¼ tsp) instant yeast

125 grams (½ c + 1 tsp) water at about 60°F (15°C)

DOUGH

425 grams (3 c + 2½ tsp) white flour, plus additional as needed for working with the dough

75 grams medium (½ c + 1½ tsp) whole wheat flour

15 grams (2½ tsp) fine sea salt

1 gram (generous ¼ tsp) instant yeast

365 grams (1½ c + 1 tsp) water at about 60°F (15°C)

Dusting Mixture (see page 35), for the lined proofing basket and the shaped loaf

FOR THE STARTER

1 Stir together the white and dark rye flours in a medium storage container. Sprinkle the yeast into the water, stir to mix, and pour over the flour. Mix with your fingers, pressing the mixture into the sides, bottom, and corners until all of the flour is wet and fully incorporated. Cover the container and let sit at room temperature for 11 to 15 hours. The starter will be at its peak at around 13 hours.

FOR THE DOUGH

1 Stir together the white and whole wheat flours, salt, and yeast in a medium bowl.

2 Pour about one-third of the water around the edges of the starter to release it from the sides of the container. Transfer the starter and water to an extra-large bowl along with the remaining water. Using a wooden spoon, break the starter up to distribute it in the water.

3 Add the flour mixture, reserving about one-sixth along the edge of the bowl (see Mixing, page 282). Continue to mix with the spoon until most of the dry ingredients have been combined with the starter mixture. Switch to a plastic bowl scraper and continue

to mix until incorporated. At this point the dough will be sticky to the touch.

4 Push the dough to one side of the bowl. Roll and tuck the dough (see Rolling and Tucking, page 284), adding the reserved flour mixture and a small amount of additional flour to the bowl and your hands as needed. Continue rolling and tucking until the dough feels stronger and begins to resist any further rolling, about 16 times. Then, with cupped hands, tuck the sides under toward the center. Place the dough, seam-side down, in a clean bowl, cover the top of the bowl with a clean kitchen towel, and let rest at room temperature for 45 minutes.

5 For the first stretch and fold (see Stretching and Folding, page 285), lightly dust the work surface and your hands with flour. Using the plastic bowl scraper, release the dough from the bowl and set it, seam-side down, on the work surface. Gently stretch it into a roughly rectangular shape. Fold the dough in thirds from top to bottom and then from left to right. With cupped hands, tuck the sides under toward the center. Place the dough in the bowl, seam-side down, cover the bowl with the towel, and let rest for 45 minutes.

6 For the second stretch and fold, repeat the steps for the first stretch and fold, then return the dough to the bowl, cover with the towel, and let rest for 45 minutes.

7 For the third and final stretch and fold, once again repeat the steps for the first stretch and fold, then return the dough to the bowl, cover with the towel, and let rest for 20 minutes.

8 Line a 9-inch (23 cm) proofing basket or bowl with a clean kitchen towel and dust the towel fairly generously with the dusting mixture.

9 Lightly dust the work surface and your hands with flour and shape the dough into a round (see Shaping a Round Loaf, page 288). Dust the sides and top of the dough with the dusting mixture, fold the edges of the towel over the top, and let rest at room temperature for 1 hour.

10 Transfer the basket to the refrigerator and chill for 14 to 18 hours.

11 Position an oven rack in the lower third of the oven. Place a covered 6-quart (5.7 L), 10-inch (25 cm) round cast-iron Dutch oven on the rack. Preheat the oven to 500°F (260°C). Remove the basket of dough from the refrigerator and let it sit at room temperature while you allow the oven to preheat for about 1 hour.

12 Using heavy-duty oven mitts or potholders, remove the Dutch oven, place it on a heatproof surface, and remove the lid.

13 Using the kitchen towel, lift and gently ease the dough out of the basket and onto a baking peel, seam-side down. Then carefully transfer it into the pot (the Dutch oven will be very hot). Score the top of the dough (see Scoring, page 290), cover the pot, and return it to the oven. Lower the oven temperature to 460°F (240°C) and bake for 30 minutes.

14 Rotate the Dutch oven and remove the lid. The loaf will already be a rich golden brown. Continue baking, uncovered, until the surface is a deep, rich brown, with some spots along the score being even slightly darker (*bien cuit*), about 20 minutes longer.

15 Loosen the edges of the loaf with a long handled spoon and then with the help of the spoon lift out of the pot onto a cooling rack. When the bottom of the loaf is tapped, it should sound hollow. If not, return it to the oven and bake directly on the rack for 5 minutes longer.

16 Let the bread cool completely before slicing and eating, at least 4 hours but preferably 8 to 24 hours.

MAKING A DUSTING MIXTURE

For most doughs—with the exception of sweeter, enriched loaves like the White Pullman Loaf (page 107)—I dust the kitchen towel, linen liner, or proofing basket, and the top and sides of the dough with a blend of semolina flour and white flour. The semolina, which is slightly coarser, helps keep the dough from sticking. Don't use this mixture during mixing, rolling and tucking, stretching and folding, or shaping, as the semolina will change the quality of the dough incorporated into it.

To make the Dusting Mixture, combine one part fine semolina flour with five parts white flour. If you bake often, mix up a large batch and keep it on hand.

PANE PUGLIESE

The most common rendition of Pane Pugliese is a rustic yeasted white bread typical of the Puglia region of Italy (which you might have guessed from its name). The version I first learned to make used wheat and potato flours and was taught to me by George DePasquale, an Italian-American baker in Seattle. I've since developed this version, which incorporates rye for a full-flavored starter. As for the potato flour, I skipped it and went straight to pieces of whole potato. As is so often the case in bread making, changing this one variable completely altered the character of the bread.

The virtue of leaving the potatoes in small chunks is both texture and flavor. And I don't peel the potatoes, because I like the texture of the skin, which dries out during roasting. In this way, the potato contributes to the final bread in the same way olives or raisins do in other breads, providing little islands of flavor and texture in the larger expanse of crumb. However, the potato's contribution really starts in during the fermentation stage. The yeast has to work harder and longer to digest the potato, and it creates new and varied flavors as it does so. But strangely, the finished loaf doesn't taste strongly of potatoes. I think what happens is that the potato starch turns into alcohol, sugars, and a multitude of flavor components as it breaks down and combines with the other ingredients. Just before baking, the finished dough smells sweet and bracing, very much like a wheat beer. One of my regular customers always buys half a loaf at a time, explaining that he's so addicted to this bread that if he bought whole loaves, he would come back for another one just as frequently, so he'd eat twice as much bread in the same amount of time. My question is, What's wrong with that?

STARTER

75 grams (½ c + ½ tsp) white rye flour
50 grams (¼ c + 2½ tbsp) dark rye flour
1 gram (generous ¼ tsp) instant yeast
125 grams (½ c + 1 tsp) water at about 60°F (15°C)

ROASTED POTATOES

400 grams (14 oz) unpeeled Yukon gold potatoes, scrubbed
    and cut into ¼-inch (6 mm) dice
9 grams (2 tsp) extra-virgin olive oil
1.5 grams (¼ tsp) flaky sea salt, preferably Maldon

Dusting Mixture (see page 35), for the lined proofing
basket and the shaped loaf

DOUGH

425 grams (3 c + 2½ tsp) white flour, plus additional as
    needed for working with the dough
75 grams (½ c + 1½ tsp) medium whole wheat flour
15 grams (2½ tsp) fine sea salt
1 gram (generous ¼ tsp) instant yeast
365 grams (1½ c + 1 tsp) water at about 60°F (15°C)

Dusting Mixture (see page 35), for the lined
    proofing basket and the shaped loaf

FOR THE STARTER

1 Stir together the white and dark rye flours in a medium storage container. Sprinkle the yeast into the water, stir to mix, and pour over the flour. Mix with your fingers, pressing the mixture into the sides, bottom, and corners until all of the flour is wet and fully incorporated. Cover the container and let sit at room temperature for 11 to 15 hours. The starter will be at its peak at around 13 hours.

FOR THE ROASTED POTATOES

1 Preheat the oven to 400°F (205°C). Put the potatoes in a bowl. Drizzle with the oil and sprinkle with the salt, then toss until evenly coated. Spread on a half sheet pan and bake until the skin is golden brown and the potatoes are tender, about 25 minutes. The potatoes will decrease in weight when roasted. You will need 200 grams (1½ c) of roasted potatoes for this recipe. Let cool completely, then refrigerate until ready to use.

FOR THE DOUGH

1 Stir together the white and whole wheat flours, salt, and yeast in a medium bowl.

2 Pour about one-third of the water around the edges of the starter to release it from the sides of the container. Transfer the starter and water to an extra-large bowl along with the remaining water. Using a wooden spoon, break the starter up to distribute it in the water.

3 Add the flour mixture, reserving about one-sixth of it along the edge of the bowl (see Mixing, page 282). Continue to mix with the spoon until most of the dry ingredients have been combined with the starter mixture. Switch to a plastic bowl scraper and continue to mix until incorporated. At this point the dough will be sticky to the touch.

4 Push the dough to one side of the bowl. Roll and tuck the dough (see Rolling and Tucking, page 284), adding the reserved flour mixture and a small amount of additional flour to the bowl and your hands as needed. Continue rolling and tucking until the dough feels stronger and begins to resist any further rolling, about 16 times. Then, with cupped hands, tuck the sides under toward the center. Place the dough, seam-side down, in a clean bowl, cover the top of the bowl with a clean kitchen towel, and let rest at room temperature for 45 minutes.

5 For the first stretch and fold (see Stretching and

Folding, page 285), lightly dust the work surface and your hands with flour. Using the plastic bowl scraper, release the dough from the bowl and set it, seam-side down, on the work surface. Gently stretch it into a rectangular shape. Fold the dough in thirds from top to bottom and then from left to right. With cupped hands, tuck the sides under toward the center. Place the dough in the bowl, seam-side down, cover the bowl with the towel, and let rest for 45 minutes.

6 For the second stretch and fold, repeat the steps for the first stretch and fold, then return the dough to the bowl, cover with the towel, and let rest for 45 minutes.

7 For the third and final stretch and fold, gently stretch the dough into a rectangle, scatter the potatoes over the top, and gently press them into the dough. (For photos of the following process, see Incorporating Add-Ins, page 292.) Roll up the dough tightly from the end closest to you; at the end of the roll the dough will be seam-side down. Turn it over, seam-side up, and gently press on the seam to flatten the dough slightly. Fold in thirds from left to right and then do one roll and tuck sequence to incorporate the potatoes. Turn the dough seam-side down and tuck the sides under toward the center. Return the dough to the bowl, cover with the towel, and let rest for 20 minutes.

8 Line a 9-inch (23 cm) proofing basket or bowl with a clean kitchen towel and dust the towel fairly generously with the dusting mixture.

9 Lightly dust the work surface and your hands with flour, and shape the dough into a round (see Shaping a Round Loaf, page 288). Dust the sides and top of the dough with the dusting mixture, fold the edges of the towel over the top, and let rest at room temperature for 1 hour.

10 Transfer the basket to the refrigerator and chill for 14 to 18 hours.

11 Position an oven rack in the lower third of the oven. Place a covered 6-quart (5.7 L), 10-inch (25 cm) round cast-iron Dutch oven on the rack. Preheat the oven to 500°F (260°C).

12 Remove the basket of dough from the refrigerator and let it sit at room temperature while you allow the oven to preheat for about 1 hour.

13 Using heavy-duty oven mitts or potholders, remove the Dutch oven, place it on a heatproof surface, and remove the lid.

14 Using the kitchen towel, lift and gently ease the dough out of the basket and onto a baking peel, seam-side down. Then carefully transfer it into the pot (the Dutch oven will be very hot). Score the top of the dough (see Scoring, page 290), cover the pot, and return it to the oven. Lower the oven temperature to 460°F (240°C) and bake for 30 minutes.

15 Rotate the Dutch oven and remove the lid. The loaf will already be a rich golden brown. Continue baking, uncovered, until the surface is a deep, rich brown, with some spots along the score being even slightly darker (*bien cuit*), about 20 minutes longer.

16 Loosen the edges of the loaf with a long handled spoon and then with the help of the spoon lift out of the pot onto a cooling rack. When the bottom of the loaf is tapped, it should sound hollow. If not, return it to the oven and bake directly on the rack for 5 minutes longer.

17 Let the bread cool completely before slicing and eating, at least 4 hours but preferably 8 to 24 hours.

KØRNTÜBERBROT

What began as a flight of fancy ended up as a wonderful bread. Peter and I were sitting around one day tasting a loaf of Pane Pugliese (page 37) that we made in the course of testing recipes. Peter asked why we couldn't try this same idea with another tuber in place of the potatoes, such as parsnips, which would bring some sweetness to the dough. Since it was summertime, I thought sweet corn would go nicely with it as well, and after trying a few approaches, I settled on the crazy idea of making my starter with minced fresh corn and cornmeal. Nowhere in all of bread lore will you find a starter made in this fashion, but that's the thing about new ideas: they're new and the good ones are begging to be tried. The name of this bread is just something silly we made up. Hey, it worked for Häagen-Dazs ice cream, which I understand is just a made-up name that looked European. We decided to give this bread a name that sounds like it's been baked in Scandinavia for the last three hundred years. People will take it more seriously that way, right?

STARTER

75 grams (½ c + 1 ½ tsp) minced raw corn kernels
    (about ¾ of a medium ear of corn)
75 grams (½ c + 1½ tsp) white flour
50 grams (¼ c + 1 tbsp) medium-grind cornmeal
1 gram (generous ¼ tsp) instant yeast
100 grams (¼ c + 3 tbsp) water at about 60°F (15°C)

ROASTED PARSNIPS

300 grams (10½ oz) peeled parsnips, cut into ¼-inch
    (6 mm) dice
9 grams (2 tsp) extra-virgin olive oil
0.3 gram (generous pinch) flaky sea salt, preferably Maldon

DOUGH

400 grams (2¾ c + 2 tbsp) white flour, plus additional
    as needed for working with the dough
100 grams (½ c + 1½ tbsp) medium-grind cornmeal
18 grams (1 tbsp) fine sea salt
1 gram (generous ¼ tsp) instant yeast
360 grams (1½ c) water at about 60°F (15°C)
25 grams (1 tbsp + 1 tsp) honey
40 grams (3 tbsp) unsalted butter, at room temperature

Dusting Mixture (see page 35), for the lined proofing
    basket and the shaped loaf

FOR THE STARTER

1 Stir together the minced corn, white flour, and cornmeal in a medium storage container. Sprinkle the yeast into the water, stir to mix, and pour over the corn mixture. Mix with your fingers, pressing the mixture into the sides, bottom, and corners until all of the flour is wet and fully incorporated. Cover the container and let sit at room temperature for 10 to 14 hours. The starter will be at its peak at around 11 hours.

FOR THE ROASTED PARSNIPS

1 Preheat the oven to 400°F (205°C). Put the parsnips in a bowl. Drizzle with the oil and sprinkle with the salt, then toss until evenly coated. Spread on a half sheet pan and bake until tender, about 25 minutes. The parsnips will decrease in weight when roasted. You will need 100 grams (1 c) of roasted parsnips for this recipe. Let cool completely, then refrigerate until ready to use.

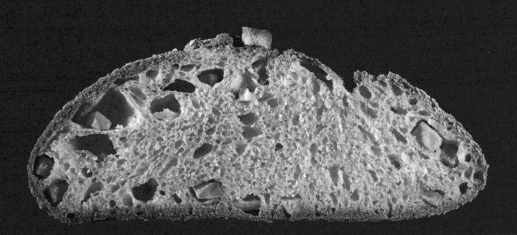

FOR THE DOUGH

1 Stir together the white flour, cornmeal, salt, and yeast in a medium bowl.

2 Pour about one-third of the water around the edges of the starter to release it from the sides of the container. Transfer the starter and water to an extra-large bowl along with the remaining water and the honey. Using a wooden spoon, break the starter up to distribute it in the liquid.

3 Add the flour mixture, reserving about one-sixth of it along the edge of the bowl (see Mixing, page 282). Continue to mix with the spoon until most of the dry ingredients have been combined with the starter mixture. Switch to a plastic bowl scraper and continue to mix until incorporated. At this point the dough will be sticky to the touch.

4 Push the dough to one side of the bowl. Roll and tuck the dough (see Rolling and Tucking, page 284), adding the reserved flour mixture and a small amount of additional flour to the bowl and your hands as needed. Continue rolling and tucking until the dough feels stronger and begins to resist any

further rolling, about 15 times. Then, with cupped hands, tuck the sides under toward the center. Place the dough, seam-side down, in a clean bowl, cover the top of the bowl with a clean kitchen towel, and let rest at room temperature for 45 minutes.

5 For the first stretch and fold (see Stretching and Folding, page 285), lightly dust the work surface and your hands with flour. Using the plastic bowl scraper, release the dough from the bowl and set it, seam-side down, on the work surface. Gently stretch it into a roughly rectangular shape. Fold the dough in thirds from top to bottom and then from left to right. With cupped hands, tuck the sides under toward the center. Place the dough in the bowl, seam-side down, cover the bowl with the towel, and let rest for 45 minutes.

6 For the second stretch and fold, gently stretch the dough into a rectangle. Pinch the butter into pieces, distributing them over the top of the dough. Using your fingers or a spatula, spread the butter across the surface of the dough. (For photos of the following process, see Incorporating Add-Ins, page 292.) Roll up the dough tightly from the end closest to you; at the end of the roll the dough will be seam-side down. Turn it over, seam-side up, and gently press on the seam to flatten the dough slightly. Fold in thirds from left to right and then do 4 to 5 roll and tuck sequences to incorporate the butter. Turn the dough seam-side down and tuck the sides under toward the center. Return the dough to the bowl, cover with the towel, and let rest for 30 minutes.

7 For the third and final stretch and fold, gently stretch the dough into a rectangle, scatter the parsnips over the top, and press them gently into the dough. Roll up the dough tightly from the end closest to you; at the end of the roll the dough will be seam-side down. Turn it over, seam-side up, and gently press on the seam to flatten the dough slightly. Fold in thirds from left to right and then do one more roll and tuck sequence to incorporate the parsnips. Turn the dough seam-side down and tuck the sides under toward the center. Return the dough to the bowl, cover with the towel, and let rest for 20 minutes.

8 Line a 9-inch (23 cm) proofing basket or bowl with a clean kitchen towel and dust the towel fairly generously with the dusting mixture.

9 Lightly dust the work surface and your hands with flour and shape the dough into a round (see Shaping a Round Loaf, page 288). Dust the sides and top of the dough with the dusting mixture, fold the edges of the towel over the top, and let rest at room temperature for 1 hour.

10 Transfer the basket to the refrigerator and chill for 24 to 28 hours.

11 Position an oven rack in the lower third of the oven. Place a covered 6-quart (5.7 L), 10-inch (25 cm) round cast-iron Dutch oven on the rack. Preheat the oven to 500°F (260°C). Remove the basket of dough from the refrigerator and let it sit at room temperature while you allow the oven to preheat for about 1 hour.

12 Using the kitchen towel, lift and gently ease the dough out of the basket and onto a baking peel, seam-side down. Then carefully transfer it into the pot (the Dutch oven will be very hot). Score the top of the dough (see Scoring, page 290), cover the pot, and return it to the oven. Lower the oven temperature to 460°F (240°C) and bake for 30 minutes.

13 Rotate the Dutch oven and remove the lid. The loaf will already be a rich golden brown. Continue baking, uncovered, until the surface is a deep, rich brown, with some spots along the score being even slightly darker (*bien cuit*), about 20 minutes longer.

14 Loosen the edges of the loaf with a long handled spoon and then with the help of the spoon lift out of the pot onto a cooling rack. When the bottom of the loaf is tapped, it should sound hollow. If not, return it to the oven and bake directly on the rack for 5 minutes longer.

15 Let the bread cool completely before slicing and eating, at least 4 hours but preferably 8 to 24 hours.

WHOLE WHEAT BREAD WITH PUMPKIN SEEDS

Toasted pumpkin seeds are proof that there is more to this giant fall vegetable than the pumpkin pie most people eat just once or twice a year. When toasted, pumpkin seeds have a distinctive flavor that marries well with the toastiness of grains. And in this recipe, because the toasted pumpkin seeds are ground to the fineness of flour, the dough is suffused with their essential oils, which have a rich and pronounced flavor that stands up well to whole wheat. Serve it as a table bread with a rich butter (for me that's the best Irish creamery kind or, failing that, any cultured butter). It's the kind of hearty combination that I think of serving in the fall, alongside upland game birds or waterfowl, such as pheasant, grouse, woodcock, duck, or wild turkey.

STARTER

250 grams (1¾ c + 1 tbsp) white flour

0.2 gram (pinch) instant yeast

250 grams (1 c + 2 tsp) water at about 60°F (15°C)

DOUGH

90 grams (½ c + 1 tbsp) pumpkin seeds

300 grams (2 c + 2 tbsp) medium whole wheat flour

200 grams (1¼ c + 3 tbsp) white flour, plus additional as needed for working with the dough

14 grams (2¼ + ⅛ tsp) fine sea salt

1 gram (generous ¼ tsp) instant yeast

400 grams (1½ c + 3 tbsp) water at about 60°F (15°C)

50 grams (¼ c) extra-virgin olive oil

Dusting Mixture (see page 35), for the lined proofing basket and the shaped loaf

FOR THE STARTER

1 Put the flour in a medium storage container. Sprinkle the yeast into the water, stir to mix, and pour over the water. Mix with your fingers, pressing the mixture into the sides, bottom, and corners until all of the flour is wet and fully incorporated. Cover the container and let sit at room temperature for 10 to 14 hours. The starter will be at its peak at around 11 hours.

FOR THE ROASTED PUMPKIN SEEDS

1 Preheat the oven to 400°F (205°C). Spread 40 grams (¼ c) of the pumpkin seeds on a quarter sheet pan and toast until slightly darker and aromatic, about 6 minutes. Let cool completely.

2 Meanwhile, process the remaining 50 grams (¼ c + 1 tbsp) of pumpkin seeds in a high-powered blender or a coffee grinder just until the texture resembles flour. Pause occasionally to be sure it is not over processing and clumping together.

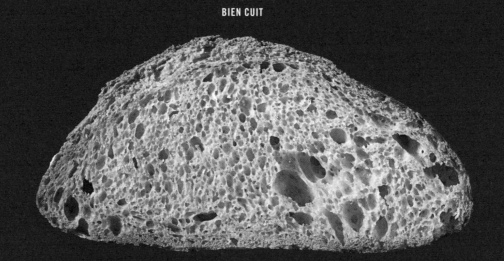

3 Stir together the whole wheat and white flours, ground pumpkin seeds, salt, and yeast in a medium bowl.

4 Pour about one-third of the water around the edges of the starter to release it from the sides of the container. Transfer the starter and water to an extra-large bowl along with the remaining water and the olive oil. Using a wooden spoon, break the starter up to distribute it in the liquid.

5 Add the flour mixture, reserving about one-sixth of it along the edge of the bowl (see Mixing, page 282). Continue to mix with the spoon until most of the dry ingredients have been combined with the starter mixture. Switch to a plastic bowl scraper and continue to mix until incorporated. At this point the dough will be pretty soft and very sticky.

6 Push the dough to one side of the bowl. Roll and tuck the dough (see Rolling and Tucking, page 284), adding the reserved flour mixture and a small amount of additional flour to the bowl and your hands as needed. You may need a bit more flour for this dough. If the dough becomes too sticky to work with at any point, let it rest for 5 minutes. Continue rolling and tucking until the dough feels stronger and begins to resist any further rolling, about 10 times. Then, with cupped hands, tuck the sides under

toward the center. Place the dough, seam-side down, in a clean bowl, cover the top of the bowlwith a clean kitchen towel, and let rest at room temperature for 45 minutes.

7 For the first stretch and fold (see Stretching and Folding, page 285), lightly dust the work surface and your hands with flour. Using the plastic bowl scraper, release the dough from the bowl and set it, seam-side down, on the work surface. Gently stretch it into a roughly rectangular shape. Fold the dough in thirds from top to bottom and then from left to right. With cupped hands, tuck the sides under toward the center. Place the dough in the bowl, seam-side down, cover the bowl with the towel, and let rest for 45 minutes.

8 For the second stretch and fold, gently stretch the dough into a rectangle, scatter the pumpkin seeds on top, and gently press them into the dough. (For photos of this process, see Incorporating Add-Ins, page 292.) Roll up the dough tightly from the end closest to you; at the end of the roll the dough will be seam-side down. Turn it over, seam-side up, and gently press on the seam to flatten the dough slightly. Fold in thirds from left to right and then roll and tuck 1 more time to incorporate the pumpkin seeds. Turn the dough seam-side down and tuck the sides under toward the center. Return the dough to the bowl, seam-side down, cover the towel, and let rest for 45 minutes.

9 For the third and final stretch and fold, repeat the steps for the first stretch and fold, then return the dough to the bowl, cover with the towel, and let rest for 20 minutes.

10 Line a 9-inch (23 cm) proofing basket or bowl with a clean kitchen towel and dust the towel fairly generously with the dusting mixture.

11 Lightly dust the work surface and your hands with flour and shape the dough into a round (see Shaping a Round Loaf, page 288). Dust the sides and top of the dough with the dusting mixture, fold the edges of the towel over the top, and let rest at room temperature for 1 hour.

12 Transfer the basket to the refrigerator and chill for 24 to 32 hours.

13 Position an oven rack in the lower third of the oven. Place a covered 6-quart (5.7 L), 10-inch (25 cm) round cast-iron Dutch oven on the rack. Preheat the oven to 500°F (260°C). Remove the basket of dough from the refrigerator and let it sit at room temperature while you allow the oven to preheat for about 1 hour.

14 Using heavy-duty oven mitts or potholders, remove the Dutch oven, place it on a heatproof surface, and remove the lid.

15 Using the kitchen towel, lift and gently ease the dough out of the basket and onto a baking peel, seam-side down. Then carefully transfer it into the pot (the Dutch oven will be very hot). Score the top of the dough (see Scoring, page 290), cover the pot, and return it to the oven. Lower the oven temperature to 460°F (240°C) and bake for 30 minutes.

16 Rotate the Dutch oven and remove the lid. The loaf will already be a rich golden brown. Continue baking, uncovered, until the surface is a deep, rich brown, with some spots along the score being even slightly darker (*bien cuit*), about 15 minutes longer.

17 Loosen the edges of the loaf with a long handled spoon and then with the help of the spoon lift out of the pot onto a cooling rack. When the bottom of the loaf is tapped, it should sound hollow. If not, return it to the oven and bake directly on the rack for 5 minutes longer.

18 Let the bread cool completely before slicing and eating, at least 4 hours but preferably 8 to 24 hours.

PORTUGUESE CORN BREAD

In coming up with the range of breads to offer at Bien Cuit, I knew I wanted to do something with cornmeal, but there didn't seem to be a compelling reason to add just another traditional corn bread to the pile. Then I heard about *broa de milho*. Where France has its rustic Country Bread (similar to my 30-Hour Sourdough Loaf, on page 129), the Portuguese incorporated corn into their peasant or farmhouse bread. It's one of the few European breads that relies on both cornmeal and wheat flour. Thanks to the cornmeal, it has a gentle, sweet nuttiness that fills the nose with a very pleasant, almost buttery aroma.

One drawback to using cornmeal in bread is that the bread tends to go stale very quickly. That's just the nature of corn. There's no way to avoid this entirely, but I reasoned if I added some milk to the dough, the lactic acid would enrich the dough, giving it a dense yet light crumb, while at the same time retarding the process of staling. To balance the acidity of the milk, I added a little honey to the dough, more as a way to boost fermentation than to actually add honeyed sweetness. A touch of olive oil also moistens this dough. In coming up with these additions, I tried to think of ingredients that were common among the Romans, who brought bread making to the Iberian Peninsula (Spain and Portugal).

The key to cracking the code for the best *broa de milho* I could imagine was including some rye flour in the cornmeal-based starter. The rate of fermentation is about the same for both grains, so I figured, *Why the hell not?* Here, as elsewhere, using a combination of grains leads to more interesting and complicated flavors. The final result is a flavor that's ultracreamy and yogurt-like. To be clear, even though the olive oil, milk, and honey make this bread slow to dry out, you really do want to eat it the day it's made—this one doesn't improve with age. Finally, and most deliciously, the brittle crunch of the crust and the sweet crumb are the perfect backdrop for butter and jam.

STARTER

225 grams (1¼ c + 1 tbsp) medium-grind cornmeal

50 grams (¼ c + 2 tbsp) white rye flour

1 gram (generous ¼ tsp) instant yeast

225 grams (¾ c + 3 tbsp) water at about 60°F (15°C)

DOUGH

400 grams (2¾ c + 2 tbsp) white flour, plus additional as needed for working with the dough

100 grams (½ c + 1½ tbsp) medium-grind cornmeal

15 grams (2½ tsp) fine sea salt

1 gram (generous ¼ tsp) instant yeast

290 grams (1 c + 2½ tbsp) cold whole milk

50 grams (¼ c) extra-virgin olive oil

40 grams (2 tbsp) honey

Dusting Mixture (see page 35), for the lined proofing basket and the shaped loaf

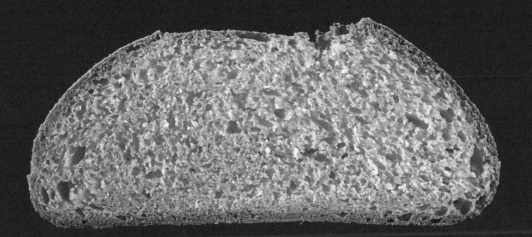

FOR THE STARTER

1 Stir together the cornmeal and rye flour in a medium storage container. Sprinkle the yeast into the water, stir to mix, and pour over the cornmeal mixture. Mix with your fingers, pressing the mixture into the sides, bottom, and corners until all of the flour is wet and fully incorporated. Cover the container and let sit at room temperature for 10 to 14 hours. The starter will be at its peak at around 11 hours.

FOR THE DOUGH

1 Stir together the white flour, cornmeal, salt, and yeast in a medium bowl.

2 Pour about one-third of the milk around the edges of the starter to release it from the sides of the container. Transfer the starter and milk to an extra-large bowl along with the remaining milk, the olive oil, and the honey. Using a wooden spoon, break the starter up to distribute it in the liquid.

3 Add the flour mixture, reserving about one-sixth of it along the edge of the bowl (see Mixing, page 282). Continue to mix with the spoon until most of the dry ingredients have been combined with the starter mixture. Switch to a plastic bowl scraper and

continue to mix until incorporated. At this point the dough will be sticky to the touch.

4 Push the dough to one side of the bowl. Roll and tuck the dough (see Rolling and Tucking, page 284), adding the reserved flour mixture and a small amount of additional flour to the bowl and your hands as needed. Continue rolling and tucking until the dough feels stronger and begins to resist any further rolling, about 18 times. Then, with cupped hands, tuck the sides under toward the center. Place the dough, seam-side down, in a clean bowl, cover the top of the bowl with a clean kitchen towel, and let rest at room temperature for 45 minutes.

5 For the first stretch and fold (see Stretching and Folding, page 285), lightly dust the work surface and your hands with flour. Using the plastic bowl scraper, release the dough from the bowl and set it, seam-side down, on the work surface. Gently stretch it into a roughly rectangular shape. Fold the dough in thirds from top to bottom and then from left to right. With cupped hands, tuck the sides under toward the center. Place the dough in the bowl, seam-side down, cover the bowl with the towel, and let rest for 45 minutes.

6 For the second stretch and fold, repeat the steps for the first stretch and fold, then return the dough to the bowl, cover with the towel, and let rest for 45 minutes.

7 For the third and final stretch and fold, once again repeat the steps for the first stretch and fold, then return the dough to the bowl, cover with the towel, and let rest for 20 minutes.

8 Line a 9-inch (23 cm) proofing basket or bowl with a clean kitchen towel and dust the towel fairly generously with the dusting mixture.

9 Lightly dust the work surface and your hands with flour and shape the dough into a round (see Shaping a Round Loaf, page 288). Dust the sides and top of the dough with the dusting mixture, fold the edges of the towel over the top, and let rest at room temperature for 1 hour.

10 Transfer the basket to the refrigerator and chill for 14 to 18 hours.

11 Position an oven rack in the lower third of the oven. Place a covered 6-quart (5.7 L), 10-inch (25 cm) round cast-iron Dutch oven on the rack. Preheat the oven to 500°F (260°C). Remove the basket of dough from the refrigerator and let it sit at room temperature while you allow the oven to preheat for about 1 hour.

12 Using heavy-duty oven mitts or potholders, re-move the Dutch oven, place it on a heatproof surface, and remove the lid.

13 Using the kitchen towel, lift and gently ease the dough out of the basket and onto a baking peel, seam-side down. Then carefully transfer it into the pot (the Dutch oven will be very hot). Score the top of the dough (see Scoring, page 290), cover the pot, and return it to the oven. Lower the oven tempera-ture to 460°F (240°C) and bake for 30 minutes.

14 Rotate the Dutch oven and remove the lid. The loaf will already be a rich golden brown. Continue baking, uncovered, until the surface is a deep, rich brown, with some spots along the score being even slightly darker (*bien cuit*), about 15 minutes longer.

15 Loosen the edges of the loaf with a long handled spoon and then with the help of the spoon lift out of the pot onto a cooling rack. When the bottom of the loaf is tapped, it should sound hollow. If not, return it to the oven and bake directly on the rack for 5 minutes longer.

16 Let the bread cool completely before slicing and eating, at least 4 hours but preferably 8 to 24 hours.

BUCKWHEAT, APRICOT, AND BLACK PEPPER BREAD

It's well known that it goes against the grain of most chefs to waste anything that can add flavor to a dish. It definitely goes against the grain—pun intended—of this bread baker. I originally tried this as a dinner roll that incorporated little pieces of baked apricot that I had soaked in water. Rather than discarding the water, I used it for the liquid in the starter. In this version, dried apricots are used instead. The result is concentrated apricot flavor from the apricot pieces set against a light wash of that same flavor in the crumb. For a contrasting, assertive flavor, I added buckwheat flour and a bit of black pepper. Used judiciously, that's a combination that can really wake up a bread. First you get the woodsy aroma of the buckwheat and the sweet fruitiness of the apricot, then a sneak attack of heat from the black pepper, and finally the pungent flavor of the pepper itself.

APRICOTS

70 grams (2.5 oz, about 10) dried apricots, preferably unsulfured
145 grams (½ c + 1½ tbsp) warm water

STARTER

120 grams (1 c) dark rye flour
0.2 gram (pinch) instant yeast
Reserved apricot soaking liquid, plus additional water as
    needed to equal 120 grams (½ c)

DOUGH

425 grams (3 c + 2½ tbsp) white flour, plus additional
    as needed for working with the dough
75 grams (½ c + 1½ tsp) buckwheat flour
15 grams (2½ tsp) fine sea salt
1 gram (generous ¼ tsp) instant yeast
365 grams (1½ c + 1 tsp) water at about 60°F (15°C)
50 grams (3½ tbsp) unsalted butter, at room temperature
2 grams (generous 1 tsp) coarsely ground black pepper

Dusting Mixture (see page 35), for the linen liner and
    shaped loaves

FOR THE APRICOTS

1 Put the apricots in a medium heatproof storage container. Pour in the water, cover, and let sit at room temperature for 8 to 12 hours.

2 Strain the soaking liquid. If the amount is less than 120 grams (½ c), add water to make up the difference. Coarsely chop the apricots. You will need 90 grams (½ c) for this recipe. Set the apricots aside in a covered storage container at room temperature until ready to use.

FOR THE STARTER

1 Put the flour in a medium storage container. Sprinkle the yeast into the apricot-soaking liquid, stir to mix, and pour over the flour. Mix with your fingers, pressing the mixture into the sides, bottom, and corners until all of the flour is wet and fully incorporated. Cover the container and let sit at room temperature for 10 to 14 hours. The starter will be at its peak at around 11 hours.

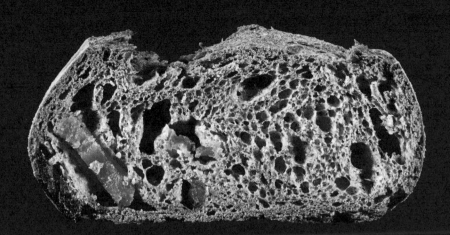

FOR THE DOUGH

1 Stir together the white and buckwheat flours, salt, and yeast in a medium bowl.

2 Pour about one-third of the water around the edges of the starter to release it from the sides of the container.

3 Transfer the starter and water to an extra-large bowl along with the remaining apricot-soaking liquid. Using a wooden spoon, break the starter up to distribute it in the liquid.

4 Add the flour mixture, reserving about one-sixth of it along the edge of the bowl (see Mixing, page 282). Continue to mix with the spoon until most of the dry ingredients have been combined with the starter mixture. Switch to a plastic bowl scraper and continue to mix until incorporated. At this point the dough will be slightly sticky to the touch.

5 Push the dough to one side of the bowl. Roll and tuck the dough (see Rolling and Tucking, page 284), adding the reserved flour mixture and a small amount of additional flour to the bowl and your hands as needed. Continue rolling and tucking until

the dough feels stronger and begins to resist any further rolling, about 8 times. Then, with cupped hands, tuck the sides under toward the center. Place the dough, seam-side down, in a clean bowl, cover the top of the bowl with a clean kitchen towel, and let rest at room temperature for 45 minutes.

6 For the first stretch and fold (see Stretching and Folding, page 285), lightly dust the work surface and your hands with flour. Using the plastic bowl scraper, release the dough from the bowl and set it, seam-side down, on the work surface. Gently stretch it into a roughly rectangular shape. Fold the dough in thirds from top to bottom and then from left to right. With cupped hands, tuck the sides under toward the center. Place the dough in the bowl, seam-side down, cover the bowl with the towel, and let rest for 45 minutes.

7 For the second stretch and fold, repeat the steps for the first stretch and fold, then return the dough to the bowl, cover with the towel, and let rest for 30 minutes.

8 For the third stretch and fold, gently stretch the dough into a rectangle. Pinch the butter into pieces, distributing them over the top of the dough. Using your fingers or a spatula, spread the butter across the surface of the dough. (For photos of the following process, see Incorporating Add-Ins, page 292.) Roll up the dough tightly from the end closest to you; at the end of the roll the dough will be seam-side down. Turn it over, seam-side up, and gently press on the seam to flatten the dough slightly. Fold in thirds from left to right and then do 4 or 5 roll and tuck sequences to incorporate the butter. Turn the dough seam-side down and tuck the sides under toward the center. Return the dough to the bowl, cover with the towel, and let rest for 30 minutes.

9 For the fourth and final stretch and fold, gently stretch the dough into a rectangle. Sprinkle the pepper evenly over the surface, then scatter the apricots on top and gently press them into the dough. Roll up the dough tightly from the end closest to you; at the end of the roll the dough will be seam-side down. Turn it over, seam-side up, and gently press on the seam to flatten the dough slightly. Fold in thirds from left to right, and then do one roll and tuck sequence to incorporate the pepper and apricots. Turn the dough seam-side down and tuck the sides under toward the center. Return the dough to the bowl, seam-side down, cover with the towel, and let rest for 20 minutes.

10 Line a half sheet pan with a linen liner and dust fairly generously with the dusting mixture.

11 Lightly dust the work surface and your hands with flour. Using a bench scraper, divide the dough into 2 equal pieces. Press each into a 7-inch (18 cm) square, then roll into a loose tube about 7 inches (18 cm) long (see Shaping a Tube or Oval Loaf, page 294). Let rest for 5 minutes. Press each piece out and then shape into a very tight tube 9 to 10 inches (23 to 25 cm) long. Transfer to the lined pan, seam-side

up, positioning the loaves lengthwise. Dust the top and sides of the loaves with flour. Fold the linen to create support walls on both sides of each loaf, then fold any extra length of the linen liner over the top or cover with a kitchen towel. Transfer the pan to the refrigerator and chill for 14 to 20 hours.

12 Set up the oven with a baking stone and a cast-iron skillet for steam (see Baking Stones and Steam, page 296), then preheat the oven to 480°F (250°C).

13 Using the linen liner, lift and gently flip the loaves off of the pan and onto a transfer peel, seam-side down. Slide the loaves, still seam-side down, onto a dusted baking peel (see Using a Transfer Peel and Baking Peel, page 311). Score the top of each (see Scoring, page 290). Working quickly but carefully, transfer the loaves to the stone using heavy-duty oven mitts or potholders. Pull out the hot skillet, add about 3 cups of ice cubes, then slide it back in and close the oven door. Immediately lower the oven temperature to 440°F (225°C). Bake, switching the positions of the loaves about two-thirds of the way through baking, until the surface is a deep, rich brown, with some spots along the scores being very dark (*bien cuit*), about 25 minutes.

14 Using the baking peel, transfer the loaves to a cooling rack. When the bottoms of the loaves are tapped, they should sound hollow. If not, return to the stone and bake for 5 minutes longer.

15 Let the bread cool completely before slicing and eating, at least 4 hours but preferably 8 to 24 hours.

AUTUMN MAPLE RYE BREAD

This is a subtle bread. It's the kind of thing I baked at Georges Perrier's restaurant Le Bec-Fin when we wanted a bread that would complement the food, but almost in a subliminal way. In this recipe, I wanted to include rye for the sweetness it adds to the final bread. For that reason, I used rye flour in the dough but not the starter, where I felt it might add some intense high notes that would overpower the subtle earthy sweetness of the maple syrup. I imagined this bread for the autumn table, when the color of maple leaves lights the New England hillsides on fire. I recommend serving it with winter squash, bitter greens, onions, and mild seafood such as trout, scallops, or flounder.

FOR THE STARTER

1 Put the flour in a medium storage container. Sprinkle the yeast into the water, stir to mix, and pour over the flour. Mix with your fingers, pressing the mixture into the sides, bottom, and corners until all of the flour is wet and fully incorporated. Cover the container and let sit at room temperature for 10 to 14 hours. The starter will be at its peak at around 11 hours.

FOR THE DOUGH

1 Stir together the white and white rye flours, salt, and yeast in a medium bowl.

2 Pour about one-third of the milk around the edges of the starter to release it from the sides of the container. Transfer the starter and milk to an extra-large bowl along with the remaining milk and the maple syrup. Using a wooden spoon, break the starter up to distribute it in the liquid.

3 Add the flour mixture, reserving about one-sixth of it along the edge of the bowl (see Mixing, page 282). Continue to mix with the spoon until most of the dry ingredients have been combined with the starter mixture. Switch to a plastic bowl scraper and continue to mix until incorporated. At this point the dough will be sticky to the touch.

STARTER

250 grams (1¾ c + 1 tbsp) white flour
0.2 gram (pinch) instant yeast
250 grams (1 c + 2 tsp) water at about 60°F (15°C)

DOUGH

350 grams (2½ c) white flour, plus additional as needed for
 working with the dough
150 grams (1 c + 1 tbsp) white rye flour
18 grams (1 tbsp) fine sea salt
1 gram (generous ¼ tsp) instant yeast
350 grams (1¼ c + 2½ tbsp) cold whole milk
85 grams (¼ c) Grade A maple syrup
25 grams (1¾ tbsp) unsalted butter, at room temperature

Dusting Mixture (see page 35), for the linen liner
 and shaped loaves

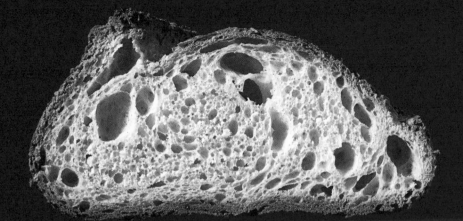

4 Push the dough to one side of the bowl. Roll and tuck the dough (see Rolling and Tucking, page 284), adding the reserved flour mixture and a small amount of additional flour to the bowl and your hands as needed. Continue rolling and tucking until the dough feels stronger and begins to resist any further rolling, about 10 times. Then, with cupped hands, tuck the sides under toward the center. Place the dough, seam-side down, in a clean bowl, cover the top of the bowl with a clean kitchen towel, and let rest at room temperature for 45 minutes.

5 For the first stretch and fold (see Stretching and Folding, page 285), lightly dust the work surface and your hands with flour. Using the plastic bowl scraper, release the dough from the bowl and set it, seam-side down, on the work surface. Gently stretch it into a roughly rectangular shape. Fold the dough in thirds from top to bottom and then from left to right. With cupped hands, tuck the sides under toward the center. Place the dough in the bowl, seam-side down, cover the bowl with the towel, and let rest for 45 minutes.

6 For the second stretch and fold, repeat the steps for the first stretch and fold, then return the dough to the bowl, cover with the towel, and let rest for 45 minutes.

7 For the third and final stretch and fold, gently stretch the dough into a rectangle. Pinch the butter into pieces, distributing them over the top of the dough. Using your fingers or a spatula, spread the butter across the surface of the dough. (For photos of the following process, see Incorporating Add-Ins, page 292.) Roll up the dough tightly from the end closest to you; at the end of the roll the dough will be seam-side down. Turn it over, seam-side up, and gently press on the seam to flatten the dough slightly. Fold in thirds from left to right and then do 4 or 5 roll and tuck sequences to incorporate the butter. Turn the dough seam-side down and tuck the sides under toward the center. Return the dough to the bowl, cover with the towel, and let rest for 20 minutes.

8 Line a half sheet pan with a linen liner and dust fairly generously with the dusting mixture.

9 Lightly dust the work surface and your hands with flour. Using a bench scraper, divide the dough into 2 equal pieces. Press each piece into an 8 by 6-inch (20 by 15 cm) rectangle, then roll into a loose tube about 8 inches (20 cm) long (see Shaping a Tube or Oval Loaf, page 294). Let rest for 5 minutes. Press each piece out again and then shape into an oval about 10 inches (25 cm) long. Transfer to the lined pan, seam-side up, positioning the loaves lengthwise. Dust the top and sides of the loaves with flour. Fold the linen to create support walls on both sides of each loaf, then fold any extra length of the linen liner over the top or cover with a kitchen towel. Transfer the pan to the refrigerator and chill for 18 to 28 hours.

10 Set up the oven with a baking stone and a cast-iron skillet for steam (see Baking Stones and Steam, page 296), then preheat the oven to 480°F (250°C).

11 Using the linen liner, lift and gently flip the loaves off the pan and onto a transfer peel, seam-side down. Slide the loaves, still seam-side down, onto a dusted baking peel (see Using a Transfer Peel and Baking Peel, page 311). Score the top of each (see Scoring, page 290). Working quickly but carefully, transfer

the loaves to the stone using heavy-duty oven mitts or potholders. Pull out the hot skillet, add about 3 cups of ice cubes, then slide it back in and close the oven door. Immediately lower the oven temperature to 440°F (225°C). Bake, switching the positions of the loaves about two-thirds of the way through baking, until the surface is a deep, rich brown, with some spots along the scores being very dark (bien cuit), about 20 minutes.

12 Using the baking peel, transfer the loaves to a cooling rack. When the bottoms of the loaves are tapped, they should sound hollow. If not, return to the stone and bake for 5 minutes longer.

13 Let the bread cool completely before slicing and eating, at least 4 hours but preferably 8 to 24 hours.

BOURBON BREAD

I am very excited about this bread, in part because I think bourbon is one of the most elegant beverages. It is simultaneously sweet and bitter, smoky and smooth, and graced with the subtle vanilla notes of oak. Because bourbon is a corn-based whiskey, I include corn in the bread—both in the starter and the dough. I had thought it was a nice accompaniment to a vegetable course or salad. Then Peter served it with a slice of Kentucky ham (which, like bourbon, is one of the glories of the Bluegrass State). It was off the charts! The only thing missing was a mint julep. My one caution in regard to baking with bourbon (or any whiskey) is that it has a bitter component that can overpower, so don't be tempted to put in a touch extra for good measure. The choice of bourbon is up to you. Common wisdom is that when cooking with wine, it's best to use a wine you would like to drink. The same holds true for baking with whiskey. My choice here is Ezra Brooks because it's pretty mellow, not overpowering, and not super expensive.

STARTER

200 grams (1 c + 3 tbsp) medium-grind cornmeal

100 grams (½ c + 3½ tbsp) white flour

0.2 gram (pinch) instant yeast

260 grams (1 c + 1½ tbsp) water at about 60°F (15°C)

DOUGH

380 grams (2½ c + 3 tbsp) white flour, plus additional as needed for working with the dough

120 grams (¾ c) medium-grind cornmeal

30 grams (2½ tbsp) granulated sugar

15 grams (2½ tsp) fine sea salt

1 gram (generous ¼ tsp) instant yeast

150 grams (½ c + 2 tbsp) water at about 60°F (15°C)

60 grams (¼ c) bourbon

25 grams (1¾ tbsp) unsalted butter, at room temperature

Dusting Mixture (see page 35), for the linen liner and shaped loaves

FOR THE STARTER

1 Stir together the cornmeal and white flour in a medium storage container. Sprinkle the yeast into the water, stir to mix, and pour over the cornmeal mixture. Mix with your fingers, pressing the mixture into the sides, bottom, and corners until all of the flour is wet and fully incorporated. Cover the container and let sit at room temperature for 10 to 14 hours. The starter will be at its peak at around 12 hours.

FOR THE DOUGH

1 Stir together the white flour, cornmeal, sugar, salt, and yeast in a medium bowl.

2 Pour about one-third of the water around the edges of the starter to release it from the sides of the container. Transfer the starter and water to an extra-large bowl along with the remaining water and the bourbon. Using a wooden spoon, break the starter up to distribute it in the liquid.

3 Add the flour mixture, reserving about one-sixth of it along the edge of the bowl (see Mixing, page

282). Continue to mix with the spoon until most of the dry ingredients have been combined with the starter mixture. Switch to a plastic bowl scraper and continue to mix until incorporated. At this point the dough will be just slightly sticky to the touch.

4 Push the dough to one side of the bowl. Roll and tuck the dough (see Rolling and Tucking, page 284), adding the reserved flour mixture and a small amount of additional flour to the bowl and your hands as needed. Continue rolling and tucking until the dough feels stronger and begins to resist any further rolling, about 8 times. Then, with cupped hands, tuck the sides under toward the center. Place the dough, seam-side down, in a clean bowl, cover the top of the bowl with a clean kitchen towel, and let rest at room temperature for 30 minutes.

5 For the first stretch and fold (see Stretching and Folding, page 285), lightly dust the work surface and your hands with flour. Using the plastic bowl scraper, release the dough from the bowl and set it, seam-side down, on the work surface. Gently stretch it into a roughly rectangular shape. Fold the dough in thirds from top to bottom and then from left to right. With cupped hands, tuck the sides under toward the center. Place the dough in the bowl, seam-side down, cover the bowl with the towel, and let rest for 30 minutes.

6 For the second stretch and fold, repeat the steps for the first stretch and fold, then return the dough to the bowl, cover with the towel, and let rest for 30 minutes.

7 For the third stretch and fold, gently stretch the dough into a rectangle. Pinch the butter into pieces, distributing them over the top of the dough. Using your fingers or a spatula, spread the butter across the surface of the dough. (For photos of the following process, see Incorporating Add-Ins, page 292.) Roll up the dough tightly from the end closest to you; at the end of the roll the dough will be seam-side down. Turn it over, seam-side up, and gently press on the seam to flatten the dough slightly. Fold in thirds from left to right and then do 4 or 5 roll and tuck sequences to incorporate the butter. Turn the dough seam-side down and tuck the sides under toward the center. Return the dough to the bowl, cover with the towel, and let rest for 30 minutes.

8 For the fourth and final stretch and fold, repeat the steps for the first stretch and fold, then return the dough to the bowl, cover with the towel, and let rest for 20 minutes.

9 Line a half sheet pan with a linen liner and dust fairly generously with the dusting mixture.

10 Lightly dust the work surface and your hands with flour. Using a bench scraper, divide the dough into 2 equal pieces. Press each into a 7-inch (18 cm) square, then roll into a loose tube about 7 inches (18 cm) long (see Shaping a Tube or Oval Loaf, page 294). Let rest for 5 minutes. Press each piece out and then shape into a very tight tube 9 to 10 inches (23 to 25 cm) long. Using a bench scraper, make 3 to 5 cuts on the diagonal down the loaf. Then, make 3 to 5 cuts in the opposite direction, crossing the first set of cuts, to make diamonds (see the photo on page 298).

11 Transfer to the lined pan, cut-side down, positioning the loaves lengthwise. Dust the top and sides of the dough with flour. Fold the linen to create support walls on both sides of each loaf, then fold any extra length of the linen liner over the top or cover with a kitchen towel. Transfer the pan to the refrigerator and chill for 16 to 22 hours.

12 Set up the oven with a baking stone and a cast-iron skillet for steam (see Baking Stones and Steam, page 296), then preheat the oven to 480°F (250°C).

13 Using the linen liner, lift and gently flip the loaves off the pan and onto a transfer peel cut-side up. Slide the loaves, still cut-side up, onto a dusted baking peel (see Using a Transfer Peel and Baking Peel, page 311). Working quickly but carefully, transfer the loaves to the stone using heavy-duty oven mitts or potholders. Pull out the hot skillet, add about 3 cups of ice cubes, then slide it back in and close the oven door. Immediately lower the oven temperature to 440°F (225°C). Bake, switching the positions of the loaves about two-thirds of the way through baking, until the surface is a deep, rich brown, with some spots a long the scores being very dark (bien cuit), about 28 minutes.

14 Using the baking peel, transfer the loaves to a cooling rack. When the bottoms of the loaves are tapped, they should sound hollow. If not, return to the stone and bake for 5 minutes longer.

15 Let the bread cool completely before slicing and eating, at least 4 hours but preferably 8 to 24 hours.

CARAMELIZED ONION BREAD

When I worked for Georges Perrier at Le Bec-Fin, they put raw onion in the sourdough, a practice that is quite common in France. I didn't like the sharp, acrid taste at all, so Georges showed me how to get serious about caramelizing onions. His method takes a long time and a lot of stirring, but it's so much better than the common shortcut of adding sugar to onions and sautéing them. I incorporated those onions into a baguette, which Georges liked a lot. Here's the secret: The onion should be neither the centerpiece nor the last thing you taste; instead, it should be a persistent note in a chorus of flavors. For this recipe, I thought the fresh and slightly cooling sensation of buckwheat would play well with the other ingredients. I also used butter because it works well with caramelized onions, and honey, to extend the sweet finish the onions elicit. Georges would serve this bread with smoked meat, especially bacon or pancetta. I love it with brisket or anything you'd serve with caramelized onions. If you make traditional French onion soup, it would be an ideal crouton.

STARTER

125 grams (¾ c + 2½ tbsp) white rye flour
0.3 gram (generous pinch) instant yeast
125 grams (½ c + 1 tsp) water at about 60°F (15°C)

DOUGH

425 grams (3 c + 2½ tsp) white flour, plus additional
    as needed for working with the dough
75 grams (½ c + 1½ tsp) buckwheat flour
15 grams (2½ tsp) fine sea salt
1 gram (generous ¼ tsp) instant yeast
350 grams (1¼ c + 3½ tbsp) water at about 60°F (15°C)
50 grams (2½ tbsp) honey
25 grams (1¾ tbsp) unsalted butter, at room temperature
50 grams (¼ c) Caramelized Onions (recipe follows)

Dusting Mixture (see page 35), for the linen liner and
    shaped loaves

FOR THE STARTER

1 Put the flour in a medium storage container. Sprinkle the yeast into the water, stir to mix, and pour over the flour. Mix with your fingers, pressing the mixture into the sides, bottom, and corners until all of the flour is wet and fully incorporated. Cover the container and let sit at room temperature for 10 to 14 hours. The starter will be at its peak at around 12 hours.

FOR THE DOUGH

1 Stir together the white and buckwheat flours, salt, and yeast in a medium bowl.

2 Pour about one-third of the water around the edges of the starter to release it from the sides of the container. Transfer the starter and water to an extra-large bowl along with the remaining water and the honey. Using a wooden spoon, break the starter up to distribute it in the water.

3 Add the flour mixture, reserving about one-sixth of it along the edge of the bowl (see Mixing, page 282).

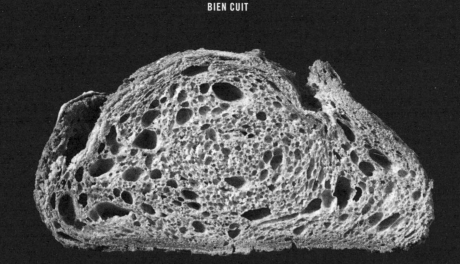

Continue to mix with the spoon until most of the dry ingredients have been combined with the starter mixture. Switch to a plastic bowl scraper and continue to mix until incorporated. At this point the dough will be sticky to the touch.

4 Push the dough to one side of the bowl. Roll and tuck the dough (see Rolling and Tucking, page 284), adding the reserved flour mixture and a small amount of additional flour to the bowl and your hands as needed. Continue rolling and tucking until the dough feels stronger and begins to resist any further rolling, about 10 times. Then, with cupped hands, tuck the sides under toward the center. Place the dough, seam-side down, in a clean bowl, cover the top of the bowl with a clean kitchen towel, and let rest at room temperature for 45 minutes.

5 For the first stretch and fold (see Stretching and Folding, page 285), lightly dust the work surface and your hands with flour. Using the plastic bowl scraper, release the dough from the bowl and set it, seam-side down, on the work surface. Gently stretch it into a roughly rectangular shape. Fold the dough in thirds from top to bottom and then from left to right. With cupped hands, tuck the sides under toward the center. Place the dough in the bowl, seam-side down, cover the bowl with the towel, and let rest for 45 minutes.

6 For the second stretch and fold, repeat the steps for the first stretch and fold, then return the dough o the bowl, cover with the towel, and let rest for 45 minutes.

7 For the third stretch and fold, gently stretch the dough into a rectangle. Pinch the butter into pieces, distributing them over the top of the dough. Using your fingers or a spatula, spread the butter across the surface of the dough. Scatter the onions on top. (For photos of the following process, see Incorporating Add-Ins, page 292.) Roll up the dough tightly from the end closest to you; at the end of the roll the dough will be seam-side down. Turn it over, seam-side up, and gently press on the seam to flatten the dough slightly. Fold in thirds from left to right and then roll and 4 or 5 roll and tuck sequences to incorporate the butter. Turn the dough seam-side down and tuck the sides under toward the center. Return the dough to the bowl, cover with the towel, and let rest for 45 minutes.

8 For the fourth and final stretch and fold, repeat the steps for the first stretch and fold, then return the dough to the bowl, cover with the towel, and let rest for 20 minutes.

9 Line a half sheet pan with a linen liner and dust fairly generously with the dusting mixture.

10 Lightly dust the work surface and your hands with flour. Using a bench scraper, divide the dough into 2 equal pieces. Press each piece into 9 by 5-inch (23 by 15 cm) rectangle, then roll into a loose tube about 9 inches (23 cm) long (see Shaping a Tube or Oval Loaf, page 294). Let rest for 5 minutes. Press each piece out again and then shape into an oval about 12 inches (30 cm) long. Transfer to the lined pan, seam-side up, positioning the loaves lengthwise. Dust the top and sides of the loaves with flour. Fold the linen to create support walls on both sides of each loaf, then fold any extra length of the linen liner over the top or cover with a kitchen towel. Transfer the pan to the refrigerator and chill for 12 to 18 hours.

11 Set up the oven with a baking stone and a cast-iron skillet for steam (see Baking Stones and Steam, page 296), then preheat the oven to 500°F (260°C).

12 Using the linen liner, lift and gently flip the loaves off the pan and onto a transfer peel, seam-side down. Slide the dough, still seam-side down, onto a dusted baking peel (see Using a Transfer Peel and Baking Peel, page 311). Score the top of each (see Scoring, page 290). Working quickly but carefully, transfer the loaves to the stone using heavy-duty oven mitts or potholders. Pull out the hot skillet, add about 3 cups of ice cubes, then slide it back in and close the oven door. Immediately lower the oven temperature to 460°F (240°C). Bake, switching the positions of the loaves about two-thirds of the way through baking, until the surface is a deep, rich brown, with some spots along the scores being very dark (*bien cuit*), about 25 minutes.

13 Using the baking peel, transfer the loaves to a cooling rack. When the bottoms of the loaves are tapped, they should sound hollow. If not, return to the stone and bake for 5 minutes longer.

14 Let the bread cool completely before slicing and eating, at least 4 hours but preferably 8 to 24 hours.

CARAMELIZED ONIONS

MAKES ABOUT 275 GRAMS (½ C) OF ONIONS AND 215 GRAMS (GENEROUS 1 C) OF ONION BUTTER

The best way to caramelize onions is the slow, low-heat method I learned from Georges Perrier. Because it takes at least an hour, do it when you're going to be in the kitchen for a while so you can return to the onions from time to time. This recipe makes quite a bit more than called for in the previous recipe. In addition to using the leftovers as a condiment, try them in omelets.

DIRECTIONS

1 Melt the butter in a small saucepan without stirring it. Skim off the foamy layer on the top and discard. Pour the clear yellow liquid into a medium sauté pan (or into a storage container if cooking the onions later), leaving the solids in the bottom behind.

2 Heat the butter over low heat until it bubbles gently (increase the heat slightly if necessary), then add the onions. After a few minutes, use a wooden spoon to gently move the onions and see the bottom of the pan. Brown bits should be starting to form. Scrape these with the spoon and incorporate them into the onions.

3 Adjusting the heat as needed to keep the contents of the pan bubbling gently, repeat the process every 15 minutes or so, scraping and incorporating the brown bits, until the onions are a rich amber color, 1 to 1½ hours. Toward the end of the process, adjust the heat so the onions don't burn and stir a bit more often, about every 5 minutes or so.

4 Set a fine-mesh strainer over a bowl or large measuring cup. Put the onions in the strainer to drain off the excess butter. Reserve 50 grams (¼ c) of the onions for Caramelized Onion Bread (page 69), 20 grams (1½ tbsp) for Alsatian Scones (page 271), or 144 grams (¾ c) for Bialys (page 243). Store the remainder in the refrigerator for up to 3 days. Refrigerate the strained butter (which has delicious flavor) in a separate container for up to 1 week.

INGREDIENTS

453 grams (1 pound) unsalted butter
907 grams (2 pounds) onions (about 4 medium), cut into ¼-inch (6 mm) dice

TOASTED OAT BREAD

Recently, in the middle of the night, I was thinking back to the farm I lived on in Oregon and about the crops we grew there. In Oregon, you can fill your personal horn of plenty better than anywhere in America. As I lay in bed running through my mental inventory of those fields and orchards, I saw stands of barley, rye, wheat, and oats—all of them grown in rotation to keep the soil healthy. I was lost in a daydream of golden grains in the fields when something about the oats made me pause and reflect.

Oats are a wonderful grain, but you don't often see them used in bakeries except for Irish soda bread and the so-called multigrain breads. And in the latter case, I think the main reason oats are used is that even though they don't provide much flavor, they make the bread look convincingly like it's brimming with healthful whole grains. If an ingredient doesn't add flavor, though, I don't see the point of using it. Yet I love oatmeal in the morning, and I started to en-vision a bread that captures that flavor. By the way, if you don't come across oat flour in the market, you can just as easily make your own by grinding up cracked oats or steel-cut oats in a spice or coffee grinder.

FOR THE STARTER

1 Preheat the oven to 425°F (220°C). Spread the oats on a half sheet pan and toast for 4 minutes. Gently shake the pan, then toast for 4 minutes longer. Shake again and toast until aromatic and evenly golden brown, 2 to 4 minutes longer. Let cool completely.

2 Transfer to a high-powered blender or a coffee grinder, and process into a fine flour. The oats will decrease slightly in weight when toasted. You will need 115 grams (1 c + 1½ tbsp) of toasted oat flour for the starter.

3 Put the oat flour in a medium storage container. Sprinkle the yeast into the water, stir to mix, and pour over the flour. Mix with your fingers, pressing the mixture into the sides, bottom, and corners until all of the flour is wet and fully incorporated. Cover the container and let sit at room temperature for 12 to 18 hours. The starter will be at its peak at around 15 hours.

STARTER

130 grams (¾ c) steel-cut oats
0.3 gram (a generous pinch) instant yeast
135 grams (½ c + 1 tbsp) water at about 60°F (15°C)

SOAKER

100 grams (½ c + 3½ tbsp) medium whole wheat flour
75 grams (¼ c + 1 tbsp) water at about 60°F (15°C)

DOUGH

400 grams (2¾ c + 2 tbsp) white flour, plus additional
    as needed for working with the dough
15 grams (2½ tsp) fine sea salt
1 gram (generous ¼ tsp) instant yeast
330 grams (1¼ c + 2 tbsp) water at about 60°F (15°C)
35 grams (1 tbsp + 2 tsp) unsulfured molasses
25 grams (1¾ tbsp) unsalted butter,
    at room temperature

Dusting Mixture (see page 35), for the lined proofing
    basket and the shaped loaf

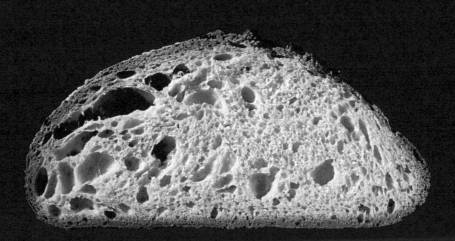

FOR THE SOAKER

1 Put the flour in a medium storage container and pour in the water. Mix with your fingers, pressing the mixture into the sides, bottom, and corners until all of the flour is wet and fully incorporated. Cover the container and let sit at room temperature for 12 to 18 hours. The soaker will be at its peak at around 15 hours.

FOR THE DOUGH

1 Stir together the flour, salt, and yeast in a medium bowl.

2 Pour about one-third of the water around the edges of the starter and another one-third around the edges of the soaker to release them from the sides of the containers. Transfer the starter, soaker, and water to an extra-large bowl along with the remaining water and the molasses. Using a wooden spoon, break the starter and soaker up into small pieces (both are fairly stiff) to distribute them in the liquid.

3 Add the flour mixture, reserving about one-sixth of it along the edge of the bowl (see Mixing, page 282). Continue to mix with the spoon until most of the dry ingredients have been combined with the starter mixture. Switch to a plastic bowl scraper and

continue to mix until incorporated. At this point the dough will be sticky to the touch.

4 Push the dough to one side of the bowl. Roll and tuck the dough (see Rolling and Tucking, page 284), adding the reserved flour mixture and a small amount of additional flour to the bowl and your hands as needed. Continue rolling and tucking until the dough feels stronger and begins to resist any further rolling, about 12 times. Then, with cupped hands, tuck the sides under toward the center. Place the dough, seam-side down, in a clean bowl, cover the top of the bowl with a clean kitchen towel, and let rest at room temperature for 1 hour.

5 For the first stretch and fold (see Stretching and Folding, page 285), lightly dust the work surface and your hands with flour. Using the plastic bowl scraper, release the dough from the bowl and set it, seam-side down, on the work surface. Gently stretch it into a roughly rectangular shape. Fold the dough in thirds from top to bottom and then from left to right. With cupped hands, tuck the sides under toward the center. Place the dough in the bowl, seam-side down, cover the bowl with the towel, and let rest for 1 hour.

6 For the second stretch and fold, gently stretch the dough into a rectangle. Pinch the butter into pieces, distributing them over the top of the dough. Using your fingers or a spatula, spread the butter across the surface of the dough. (For photos of the following process, see Incorporating Add-Ins, page 292.) Roll up the dough tightly from the end closest to you; at the end of the roll the dough will be seam-side down. Turn it over, seam-side up, and gently press on the seam to flatten the dough slightly. Fold in thirds from left to right and then do 4 or 5 roll and tuck sequences to incorporate the butter. Turn the dough seam-side down and tuck the sides under toward the center. Return the dough to the bowl, cover with the towel, and let rest for 1 hour.

7 For the third and final stretch and fold, repeat the steps for the first stretch and fold, then return the dough to the bowl, cover with the towel, and let rest for 30 minutes.

8 Line a 9-inch (23 cm) proofing basket or bowl with a clean kitchen towel and dust the towel fairly generously with the dusting mixture.

9 Lightly dust the work surface and your hands with flour and shape the dough into a round (see Shaping a Round Loaf, page 288). Dust the sides and top of the dough with the dusting mixture, fold the edges of the towel over the top, and transfer the basket or bowl to the refrigerator and chill for 16 to 20 hours.

10 Position an oven rack in the lower third of the oven. Place a covered 6-quart (5.7 L), 10-inch (25 cm) round cast-iron Dutch oven on the rack. Preheat the oven to 500°F (260°C). Remove the basket of dough from the refrigerator and let it sit at room temperature while you allow the oven to preheat for about 1 hour.

11 Using heavy-duty oven mitts or potholders, remove the Dutch oven, place it on a heatproof surface, and remove the lid.

12 Using the kitchen towel, lift and gently ease the dough out of the basket and onto a baking peel, seam-side down. Then carefully transfer it into the pot (the Dutch oven will be very hot). Score the top of the dough (see Scoring, page 290), cover the pot, and return it to the oven. Lower the oven temperature to 460°F (240°C) and bake for 30 minutes.

13 Rotate the Dutch oven and remove the lid. The loaf will already be a rich golden brown. Continue baking, uncovered, until the surface is a deep, rich brown, with some spots along the score being even slightly darker (*bien cuit*), 20 minutes longer.

14 Loosen the edges of the loaf with a long handled spoon and then with the help of the spoon lift out of the pot onto a cooling rack. When the bottom of the loaf is tapped, it should sound hollow. If not, return it to the oven and bake directly on the rack for 5 minutes longer.

15 Let the bread cool completely before slicing and eating, at least 4 hours but preferably 8 to 24 hours.

TRULY WHOLE WHEAT BREAD WITH TOASTED FARRO

Since I opened Bien Cuit, the most-requested loaf that we don't offer has been whole wheat, so I took the opportunity afforded by this book to come up with one. Although I started to develop this recipe more out of a sense of duty ("Ya gotta have whole wheat") than a true belief that the bread would be a winner, the result surprised me. It has a tremendous depth of flavor and, at long last, makes the words "whole wheat" sound not only healthy, but appetizing as well.

STARTER

200 grams (1¼ c + 3 tbsp) medium whole wheat flour
0.8 gram (¼ tsp) instant yeast
200 grams (¾ c + 1½ tbsp) water at about 60°F (15°C)

WHOLE WHEAT SOAKER

320 grams (2¼ c + 1¾ tsp) medium whole wheat flour
240 grams (1 c) water at about 60°F (15°C)

FARRO SOAKER

40 grams (1 tbsp + 2 tsp) farro or emmer berries (not sprouted)
24 grams (1 tbsp + 2 tsp) water at about 60°F (15°C)

DOUGH

80 grams (½ c + 1 tbsp) medium whole wheat flour
12 grams (2 tsp) fine sea salt
0.8 gram (¼ tsp) instant yeast
80 grams (¼ c + 1½ tbsp) water at about 60°F (15°C)
20 grams (1 tbsp) unsulfured molasses

White flour, as needed for working with the dough
Dusting Mixture (see page 35), for the lined proofing basket and the shaped loaf

FOR THE STARTER

1 Put the flour in a medium storage container. Sprinkle the yeast into the water, stir to mix, and pour over the flour. Mix with your fingers, pressing the mixture into the sides, bottom, and corners until all of the flour is wet and fully incorporated. Cover the container and let sit at room temperature for 10 to 14 hours. The starter will be at its peak at around 12 hours.

FOR THE WHEAT SOAKER

1 Put the flour in a large storage container and pour in the water. Mix with your fingers, pressing the mixture into the sides, bottom, and corners until all of the flour is wet and fully incorporated. Cover the container and let sit at room temperature for 10 to 14 hours. The soaker will be at its peak at around 12 hours.

FOR THE FARRO SOAKER

1 Preheat the oven to 400°F (205°C). Spread the farro on a quarter sheet pan and bake until toasted, about 8 minutes. Let cool completely.

2 Put the farro in a medium storage container and pour in the water. Cover with the lid, and let sit at room temperature for 6 hours. (If need be, the farro can soak for up to 10 hours, but it will have a bit less of a firm bite in the final loaf.)

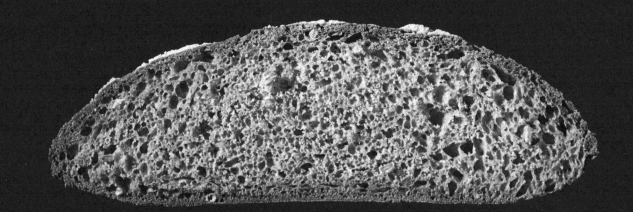

FOR THE DOUGH

1 Stir together the flour, salt, and yeast in a small bowl.

2 Pour about one-third of the water around the edges of the starter to release it from the sides of the container. Transfer the starter and water into an extra-large bowl. If need be, use a little of the remaining water to loosen the whole wheat soaker from its container. Carefully pour the whole wheat soaker into the bowl; it's dense and will splash if it goes in too quickly. Add the remaining water and the molasses. Using a wooden spoon, break the starter and soaker up as best you can to distribute them in the liquid. The mixture will be very thick.

3 Add the farro and its soaking water and all of the flour mixture; unlike most of the doughs in this book, where one-sixth of the flour is reserved at the side of the bowl, in this recipe it is all added at once. Mix with the spoon until all of the ingredients are evenly combined. Switch to a plastic bowl scraper and continue to mix until the farro is evenly distributed. At this point the dough will be very sticky to the touch.

4 Push the dough to one side of the bowl. With this dough, try to resist the urge to add too much white flour for dusting in the beginning; it will firm up considerably after the first 5 to 10 roll and tuck sequences. Roll and tuck the dough (see Rolling and Tucking, page 284), adding a small amount of white flour to the bowl and your hands as needed. Continue rolling and tucking until the dough feels stronger and begins to resist any further rolling, about 16 times. Then, with cupped hands, tuck the sides under toward the center. Place the dough, seam-side down, in a clean bowl, cover the top of the bowl with a clean kitchen towel, and let rest at room temperature for 1 hour.

5 For the first stretch and fold (see Stretching and Folding, page 285), lightly dust the work surface and your hands with flour. Using the plastic bowl scraper, release the dough from the bowl and set it, seam-side down, on the work surface. Gently stretch it into a roughly rectangular shape. Fold the dough in thirds from top to bottom and then from left to right. With cupped hands, tuck the sides under toward the center. Place the dough in the bowl, seam-side down, cover the bowl with the towel, and let rest for 1 hour.

6 For the second stretch and fold, repeat the steps for the first stretch and fold, then return the dough to the bowl, cover with the towel, and let rest for 1 hour.

7 For the third and final stretch and fold, once again repeat the steps for the first stretch and fold, then return the dough to the bowl, cover with the towel, and let rest for 20 minutes.

8 Line a 9-inch (23 cm) proofing basket or bowl with a clean kitchen towel and dust the towel fairly generously with the dusting mixture.

9 Lightly dust the work surface and your hands with flour and shape the dough into a round (see Shaping a Round Loaf, page 288). Dust the sides and top of the dough with the dusting mixture, fold the edges of the towel over the top, and transfer the basket or bowl to the refrigerator and chill for 16 hours.

10 Position an oven rack in the lower third of the oven. Place a covered 6-quart (5.7 L), 10-inch (25 cm) round cast-iron Dutch oven on the rack. Preheat the oven to 500°F (260°C). Remove the basket of dough from the refrigerator and let it sit at room temperature while you allow the oven to preheat for about 1 hour.

11 Using heavy-duty oven mitts or potholders, remove the Dutch oven, place it on a heatproof surface, and remove the lid.

12 Using the kitchen towel, lift and gently ease the dough out of the basket and onto a baking peel, seam-side down. This dough is fairly delicate. Then carefully transfer it into the pot (the Dutch oven will be very hot). Score the top of the dough (see Scoring, page 290), cover the pot, and return it to the oven. Bake for 5 minutes.

13 Lower the oven temperature to 460°F (240°C) and bake for 15 minutes.

14 Rotate the Dutch oven, keeping the lid on, and bake for 10 minutes longer. Remove the lid. The loaf will already be a rich golden brown. Continue baking, uncovered, until the surface is a deep, rich brown, with some spots along the score being even slightly darker (*bien cuit*), about 5 minutes longer.

15 Loosen the edges of the loaf with a long handled spoon and then with the help of the spoon lift out of the pot onto a cooling rack. When the bottom of the loaf is tapped, it should sound hollow. If not, return it to the oven and bake directly on the rack for 5 minutes longer.

16 Let the bread cool completely before slicing and eating, at least 4 hours but preferably 8 to 24 hours.

SOAKERS

Soaking whole grains for a good long while before adding them to dough accomplishes a few things. First, the hard grains soften, so you won't have little hard bits in your dough. But more importantly, soaking (and the extra hydration it contributes) activates enzymes in the grain, beginning the process of breaking down its starches into the sugars that provide food for the yeast. Then, when you incorporate the soaked grain into the dough, you will have already lined things up to jumpstart the fermentation process. In the course of writing this book, I discovered that making soakers with flour or ground nuts, sometimes using milk for the liquid, allows these ingredients to contribute their own unique and tasty qualities during fermentation.

PANE FRANCESE

I first tasted a bread like this when I was a *stagiaire* (a kind of a low-level apprentice) in the town of Blois in France's Loire Valley. Like most young, aspiring chefs, I rarely had the time or money to take advantage of being in such a legendary dining country. Most days I ate dinner with a local family who took in paying dinner guests. Breakfast was at the bakery, usually black tea and left-over brioche from the day before. That's what our chef ate, so that's what we ate. When I had a few extra Euros, which wasn't often, my other meals were some combination of goat cheese, local wine, lots of ratatouille, and bread.

There were three or four bakeries in town. They were good but not extraordinary, except for one bakery that made one special bread, which was creamy tasting and soft textured, thanks to a good amount of olive oil in the dough. It looked like a baguette and tasted like ciabatta (hence the Italian name by which it was known in France), but its shape was a little flatter. These breads were so good that I often consumed them en route to my room. Living as I did, in very modest circumstances, I appreciated simple pleasures when they came my way.

STARTER

300 grams (2 c + 2 tbsp) white flour
0.2 gram (pinch) instant yeast
300 grams (1¼ c) water at about 60°F (15°C)

DOUGH

500 grams (3½ c + 1 tbsp) white flour, plus additional
  as needed for working with the dough
20 grams (1 tbsp + ¼ tsp) fine sea salt
1 gram (generous ¼ tsp) instant yeast
235 grams (¾ c + 3 tbsp) cold whole milk
70 grams (¼ c + 1½ tbsp) extra-virgin olive oil

Dusting Mixture (see page 35), for the lined proofing
  basket and the shaped loaf

FOR THE STARTER

1 Put the flour in a medium storage container. Sprinkle the yeast into the water, stir to mix, and pour over the flour. Mix with your fingers, pressing the mixture into the sides, bottom, and corners until all of the flour is wet and fully incorporated. Cover the container and let sit at room temperature for 12 to 15 hours. The starter will be at its peak at around 13 hours.

FOR THE DOUGH

1 Stir together the flour, salt, and yeast in a medium bowl.

2 Pour about one-third of the milk around the edges of the starter to release it from the sides of the container. Transfer the starter and milk to an extra-large bowl along with the remaining milk and the olive oil. Using a wooden spoon, break the starter up to distribute it in the liquid.

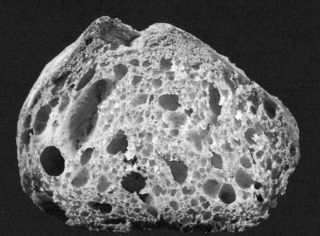

3 Add the flour mixture, reserving about one-sixth of it along the edge of the bowl (see Mixing, page 282). Continue to mix with the spoon until most of the dry ingredients have been combined with the starter mixture. Switch to a plastic bowl scraper and continue to mix until incorporated. At this point the dough will be sticky to the touch.

4 Push the dough to one side of the bowl. Roll and tuck the dough (see Rolling and Tucking, page 284), adding the reserved flour mixture and a small amount of additional flour to the bowl and your hands as needed. Continue rolling and tucking until the dough feels stronger and begins to resist any further rolling, about 10 times. Then, with cupped hands, tuck the sides under toward the center. Place the dough, seam-side down, in a clean bowl, cover the top of the bowl with a clean kitchen towel, and let rest at room temperature for 1 hour.

5 For the first stretch and fold (see Stretching and Folding, page 285), lightly dust the work surface, your hands, and a 9 by 13-inch (23 by 33 cm) baking pan with flour. Using the plastic bowl scraper, release the dough from the bowl and set it, seam-side down, on the work surface. Gently stretch it into a roughly rectangular shape. Fold the dough in thirds from top to bottom and then from left to right. With cupped

hands, tuck the sides under toward the center. Place the dough, seam-side down, in the floured baking pan, cover the pan with the towel or plastic wrap stretched tight, and let rest for 1 hour.

6 For the second and final stretch and fold, repeat the steps for the first stretch and fold, then return the dough to the pan, cover with the towel or plastic wrap, and let rest for 1 hour.

7 Line a half sheet pan with a linen liner and dust fairly generously with the dusting mixture.

8 Lightly dust the work surface and your hands with flour. Turn the dough out onto the work surface and let it spread, then gently stretch to form a 9 by 7-inch (23 by 18 cm) rectangle. Using a bench scraper, divide the dough into 4 equal pieces, each measuring about 2¼ by 7 (5.5 by 18 cm) inches. Gently stretch each into a rectangle measuring about 2 by 12 (5 by 30 cm) inches. Transfer to the lined pan, positioning the loaves across the width, rather than lengthwise. Dust the top and sides of the loaves with the dusting mixture. Fold the linen to create support walls on both sides of each loaf, then fold any extra length of the linen liner over the top or cover with a kitchen towel. Let rest at room temperature for 30 minutes.

9 Transfer the pan to the refrigerator and chill for 12 to 16 hours.

10 Set up the oven with a cast-iron skillet for steam (see Baking Stones and Steam, page 296), then preheat the oven to 500°F (260°C).

11 Using the linen liner, lift and gently flip the loaves off of the pan and onto a transfer peel. Slide the loaves onto a dusted baking peel (see Using a Transfer Peel and Baking Peel, page 311). (These loaves are not scored.) Working quickly but carefully, transfer the loaves to the stone using heavy-duty oven mitts or potholders. Pull out the hot skillet, add about 3 cups of ice cubes, then slide it back in and close the oven door. Immediately lower the oven tempera-ture to 460°F (240°C). Bake, switching the positions of the loaves about two-thirds of the way through baking, until their surface is golden brown, about 25 minutes.

12 Using the baking peel, transfer the loaves to a cooling rack. When the bottoms of the loaves are tapped, they should sound hollow. If not, return to the stone and bake for 5 minutes longer.

13 Let the bread cool completely before slicing and eating, at least 4 hours but preferably 8 to 24 hours.

If you are not comfortable working with the baguette shape, you may bake this as a round loaf in a Dutch oven.

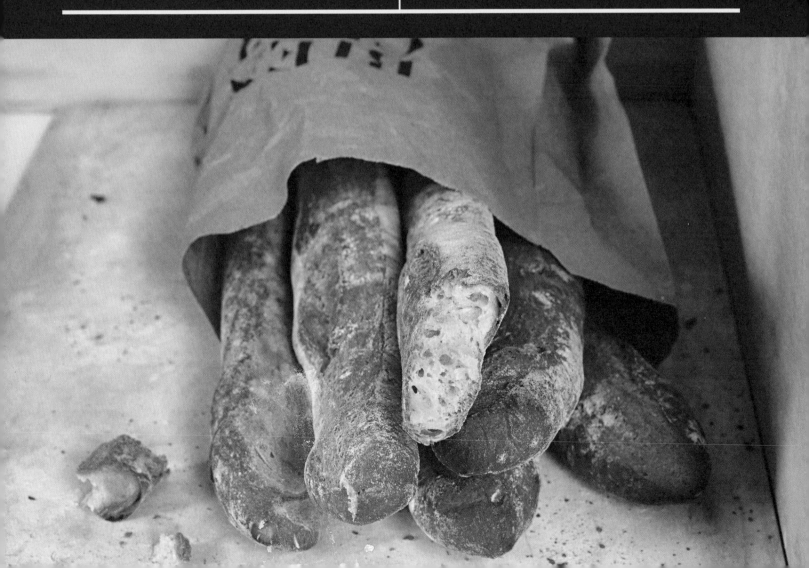

-BREAD QUEST-
LARD BREAD

Also called prosciutto bread, this delicious calorie bomb is a reliable old warhorse at Sicilian-American bakeries all over Brooklyn. I first tasted it when Peter took me to the nearby neighborhood of Carroll Gardens, where Mazzola Bakery has occupied a corner for over eighty years. On Peter's advice we bought two loaves. "We're going to devour one on the way home, so you might as well have another on hand to analyze." Then, like generations of Brooklynites, we parked ourselves on the stoop of a nearby brownstone for a munch break. I ripped off a piece and handed the bag over to Peter, who did the same. The bag already had some spots on it where the lard had seeped through.

As we sat and ate and chatted and watched the world go by, like generations of stoop sitters before us, four of NYPD's finest in a squad car from the nearby Seventy-Sixth Precinct stopped to pick up some coffee and a few pastries. Young mothers pushing strollers the size of small SUVs threaded their way behind a line of customers. By the time we had finished chatting and people watching, we had eaten our way down to the end of that first loaf, and we were as full as you feel after a second helping on Thanksgiving.

Over the next few months, we sampled more lard breads. At Caputo's Bake Shop on Court Street—which, like Mazzola's, always has a line of customers stocking up on semolina loaves and chewy onion rolls—we found a bread that was less larded and too "breadish."

Peter suggested a trip to Villabate Alba, his favorite Italian bakery, located in Bensonhurst, an old middle-to-working-class neighborhood that had not yet been gentrified into a mix of espresso bars and expensive clothing stores.

Dark wood accents everywhere, brightly lit glass cases and equally brightly colored pastries dazzle you as you pass over the threshold from the workaday neighborhood into a store that looks like nothing so much as the inside of a jewel box: creamy cannoli, mini pies filled with apricot preserves and topped with toasted pine nuts, colorful cakes topped with marzipan replicas of fresh fruits as well executed as any old master's still life, and, almost hidden in the bread section, a lard loaf which, though delicious, was not much different than the breads we had already tasted.

We got closer to the secret at G. Esposito & Sons Jersey Pork Store on Court Street. In front of the store stood a statue of a smiling and very plump pig, a giveaway that there are pork products to be had here. Salami, prosciutto, and mortadella hung in profusion from the ceiling. Pork products also filled the showcase—as did lard bread.

I asked the proprietor about those little bits of meat, largely unidentifiable, that studded the best lard breads. "I think it's called *ciccoro*," he said.

"What is it? How do they make it?"

"Not sure," he said, either because he truly wasn't sure or because you don't reveal secrets.

But *ciccoro* was all I needed to hear. Within minutes I was Googling the word on my phone. No luck. I tried "chicorro." Then "cichorro." Three strikes.

As a Hail Mary, we fired off an email to Mario Batali, who is most obliging when it comes to questions of la cucina Italiana.

"Is it *ciccioli*?" he replied, signing off with "peace thru pasta."

This time Google paid off. Ciccioli is made by rendering the fat of leftover cold cuts along with pork belly—it is essentially a kind of confit in which the bits are pressed into a cake. If you want to make an authentic old-style lard bread, you can't go to the supermarket and pick up a package in the ciccioli aisle. This is strictly a homegrown product, but well worth the trouble required to make it. The recipe below yields a bit more ciccioli than you'll need for the bread. You can use the remainder in a frittata or omelet or as a pizza topping.

CICCIOLI

One 300-gram (10½ oz) piece raw pork belly
One 225-gram (8 oz) piece prosciutto
One 225-gram (8 oz) piece uncured salami
One 150-gram (5¼ oz) piece Genoa salami
15 grams (2½ tsp) fine sea salt

STARTER

135 grams (¾ c + 3½ tbsp) buckwheat flour
0.3 gram (generous pinch) instant yeast
135 grams (½ c + 1 tbsp) water at about 60°F (15°C)

DOUGH

245 grams (1¾ c) white flour, plus additional as needed
    for working with the dough
75 grams (½ c + 1½ tsp) buckwheat flour
16 grams (1½ tbsp) medium whole wheat flour
11 grams (1¾ tsp) fine sea salt
1.5 grams (½ tsp) instant yeast
215 grams (¾ c + 2½ tbsp) water at about 60°F (15°C)
40 grams (¼ c) grated Parmigiano-Reggiano cheese

TO FILL

320 grams (11 oz) Taleggio cheese, cut into ½-inch (1.5 cm)
    chunks (no need to remove the rind)

Dusting Mixture (see page 35), for the linen liner
    and shaped loaves

FOR THE CICCIOLI

1 It will be easiest to prepare the meat if it's quite cold. If at any point it becomes difficult to cut, refrigerate it or briefly freeze it to make it easier to work with. Remove the skin from the pork belly. This can be difficult, but a sharp, serrated blade will help. Cut the pork belly into ³⁄₈-inch (1 cm) dice. Cut the prosciutto into to ¼-inch (6 mm) dice. Remove the casings from the salami and cut it into ¼-inch (6 mm) dice as well.

2 Put the pork belly in a large skillet over low heat and sprinkle with the salt. Cook, stirring frequently, to render the fat until it pools in the bottom, about 8 minutes. Add the prosciutto and continue to cook and stir until the fat on the pieces of pork belly is translucent and there is additional rendered fat from the prosciutto, about 5 minutes. Increase the heat to medium and continue to cook and stir until the meats are browned and beginning to crisp, about 8 minutes. Stir in the salami, making sure that all of the meat is cooking in the fat, preferably in an even layer. Continue to cook, scraping up and incorporating any browned bits that form on the bottom of the pan, for 8 minutes longer.

3 Remove the pan from the heat. Using a slotted spoon, transfer the meat to a storage container. You should have about 470 grams (3 c) of cooked meat, but the yield will vary depending on how much fat is in the pork belly. You will need 400 grams (about 2²⁄₃ c) of the cooked meat for this recipe. Store the remainder in the refrigerator for another use.

4 Measure the fat (from here forward called lard) remaining in the pan. You will need 45 grams (3 tbsp + 2¼ tsp) for spreading on the dough. Set that aside in a separate container. Stir the remaining lard, about 35 grams (3 tbsp), into the 400 grams (about 2²⁄₃ c) of cooked meat; this is the *ciccioli*. Refrigerate both the *ciccioli* and the lard until ready to use.

FOR THE STARTER

1 Put the flour in a medium storage container. Sprinkle the yeast into the water, stir to mix, and pour over the flour. Mix with your fingers, pressing the mixture into the sides, bottom, and corners until all of the flour is wet and fully incorporated. Cover the container and let sit at room temperature for 12 to 16 hours. The starter will be at its peak at around 14 hours.

FOR THE DOUGH

1 Stir together the white, buckwheat, and whole wheat flours, salt, and yeast in a medium bowl.

2 Pour about one-third of the water around the edges of the starter to release it from the sides of the container. Transfer the starter and water to an extra-large bowl along with the remaining water. Using a wooden spoon, break the starter up to distribute it in the water.

3 Add the flour mixture, reserving about one-sixth of it along the edge of the bowl (see Mixing, page 282). Continue to mix with the spoon until most of the dry ingredients have been combined with the starter mixture. Switch to a plastic bowl scraper and continue to mix until incorporated. At this point the dough will be just a bit sticky to the touch.

4 Push the dough to one side of the bowl. Roll and tuck the dough (see Rolling and Tucking, page 284), adding the reserved flour mixture and a small amount of additional flour to the bowl and your hands as needed. Continue rolling and tucking until the dough feels stronger and begins to resist any further rolling, about 12 times. Then, with cupped hands, tuck the sides under toward the center. Place the dough, seam-side down, in a clean bowl, cover the top of the bowl with a clean kitchen towel, and let rest at room temperature for 45 minutes.

5 For the first stretch and fold (see Stretching and Folding, page 285), lightly dust the work surface and your hands with flour. Using the plastic bowl scraper, release the dough from the bowl and set it, seam-side down, on the work surface. Gently stretch it into a roughly rectangular shape. Fold the dough in thirds from top to bottom and then from left to right.

With cupped hands, tuck the sides under toward the center. Place the dough in the bowl, seam-side down, cover the bowl with the towel, and let rest for 45 minutes.

6 Remove the *ciccioli* and the reserved 45 grams (3 tbsp + 2¼ tsp) of lard from the refrigerator. Keep an eye on both. The lard should be soft enough to spread, but not completely liquefied. The *ciccioli* should have a cakey consistency with the lard distributed evenly throughout. If necessary, the meat can be loosened by dipping the bottom of the container in warm water. Just be sure to stir it from time to time to keep the consistency even.

7 For the second stretch and fold, repeat the steps for the first stretch and fold, then return the dough to the bowl, cover with the towel, and let rest for 30 minutes.

8 For the third and final stretch and fold, gently stretch the dough into a rectangle measuring about 9 by 12 inches (23 by 30 cm). Spread the lard across the surface of the dough with a small spatula, and sprinkle the Parmigiano-Reggiano on top. (For photos of the following process, see Incorporating Add-Ins, page 292.) Roll up the dough tightly from the end closest to you; at the end of the roll the dough will be seam-side down. Turn it over, seam-side up, and gently press on the seam to flatten the dough slightly. Fold in thirds from left to right and then do about 10 more roll and tuck sequences to incorporate the lard and cheese. The dough will feel stiff for the first few roll and tuck sequences, but it will loosen as the lard is incorporated. Turn the dough seam-side down and tuck the sides under toward the center. Return the dough to the bowl, cover with the towel, and let rest for 30 minutes.

TO FILL, SHAPE, AND BAKE THE DOUGH

1 Line a half sheet pan with a silicone baking mat or parchment paper. (Cleanup will be easier with the silicone mat. This loaf will not be transferred to a different pan before baking.)

2 Lightly dust the work surface and your hands with flour. Using a bench scraper, divide the dough into 4 equal pieces. Press each into an 8-inch (20 cm) square. Spoon 100 grams (about ⅔ c) of the *ciccioli* evenly over the top of each, then scatter 80 grams (about ½ c) of the diced Taleggio over each piece of dough.

3 Working with one square at a time, start at the top and roll the dough over on itself about a quarter of the way down the square. Roll two more times, ending with the dough seam-side down. Carefully move the square to another floured spot on the work surface to be sure it isn't sticking. Gently press the top of the dough to form a rectangle measuring about 4 by 8 inches (10 by 20 cm); it's okay if some of the filling breaks through as you do so. Starting again at the top, make one fold along the length of the rectangle, folding the dough in half and ending with the seams touching. Transfer to the lined pan and repeat with the remaining rectangles. Dust the top of the loaves with the dusting mixture, then cover with a clean kitchen towel. Transfer the pan to the refrigerator and chill for 12 to 20 hours.

4 Set up the oven with a cast-iron skillet for steam (see Baking Stones and Steam, page 296), then preheat the oven to 450°F (230°C).

5 Transfer the sheet pan to the oven. (These loaves are not scored.) Using heavy-duty oven mitts or potholders, pull out the hot skillet, add about 3 cups of ice cubes, then slide it back in and close the oven door. Bake, rotating the pan about two-thirds of the way through baking, until the tops are dark and crispy, about 20 minutes. (If you used a dark buckwheat flour, it may be hard to gauge much of a color difference, but the appearance will no longer be raw.)

6 Set the sheet pan on a cooling rack. It's very likely that some cheese will have escaped during baking. Don't worry about it. If it has, give it a couple of minutes to cool. Then lift the loaves from the pan. The cheese can be pressed back onto the loaves or kept as a quick snack for the cook.

7 Let the bread cool completely before eating, about 2 hours. This bread is best eaten the day it is baked.

CIABATTA

Here is the origin story of ciabatta that I learned early in my career. According to legend, ciabatta was the bread Roman legionnaires ate just before they headed into battle. The dough was mixed by slaves treading in a trough full of flour, water, and verjus (the supertart juice of unripe grapes). The loaves themselves looked very much like a slipper—*batta* in Italian—and were said to be the same size as the sandal of a Roman soldier.

That should have been the tip-off. Look at your average ciabatta, then look at your foot. The ciabatta is bigger, right? Roman soldiers would have had to have enormous feet to fill a loaf.

It turns out that—as is often the case with food origin stories—the slave-treaded, verjus-laced ciabatta actually has less colorful and more recent roots. What appears to have happened is that French baguettes were making big inroads into the Italian bread market. Rather than surrender the Italian sandwich to the Northern invaders, a miller and baker named Arnaldo Cavallari experimented with a lot of flours and doughs before landing on a high-gluten dough based on a stiff pre-ferment. The result was the snack bread he named ciabatta.

If you want to test your skill with a goopy dough, here's your chance. That said, ciabatta looks a lot harder to work with than it really is, although patience is required for a successful outcome. You will definitely need to use a bit more flour during the stretch and fold and shaping phases. Then, for the final stages of fermentation, this dough sits at room temperature for 3 hours, a step that's best done on a floured wooden board.

STARTER

250 grams (1¾ c + 1 tbsp) white flour
0.2 gram (pinch) instant yeast
250 grams (1 c + 2 tsp) water at about 60°F (15°C)

DOUGH

500 grams (3½ c + 1 tbsp) white flour, plus additional
as needed for working with the dough
20 grams (1 tbsp + ¼ tsp) fine sea salt
2 grams (½ tsp) instant yeast
450 grams (1¾ c + 2 tbsp) water at about 60°F (15°C)
25 grams (1 tbsp + 1 tsp) honey
25 grams (2 tbsp) extra-virgin olive oil

Dusting Mixture (see page 35), for the sheet pans

FOR THE STARTER

1 Put the flour in a medium storage container. Sprinkle the yeast into the water, stir to mix, and pour over the flour. Mix with your fingers, pressing the mixture into the sides, bottom, and corners until all of the flour is wet and fully incorporated. Cover the container and let sit at room temperature for 10 to 15 hours. The starter will be at its peak at around 12 hours.

FOR THE DOUGH

1 Spray two large storage containers, each about 2 quarts (1.9 L) and preferably round, generously with nonstick cooking spray, or oil them generously with a neutral oil.

2 Stir together the flour, salt, and yeast in a medium bowl.

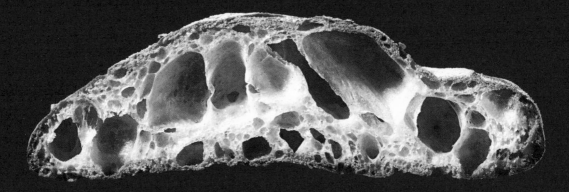

3 Pour about one-third of the water around the edges of the starter to release it from the sides of the container. Transfer the starter and water to an extra-large bowl along with the remaining water, the honey, and the oil. Using a wooden spoon, break the starter up to distribute it in the liquid. Add the flour mixture and stir vigorously with a wooden spoon for 1 minute.

4 Pour the dough, which will have a texture a little thicker than pancake batter, into one of the sprayed containers. Cover the container and let the dough rest for 45 minutes.

5 For the first stretch and fold (see Stretching and Folding, page 285), generously dust the work surface, the plastic bowl scraper, and your hands with flour. Using the scraper, release the batter-like dough from the bowl and onto the work surface. Lightly dust the second storage container with flour.

6 With the scraper (and your hands, if needed), do your best to fold the dough in thirds from top to bottom and then from left to right. This fold may be difficult with the batter still being soupy, but it should have enough stretch that it's manageable. With the scraper, tuck the sides under toward the center and then lift the dough, placing it seam-side down in the

second prepared container. Cover the container and let the dough rest for 45 minutes.

7 For the second stretch and fold, repeat the steps for the first stretch and fold, then return the dough to the container, cover, and let rest for 45 minutes.

8 For the third stretch and fold, once again repeat the steps for the first stretch and fold, then return the dough to the container, cover, and let rest for 45 minutes.

9 For the fourth and final stretch and fold, repeat the steps for the first stretch and fold, then return the dough to the container, cover, and let rest for 30 minutes.

10 Transfer the container to the refrigerator and chill for 12 to 18 hours.

11 Using a plastic bowl scraper, turn the dough out onto a generously floured work surface (for these loaves, preferably a butcher block or large wooden board). The dough will spread on its own. Divide the dough into 2 equal pieces and gently coax each piece into a rough rectangle. Cover the loaves, preferably with a plastic tub or a clean cardboard box; if neither is available, spray plastic wrap with nonstick cooking spray or oil it and lay it over the loaves (at the end of the final fermentation, be sure to remove the plastic carefully so as to not deflate the dough).

12 Let the dough rest until the loaves have increased substantially in volume (about doubled in size), about 3 hours. (The amount of time can vary significantly depending on the temperature of the room.) Dust one finger with flour and press it into the dough. The imprint should remain. If it doesn't, leave the dough to ferment until it does. If fermenting under a tub, check from time to time to make sure the top of the dough is soft. If at any point a skin begins to form, give it a light spritz of water with a spray bottle.

13 Set up the oven with a cast-iron skillet for steam (see Baking Stones and Steam, page 296, being sure to read about baking multiple loaves), then preheat the oven to 480°F (250°C).

14 Line two half sheet pans with parchment paper and dust with the dusting mixture. Position the first lined pan close to one piece of the dough. Uncover that piece of dough, leaving the second piece covered.

15 The next steps are done as a series of consecutive events. Gently flip the first piece of dough over onto your hands. Bring your thumbs and fingers together and gently stretch the width of the dough from top to bottom to make a rectangle about 1½ inches (4 cm) thick; the exact size doesn't matter as much as the thickness. Place it on a sheet pan. Be sure to keep the second piece of dough covered while the first one bakes.

16 Put the pan in the oven. Using heavy-duty oven mitts or potholders, pull out the hot skillet, add about 3 cups of ice cubes, then slide it back in and close the oven door. Immediately lower the oven temperature to 440°F (225°C) and bake the first loaf, rotating the pan about two-thirds of the way through baking, until golden brown, about 20 minutes.

17 Carefully transfer the loaf to a cooling rack. When the bottom of the loaf is tapped, it should sound hollow. If not, return it to the oven and bake directly on the rack for 5 minutes longer.

18 Carefully remove the skillet and pour out any remaining water. Set the skillet back on the lower rack and let the oven temperature return to 480°F (250°C). Bake the second loaf in the same way, again using about 3 cups of ice to create steam.

19 Let the bread cool completely before slicing and eating, at least 2 hours. This bread is best eaten the day it is baked.

PANE DOLCE

Like all chefs (and business owners), I can't stand waste, but waste is what you inevitably get when you make croissants. Because of the way they are shaped and rolled, there will always be less-than-perfect-looking ends. Instead of throwing them away, we use that rich, yeasty dough to make the starter we use for the next day's croissants. However, it doesn't take much of this dough to start a batch of croissants, so I still had excess that was going to waste.

This kept nagging at me until I came up with the idea of using the dough to make a sweet bread. I approached one of my bakers, a Uruguayan named Walter, and asked him to shape the leftover croissant dough into long tubes. I knew this dough could benefit from even more fermentation, and my guess was that the added fermentation time would provide a big boost in flavor, both from the yeast and from the lactic acid in the milk.

So Walter gave the tube-shaped loaves another 15 hours of fermenting time. The bakery smelled like a cross between a ripe banana and an open bottle of rum: yeast and alcohol pushed to their practical limit. Once baked, the result was a deliciously addictive bread I wanted to call *pain sucrée* or "sweet bread." Walter, on the other hand, was in love with all things Italian and lobbied for *pane dolce*. As I thought about it, the bread was soft and sweet, like many Italian breads, so Walter won the day.

If you don't have leftover croissant dough on hand, the second starter in this recipe works just as well. One final note: As you'll see, this recipe employs two different starters, with varying amounts of water, flour, and yeast. This approach yields breads with a fuller flavor profile than those made with a single starter.

STARTER

75 grams (½ c + 1½ tsp) white flour
0.2 gram (pinch) instant yeast
75 grams (¼ c + 1 tbsp) water at about 60°F (15°C)

SECOND STARTER

50 grams (¼ c + 2 tbsp) white flour
5 grams (1¼ tsp) granulated sugar
1 gram (generous ⅛ tsp) fine sea salt
0.2 gram (pinch) instant yeast
44 grams (2 tbsp + 2¼ tsp) cold whole milk

DOUGH

500 grams (3½ c + 1 tbsp) white flour, plus additional
    as needed for working with the dough, and for the
    linen liner and shaped loaves
100 grams (½ c) granulated sugar
13 grams (2¼ tsp) fine sea salt
4 grams (1¼ tsp) instant yeast
150 grams (½ c + 1½ tbsp) cold whole milk
150 grams (½ c + 1½ tbsp) eggs, lightly beaten
100 grams (7 tbsp) unsalted butter, at room temperature

EGG WASH

1 large egg (about 50 grams)
2 grams (¼ + ⅛ tsp) fine sea salt
20 grams (1 tbsp + 1 tsp) water

30 grams (3 tbsp) pearl sugar or other sugar with
    large granules, such as turbinado

FOR THE STARTER

1 Put the flour in a medium storage container. Sprinkle the yeast into the water, stir to mix, and pour over the flour. Mix with your fingers, pressing the mixture into the sides, bottom, and corners until all of the flour is wet and fully incorporated. Cover the container and let sit at room temperature for 12 to 15 hours. The starter will be at its peak at around 13 hours.

FOR THE SECOND STARTER

1 Stir together the flour, sugar, salt, and yeast in a medium storage container. Pour in the milk. Mix with your fingers, pressing the mixture into the sides, bottom, and corners until all of the flour is wet and fully incorporated. This starter is best if covered and left at room temperature for 6 hours, then chilled in the refrigerator for 6 hours. But if the timing is better, you can also leave it at room temperature for 2 to 3 hours and then move it to the refrigerator to chill for 9 to 12 hours.

FOR THE DOUGH

1 Stir together the flour, sugar, salt, and yeast in a medium bowl.

2 Pour about one-third of the milk around the edges of each of the starters to release them from the sides of the containers. Transfer the starters and milk to an extra-large bowl along with the remaining milk and the eggs. Using a wooden spoon, break up the starters to distribute them in the liquid.

3 Add the flour mixture, reserving about one-sixth of it along the edge of the bowl (see Mixing, page 282). Continue to mix with the spoon until most of the dry ingredients have been combined with the starter mixture. Switch to a plastic bowl scraper and continue to mix until incorporated. At this point the dough will be slightly sticky to the touch.

4 Push the dough to one side of the bowl. Roll and tuck the dough (see Rolling and Tucking, page 284), adding the reserved flour mixture and a small amount of additional flour to the bowl and your hands as needed. Continue rolling and tucking until the dough feels stronger and begins to resist any further rolling, about 12 times. Then, with cupped hands, tuck the sides under toward the center. Place the dough, seam-side down, in a clean bowl, cover the top of the bowl with a clean kitchen towel, and let rest at room temperature for 45 minutes.

5 For the first stretch and fold (see Stretching and Folding, page 285), lightly dust the work surface and your hands with flour. With the plastic bowl scraper, release the dough from the bowl and set it, seam-side down, on the work surface. Gently stretch it into a roughly rectangular shape. Fold the dough in thirds from top to bottom and then from left to right. With cupped hands, tuck the sides under toward the center. Place the dough in the bowl, seam-side down, cover the bowl with the towel, and let rest for 45 minutes.

6 For the second stretch and fold, repeat the steps for the first stretch and fold, then return the dough to the bowl, cover with the towel, and let rest for 45 minutes.

7 For the third stretch and fold, gently stretch the dough into a rectangle. Pinch the butter into pieces, distributing them over the top of the dough. Using your fingers or a spatula, spread the butter across the surface of the dough. (For photos of the following process, see Incorporating Add-Ins, page 292.) Roll up the dough tightly from the end closest to you; at the end of the roll the dough will be seam-side down. Turn it over, seam-side up, and gently press on the seam to flatten the dough slightly. Fold in thirds from left to right and then do 4 or 5 roll and tuck sequences to incorporate the butter. Turn the dough seam-side down and tuck the sides under toward the center. Return the dough to the bowl, cover with the towel, and let rest for 45 minutes.

8 For the fourth and final stretch and fold, repeat the steps for the first stretch and fold, then return

the dough to the bowl, cover with the towel, and let rest for 20 minutes.

9 Line a half sheet pan with a linen liner and dust fairly generously with white flour.

10 Lightly dust the work surface and your hands with flour. Using a bench scraper, divide the dough into 3 equal pieces. Press each into a 6-inch (15 cm) square, then roll into a loose tube about 6 inches (15 cm) long (see Shaping a Tube or Oval Loaf, page 294). Let rest for 5 minutes. Press each piece out again and then shape into a very tight tube about 9 inches (23 cm) long. Transfer to the lined pan, seam-side up, positioning the loaves across the width of the pan, rather than lengthwise. Dust the top and sides of the loaves with flour. Fold the linen to create support walls on both sides of each loaf, then fold any extra length of the linen liner over the top or cover with a kitchen towel. Transfer the pan to the refrigerator and chill for 16 to 24 hours.

11 About 1 hour before baking, set up the oven with a baking stone and a cast-iron skillet for steam (see Baking Stones and Steam, page 296), then preheat the oven to 460°F (240°C).

12 Using the linen liner, lift and gently flip the loaves off the pan onto a transfer peel, seam-side down. Slide the loaves, still seam-side down, onto a dusted baking peel (see Using a Transfer Peel and Baking Peel, page 311). Score the top of each (see Scoring, page 290); these loaves should be scored more deeply than usual: about ¾ inch (6 mm) deep. Brush the tops of the loaves with the egg wash, then sprinkle 10 grams (1 tbsp) of the pearl sugar over each loaf. Working quickly but carefully, transfer the loaves to the stone using heavy-duty oven mitts or potholders. Pull out the hot skillet, add about 3 cups of ice cubes, then slide it back in and close the oven door. Immediately lower the oven temperature to 400°F (205°C). Bake, switching the positions of the loaves about two-thirds of the way through baking, until the crust is rich golden brown, about 25 minutes.

13 Using the baking peel, transfer the loaves to a cooling rack. When the bottoms of the loaves are tapped, they should sound hollow. If not, return to the stone and bake for 5 minutes longer.

14 Let the bread cool completely before slicing and eating, at least 4 hours but preferably 8 to 24 hours.

FOR THE EGG WASH

1 In a small bowl, beat together the egg, salt, and water. Let sit at room temperature for 1 hour, then refrigerate until ready to use (overnight is fine). Give the egg wash a quick stir before using it.

2 Remove the sheet pan from the refrigerator and let the loaves sit at room temperature for 1½ hours.

WHITE PULLMAN LOAF

I think of my Pullman Loaf as what white bread could be if it had the maximum amount of flavor it could aspire to. Much of that comes from the fact that the dough is highly enriched with milk and eggs, making for very full flavor and velvety soft crumb. Underneath the soft texture and light sweetness, you will detect a pleasant hint of sharpness that comes from the fermented milk. That's a good thing. It gives the taste some structure and character instead of being the mushy experience typical of so many white breads. The element that truly elevates this white bread is the starter. In my bakery, we use leftover dough from the previous day's croissants (in French baking parlance, old dough used in this way is known as *pâte fermentée*). However, if you haven't made any croissants lately, you can easily mix up the starter in this recipe.

Note: I don't take the temperature of the milk in this recipe. I measure and cover it and let it sit in the kitchen for about an hour before I begin to scale the ingredients for the dough.

STARTER

50 grams (¼ c + 2 tbsp) white flour
5 grams (1¼ tsp) granulated sugar
1 gram (generous ⅛ tsp) fine sea salt
0.2 gram (pinch) instant yeast
44 grams (2 tbsp + 2¼ tsp) cold whole milk

DOUGH

500 grams (3½ c + 1 tbsp) white flour, plus additional
    as needed for working with the dough
50 grams (¼ c) granulated sugar
9 grams (1½ tsp) fine sea salt
4 grams (1¼ tsp) instant yeast
325 grams (1¼ c + 2 tbsp) cold whole milk,
    plus additional for brushing the top of the dough
75 grams (¼ c + 2¼ tsp) eggs, lightly beaten
50 grams (7 tbsp) unsalted butter, at room temperature,
    plus additional for the pan and brushing the
    top of the dough

FOR THE STARTER

1 Stir together the flour, sugar, salt, and yeast in a medium storage container. Pour in the milk. Mix with your fingers, pressing the mixture into the sides, bottom, and corners until all of the flour is wet and fully incorporated. This starter is best if covered and left at room temperature for 6 hours, then chilled in the refrigerator for 6 hours. But if the timing is better, you can also leave it at room temperature for 2 to 3 hours and then move it to the refrigerator to chill for 9 to 12 hours.

FOR THE DOUGH

1 Stir together the flour, sugar, salt, and yeast in a medium bowl.

2 Pour about one-third of the milk around the edges of the starter to release it from the sides of the container. Transfer the starter and milk to an extra-large bowl along with the remaining milk and the eggs. Using a wooden spoon, break the starter up to distribute it in the liquid.

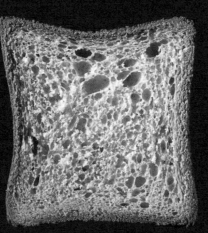

3 Add the flour mixture, reserving about one-sixth of it along the edge of the bowl (see Mixing, page 282). Continue to mix with the spoon until most of the dry ingredients have been combined with the starter mixture. Switch to a plastic bowl scraper and continue to mix until incorporated. At this point the dough will be slightly sticky to the touch.

4 Push the dough to one side of the bowl. Roll and tuck the dough (see Rolling and Tucking, page 284), adding the reserved flour mixture and a small amount of additional flour to the bowl and your hands as needed. Continue rolling and tucking until the dough feels stronger and begins to resist any further rolling, about 15 times. Then, with cupped hands, tuck the sides under toward the center. Let rest for 5 minutes.

5 For the first stretch and fold (see Stretching and Folding, page 285), lightly dust the work surface and your hands with flour. Gently stretch the dough into a rectangle. Pinch the butter into pieces, distributing them over the top of the dough. Using your fingers or a spatula, spread the butter across the surface of the dough. (For photos of the following process, see Incorporating Add-Ins, page 292.) Roll up the dough tightly from the end closest to you; at the end of the roll the dough will be seam-side down. Turn it over,

seam-side up, and gently press on the seam to flatten the dough slightly. Fold in thirds from left to right and then do 4 or 5 roll and tuck sequences to incorporate the butter. Turn the dough seam-side down and tuck the sides under toward the center. Place the dough, seam-side down, in a clean bowl, cover the top of the bowl with a clean kitchen towel, and let rest at room temperature for 45 minutes.

6 For the second stretch and fold, use the plastic bowl scraper to release the dough from the bowl and set it, seam-side down, on the work surface. Gently stretch it into a roughly rectangular shape. Fold the dough in thirds from top to bottom and then from left to right. With cupped hands, tuck the sides under toward the center. Place the dough in the bowl, seam-side down, cover the bowl with the towel, and let rest for 45 minutes.

7 For the third and final stretch and fold, once again repeat the steps for the first stretch and fold, then return the dough to the bowl, cover with the towel, and let rest for 45 minutes.

8 Butter the bottom and sides of a 13 by 4 by 4-inch (33 by 10 by 10 cm) Pullman loaf pan.

9 Lightly dust the work surface and your hands with flour. Press the dough into a 10-inch (25 cm) square and then roll into a loose tube about 10 inches (25 cm) long (see Shaping a Tube or Oval Loaf, page 294). Let rest for 5 minutes. Press the dough out again and then shape into a tight tube about 12 inches (30 cm) long. Place the tube, seam-side down, in the prepared pan. Spread some butter over the top of the dough and cover the top of the pan with plastic wrap. Let ferment at room temperature until the dough rises to about ½ inch (1.5 cm) from the top of the pan, 3½ to 4 hours.

10 Position an oven rack in the center of the oven, then preheat the oven to 425°F (220°C).

11 Gently brush milk across the top of the dough and bake for 10 minutes. Lower the oven temperature to 380°F (195°C) and bake for 10 minutes. Rotate the pan and bake for 10 minutes longer.

12 Remove the pan from the oven. Carefully turn the bread out of the pan, then return the loaf to the oven and bake directly on the rack to brown the sides a bit more, about 5 minutes.

13 Transfer the bread to a cooling rack and let cool completely before slicing and eating, at least 4 hours but preferably 8 to 24 hours.

HAZELNUT BREAD

As with many of my recipes, this one started out as a daydream. Shortly after I opened Bien Cuit, the oven gave us some problems. A French-Russian immigrant named Serge was able to repair it and got us up and running with minimal pain to the business and my psyche. We really hit it off, and when my daughter was born, Serge, who is a thoughtful guy, gave me a bottle of walnut wine.

   With the clarity brought on by a few glasses of Serge's walnut wine came an idea: Fermented walnuts…Now there's a concept! Then, realizing that all nuts can be fermented, I landed on hazelnuts for this bread. I soaked chopped hazelnuts in water for 36 hours to allow ample time for fermentation before blending them to make hazelnut milk. I hit upon the further notion of adding toasted hazelnut flour, sugar, and cow's milk to the dough and letting it continue to ferment for a good long time. So in this recipe, you have all kinds of ingredients fermenting at different rates and then coming together for a broad, balanced, and truly exquisite bread.

HAZELNUT MILK

100 grams (½ c + 3 tbsp) skinned hazelnuts
200 grams (¾ c + 1½ tbsp) warm water

STARTER

50 grams (¼ c + 2 tbsp) white flour
5 grams (1¼ tsp) granulated sugar
1 gram (generous ⅛ tsp) fine sea salt
0.2 gram (pinch) instant yeast
44 grams (2 tbsp + 2¼ tsp) cold whole milk

DOUGH

115 grams (1 c + 1½ tsp) hazelnut flour or meal
400 grams (2¾ c + 2 tbsp) white flour, plus additional
      as needed for working with the dough, and for the
      linen liner and shaped loaves
60 grams (¼ c + 2½ tsp) granulated sugar
15 grams (2½ tsp) fine sea salt
2 grams (½ tsp) instant yeast
75 grams (¼ c + 2 tsp) cold whole milk
50 grams (3½ tbsp) unsalted butter, at room temperature

FOR THE HAZELNUT MILK

1 Put the hazelnuts in a medium heatproof container. Add the water, cover the container, and let sit at room temperature for 24 hours.

FOR THE STARTER

1 Stir together the flour, sugar, salt, and yeast in a medium storage container. Pour in the milk. Mix with your fingers, pressing the mixture into the sides, bottom, and corners until all of the flour is wet and fully incorporated. This starter is best if covered and left at room temperature for 6 hours, then chilled in the refrigerator for 6 hours. But if the timing is better, you can also leave it at room temperature for 2 to 3 hours and then move it to the refrigerator to chill for 9 to 12 hours.

FOR THE DOUGH

1 Preheat the oven to 425°F (220°C). Spread the hazelnut flour on a half sheet pan and toast until golden brown and aromatic, 5 to 6 minutes. Let cool completely. The flour will decrease slightly in weight

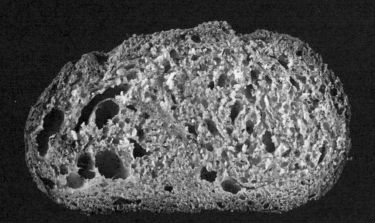

when toasted. You will need 100 grams (1 cup) for this recipe.

2 Transfer the hazelnuts and their soaking water to a blender, preferably a high-powered one, and process into a smooth puree.

3 Stir together the white and toasted hazelnut flours, sugar, salt, and yeast in a medium bowl.

4 Pour the cold whole milk around the edges of the starter to release it from the sides of the container. Transfer the starter and milk to an extra-large bowl along with the hazelnut milk. Using a wooden spoon, break the starter up to distribute it in the liquid.

5 Add the flour mixture, reserving about one-sixth of it along the edge of the bowl (see Mixing, page 282). Continue to mix with the spoon until most of the dry ingredients have been combined with the starter mixture. Switch to a plastic bowl scraper and continue to mix until incorporated. At this point the dough will be very sticky to the touch.

6 Push the dough to one side of the bowl. Roll and tuck the dough (see Rolling and Tucking, page 284), adding the reserved flour mixture and a small amount of additional flour to the bowl and your

hands as needed. Continue rolling and tucking until the dough feels stronger and begins to resist any further rolling, about 12 times. Then, with cupped hands, tuck the sides under toward the center. Place the dough, seam-side down, in a clean bowl, cover the top of the bowl with a clean kitchen towel, and let rest at room temperature for 45 minutes.

7 For the first stretch and fold (see Stretching and Folding, page 285), lightly dust the work surface and your hands with flour. Using the plastic bowl scraper, release the dough from the bowl and set it, seam-side down, on the work surface. The dough will be slightly sticky for this fold (as well as the others, but slightly less each time). Gently stretch it into a roughly rectangular shape. Fold the dough in thirds from top to bottom and then from left to right. With cupped hands, tuck the sides under toward the center. Place the dough in the bowl, seam-side down, cover the bowl with the towel, and let rest for 45 minutes.

8 For the second stretch and fold, repeat the steps for the first stretch and fold, then return the dough to the bowl, cover with the towel, and let rest for 30 minutes.

9 For the third and final stretch and fold, gently stretch the dough into a rectangle. Pinch the butter into pieces, distributing them over the top of the dough. Using your fingers or a spatula, spread the butter across the surface of the dough. (For photos of the following process, see Incorporating Add-Ins, page 292.) Roll up the dough tightly from the end closest to you; at the end of the roll the dough will be seam-side down. Turn it over, seam-side up, and gently press on the seam to flatten the dough slightly. Fold in thirds from left to right and then do 4 or 5 roll and tuck sequences to incorporate the butter. Turn the dough seam-side down and tuck the sides under toward the center. Return the dough to the bowl, cover with the towel, and let rest for 20 minutes.

10 Line a half sheet pan with a linen liner and dust fairly generously with white flour.

11 Lightly dust the work surface and your hands with flour. Using a bench scraper, divide the dough into 4 equal pieces. Press each piece into a 5-inch (13 cm) square, then roll into a loose tube about 5 inches (13 cm) long (see Shaping a Tube or Oval Loaf, page 294). Let rest for 5 minutes. Press each piece out again and then shape into a very tight tube about 8 inches (20 cm) long. Transfer to the lined pan, seam-side up, positioning the loaves across the width of the pan, rather than lengthwise. Dust the top and sides of the loaves with flour. Fold the linen to create support walls on both sides of each loaf, then fold any extra length of the linen liner over the top or cover with a kitchen towel. Let rest at room temperature for 1 hour.

12 Transfer the bowl to the refrigerator and chill for 12 to 16 hours.

13 Set up the oven with a baking stone and a cast-iron skillet for steam (see Baking Stones and Steam, page 296), then preheat the oven to 480°F (250°C).

14 Using the linen liner, lift and gently flip the loaves off the pan and onto a transfer peel, seam-side down. Slide the loaves, still seam-side down, onto a dusted baking peel (see Using a Transfer Peel and Baking Peel, page 311). Score the top of each (see Scoring, page 290). Working quickly but carefully, transfer the loaves to the stone using heavy-duty oven mitts or potholders. Pull out the hot skillet, add about 3 cups of ice cubes, then slide it back in and close the oven door. Immediately lower the oven temperature to 410°F (210°C). Bake, switching the positions of the loaves about two-thirds of the way through baking, until the crust is a rich golden brown, about 40 minutes.

15 Using the baking peel, transfer the loaves to a cooling rack. When the bottoms of the loaves are tapped, they should sound hollow. If not, return to the stone and bake for 5 minutes longer.

16 Let the bread cool completely before slicing and eating, at least 4 hours but preferably 8 to 24 hours.

CHESTNUT HOLIDAY BREAD

Through much of Europe, especially in antiquity, chestnuts were an important source of starch and protein before the introduction of wheat and, later, potatoes. This is not the cheapest bread in the book, simply because a can or jar of peeled chestnuts costs more than typical baking ingredients. However, you might find it a bit of a pain to roast and peel chestnuts. (I definitely do.) If you purchase peeled chestnuts, it becomes a simple dump and stir process.

As in the Hazelnut Bread (page 111), for this recipe I use a nut puree with milk, which ferments alongside a more traditional starter. Then, as I do in my Pan Pugliese (page 37) and Kørntüberbrot (page 41), I incorporate chunks of the featured ingredient (in this case, chestnuts) into the dough to create islands of contrasting texture and flavor in the finished loaf. As for the currants, well, those seemed appropriate for a holiday-themed bread. Come to think of it, while I'm doing this mini inventory of the inspirations for this bread, they're informed by an impulse similar to that behind my Raisin Walnut Bread (page 132), only sweeter and with a softer crumb.

STARTER

50 grams (¼ c + 2 tbsp) white flour

5 grams (1¼ tsp) granulated sugar

1 gram (generous ⅛ tsp) fine sea salt

0.2 gram (pinch) instant yeast

44 grams (2 tbsp + 2¼ tsp) cold whole milk

CHESTNUT MILK

150 grams (½ c + 2 tbsp) chestnut puree

350 grams (1¼ c + 2½ tbsp) cold whole milk

0.2 gram (pinch) fine sea salt

DOUGH

500 grams (3½ c + 1 tbsp) white flour, plus additional
as needed for working with the dough, and for the linen
liner and shaped loaves

40 grams (3½ tbsp) granulated sugar

15 grams (2½ tsp) fine sea salt

5 grams (1½ tsp) instant yeast

60 grams (3½ tbsp) cold whole milk

45 grams (2 tbsp) Grade A maple syrup

150 grams (1 c) coarsely chopped roasted chestnuts

75 grams (¼ c + 3½ tbsp) dried currants

FOR THE STARTER

1 Stir together the flour, sugar, salt, and yeast in a medium storage container. Pour in the milk. Mix with your fingers, pressing the mixture into the sides, bottom, and corners until all of the flour is wet and fully incorporated. This starter is best if covered and left at room temperature for 6 hours, then chilled in the refrigerator for 6 hours. But if the timing is better, you can also leave it at room temperature for 2 to 3 hours and then move it to the refrigerator to chill for 9 to 12.

FOR THE CHESTNUT MILK

1 Whisk the chestnut puree, milk, and salt together in a medium saucepan and heat, stirring often, until steaming but not simmering, about 164°F (73°C). Remove from the heat and let cool to room temperature. Whisk again and refrigerate until ready to use.

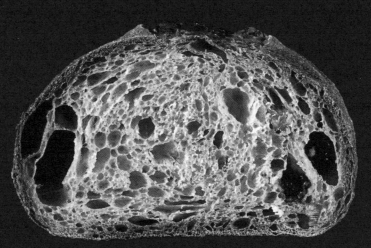

FOR THE DOUGH

1 Stir together the flour, sugar, salt, and yeast in a medium bowl.

2 Whisk the chestnut milk, then pour about one-third of it around the edges of the starter to release it from the sides of the container. Transfer the starter and chestnut milk to an extra-large bowl along with the remaining chestnut milk, the milk, and the maple syrup. Using a wooden spoon, break the starter up to distribute it in the liquid.

3 Add the flour mixture, reserving about one-sixth of it along the edge of the bowl (see Mixing, page 282). Continue to mix with the spoon until most of the dry ingredients have been combined with the starter mixture. Switch to a plastic bowl scraper and continue to mix until incorporated. At this point the dough will be very sticky to the touch and have an almost gluey texture.

4 Push the dough to one side of the bowl. Roll and tuck the dough (see Rolling and Tucking, page 284), adding the reserved flour mixture and a small amount of additional flour to the bowl and your hands as needed, until the dough feels stronger and begins to resist any further rolling, about 16 times.

Then, with cupped hands, tuck the sides under toward the center. Place the dough, seam-side down, in a clean bowl, cover the top of the bowl with a clean kitchen towel, and let rest at room temperature for 45 minutes.

5 For the first stretch and fold (see Stretching and Folding, page 285), lightly dust the work surface and your hands with flour. Using the plastic bowl scraper, release the dough from the bowl and set it, seam-side down, on the work surface. Gently stretch it into a roughly rectangular shape. Fold the dough in thirds from top to bottom and then from left to right. With cupped hands, tuck the sides under toward the center. Place the dough in the bowl, seam-side down, cover the bowl with the towel, and let rest for 45 minutes.

6 For the second stretch and fold, gently stretch the dough into a rectangle, scatter the chopped chestnuts and the currants evenly over the top, and press them gently into the dough. (For photos of the following process, see Incorporating Add-Ins, page 292.) Roll up the dough tightly from the end closest to you; at the end of the roll the dough will be seam-side down. Turn it over, seam-side up, and gently press on the seam to flatten the dough slightly. Fold in thirds from left to right and then do 1 roll and tuck sequence to incorporate the chestnuts and currants. Turn the dough seam-side down and tuck the sides under toward the center. Return the dough to the bowl, cover with the towel, and let rest for 45 minutes.

7 For the third and final stretch and fold, repeat the steps for the first stretch and fold, then return the dough to the bowl, cover with the towel, and let rest for 30 minutes.

8 Line a half sheet pan with a linen liner and dust fairly generously with white flour.

9 Lightly dust the work surface and your hands with flour. Using a bench scraper, divide the dough into 4 equal pieces. Press each piece into a 5-inch (13 cm) square, then roll into a loose tube about 5 inches (13 cm) long (see Shaping a Tube or Oval Loaf, page 294). Let rest for 5 minutes. Press each piece out again and then shape into a very tight tube about 8 inches (20 cm) long. Transfer to the lined pan, seam-side up, positioning the loaves across the width of the pan, rather than lengthwise. Dust the top and sides of the loaves with flour. Fold the linen to create support walls on both sides of each loaf, then fold any extra length of the linen liner over the top or cover with a kitchen towel. Transfer the pan to the refrigerator and chill for 14 to 20 hours.

10 Set up the oven with a baking stone and a cast-iron skillet for steam (see Baking Stones and Steam, page 296), then preheat the oven to 480°F (250°C).

11 Using the linen liner, lift and gently flip the loaves off the pan and onto a transfer peel, seam-side down. Slide the loaves, still seam-side down, onto a dusted baking peel (see Using a Transfer Peel and Baking Peel, page 311). Score the top of each (see Scoring, page 290). Working quickly but carefully, transfer the loaves to the stone using heavy-duty oven mitts or potholders. Pull out the hot skillet, add about 3 cups of ice cubes, then slide it back in and close the oven door. Immediately lower the oven temperature to 410°F (210°C). Bake, switching the positions of the loaves about two-thirds of the way through baking, until the crust is a rich golden brown, about 40 minutes.

12 Using the baking peel, transfer the loaves to a cooling rack. When the bottoms of the loaves are tapped, they should sound hollow. If not, return to the stone and bake for 5 minutes longer.

13 Let the bread cool completely before slicing and eating, at least 4 hours but preferably 8 to 24 hours.

MEDITERRANEAN MARINER BREAD

When I worked in Las Vegas, there were two Italian chefs who served my breads. One of them, a very food-wise Tuscan, caught my imagination with an old sea tale. He'd heard a myth that Mediterranean fisherman on longer voyages made a bread with the liquid used for curing anchovies in place of salt. An email to Mario Batali produced a reference to *Apicius*, an ancient collection of Roman recipes. Nosing around the Internet led me to a mention of a medieval manuscript that recommended bread seasoned with *colatura di alici*, a liquid pressed from salted anchovies. This idea remained stuck in my head as something I'd do when I had the time.

When we started this book, Peter asked me if there was one bread that I had thought about making but had never got around to. The mariner's bread popped up immediately in my mental file cabinet. This book was all the excuse I needed to take a few days to perfect a recipe, though it did require testing thirteen different iterations before I hit on the formula in this recipe. It has the soft crumb of a sweet bread, but all the savoriness of anchovies—tightly focused by the addition of a barely noticeable trace of cloves, a favorite ingredient in Italian food in olden days. Try this bread toasted and topped with a roasted red bell pepper and a couple of anchovy fillets, or with a slice of cold lamb or roast beef. When eaten with other foods, the fish flavor recedes and serves as an excellent seasoning.

I found *colatura di alici* at Il Buco Alimentari e Vineria, a wonderful restaurant and provisions shop in Manhattan. But you can also order it from better Italian food stores or from Amazon.com. (The main brand appears to be Colatura di Alici di Cetara.) In addition to being useful in the occasional bread, it's lovely in pasta sauce, on vegetables such as cauliflower, and drizzled on a pan-roasted steak or lamb chop.

Even though this bread has a salty flavor from the *colatura di alici*, the salt on top is a nice addition. Maldon, a flaky salt from Britain, gives a textural contrast to the soft bread, but any sea salt or even kosher salt will do the trick. Just don't used iodized table salt.

STARTER

100 grams (½ c + 3½ tbsp) white flour

0.2 gram (pinch) instant yeast

100 grams (¼ c + 3 tbsp) water at about 60°F (15°C)

DOUGH

125 grams (¾ c + 2½ tbsp) white flour, plus additional as needed for working with the dough

100 grams (½ c + 3½ tbsp) medium whole wheat flour

25 grams (¾ c + 1½ tbsp) white rye flour

5 grams (1½ tsp) instant yeast

0.2 gram (pinch) ground cloves

225 grams (¾ c + 3 tbsp) water at about 60°F (15°C)

55 grams (3 tbsp) anchovy juice (*colatura di alici*) (anchovy syrup)

13 grams (1 tbsp) extra-virgin olive oil, plus additional for the pan and dough

6 to 9 grams (1 to 1½ tsp) flaky sea salt, preferably Maldon, for sprinkling on top

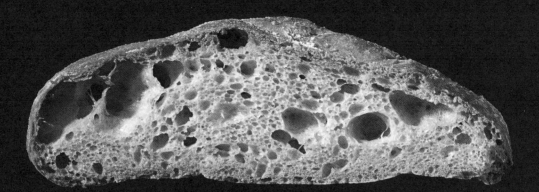

FOR THE STARTER

1 Put the flour in a medium storage container. Sprinkle the yeast into the water, stir to mix, and pour over the flour. Mix with your fingers, pressing the mixture into the sides, bottom, and corners until all of the flour is wet and fully incorporated. Cover the container and let sit at room temperature for 10 to 14 hours. The starter will be at its peak at around 12 hours.

FOR THE DOUGH

1 Spray 2 large storage containers, each about 2½ quarts (2.4 L) and preferably round, generously with nonstick cooking spray, or oil them generously with any neutral oil.

2 Stir together the white, whole wheat, and white rye flours, yeast, and cloves in a small bowl.

3 Pour about one-third of the water around the edges of the starter to release it from the sides of the container. Transfer the starter and water to an extra-large bowl along with the remaining water, the anchovy juice, and the oil. Using a wooden spoon, break the starter up to distribute it in the liquid. Add

the flour mixture and stir vigorously with a wooden spoon for 1 minute.

4 Pour the dough, which will have a texture a little thicker than pancake batter, into the sprayed container. Cover and let the dough rest for 45 minutes.

5 For the first stretch and fold (see Stretching and Folding, page 285) generously dust the work surface, the plastic bowl scraper, and your hands with flour. Using the scraper, release the batter-like dough from the bowl and onto the work surface. It will spread easily on its own. Lightly dust the second storage container with flour.

With the scraper (and your hands, if needed), do your best to fold the dough in thirds from top to bottom and then from left to right. This fold may be difficult with the batter still being soupy, but it should enough stretch that it's manageable. Repeat the folds in both directions. With the scraper, tuck the sides under toward the center, and then lift the dough, placing it seam-side down in the second prepared container. Cover the container and let the dough rest for 45 minutes.

6 For the second stretch and fold, repeat the steps for the first stretch and fold (both ways twice), then return the dough to the container, cover, and let rest for 45 minutes.

7 For the third and final stretch and fold, clean the first container and oil it again. This time, the steps for stretching and folding only need to be done once in each direction. Return the dough to the container, cover, and transfer to the refrigerator to chill for 16 to 20 hours.

8 Set up the oven with a cast-iron skillet for steam (see Baking Stones and Steam page 296), then pre-heat the oven to 480°F (250°C). Oil a half sheet pan with about 20 grams (1 tbsp + 1 ½ tsp) of olive oil.

9 Using the scraper (and your fingertips, if needed), gently release the dough onto the oiled pan. Bring your thumbs and fingers together under the dough and gently stretch the dough to form an oval measuring about 8 by 12 inches (20 by 30 cm). Gently brush the top of the dough with a bit more oil and sprinkle with the flaky sea salt.

10 Working quickly but carefully, put the pan in the oven using heavy-duty oven mitts or potholders. Pull out the hot skillet, add about 3 cups of ice cubes, then slide it back in and close the oven door. Immediately lower the oven temperature to 440°F (225°C). Bake, rotating the pan about two-thirds of the way through baking, until the crust is a warm golden brown, about 20 minutes.

11 Carefully transfer the pan to a cooling rack and let cool completely, about 2 hours. This bread is best eaten the day it's baked.

SOURDOUGH STARTER

makes **300** grams (10 ½ oz)

The next few recipes require the longest fermentation. In the process, they develop deep, deep flavor, a creamy texture, a beautifully textured crumb, and a crackling crust. To make them, first you need to make a sourdough starter, which is a bit of a project. Other books will tell you that you can make a great starter in less time. I would say that with shorter methods you can make a good starter, but not a great one. This formula, which requires at least 24 days to mature, takes long, cold fermentation to new heights, and that difference shows in the bread.

You read it right. I find that it takes 24 days for my sourdough starter (in baker speak, a levain) to be really good. If that sounds daunting, look at it his way: you only have to make a sourdough starter once, and then you only have to feed it every few days, just like you'd water a house-plant. With proper care and feeding, a sourdough "mother" can last forever. If you continue to maintain it properly, by the end of about three months you will notice even more improvement in flavor, texture, and the leavening power. I wanted to recommend letting it develop for a full 90 days, but it seemed cruel to ask you to wait that long. It will be nicely bake-able at 24 days, but a more mature sourdough will give more delicious results.

I call for local organic grapes because they don't require rinsing, which would wash away the wild yeasts that naturally occur on grape skins. And, of course, the activity of yeast is ultimately what makes a starter.

DAY 1

250 grams (8.8 oz) organic grapes (seeded or seedless)
    preferably locally grown
125 grams (½ c + 3 tbsp) whole rye berries, ground
    into flour, or 125 grams (1 c + 1½ tsp) dark rye flour

DAYS 3 THROUGH 6

400 grams (2½ c) dark rye flour
400 grams (1½ c + 3 tbsp) water at about 60°F (15°C)

DAYS 7 THROUGH 9

225 grams (1½ c + 1½ tbsp) medium whole wheat flour
225 grams (¾ c + 3 tbsp) water at about 60°F (15°C)

DAYS 10 THROUGH 20

1,650 grams (11¾ c + 1 tbsp) medium whole wheat flour
1,650 grams (6¾ c + 2 tbsp) water at about 60°F (15°C)

DAY 21

150 grams (1 c + 1 tbsp) medium whole wheat flour
100 grams (¼ c + 3 tbsp) water at about 60°F (15°C)

DAY 1

1 Wipe any dirt from the grapes, but don't immerse them in water. Puree in a blender or food processor. Transfer to a medium storage container, preferably one with high sides, and add the rye. Mix with your fingers, pressing the mixture into the sides, bottom, and corners until all of the flour is wet and fully incorporated. Cover and let sit at room temperature for 48 hours.

DAYS 3 THROUGH 6

1 In a clean, high-sided storage container, combine 100 grams (¾ c + 1½ tbsp) of the flour and 100 grams (¼ c + 3 tbsp) of the water.

Add 100 grams (¼ c + 2½ tbsp) of the Day 1 starter and discard the rest. Cover and let sit at room temperature.

2 Repeat the feeding every 24 hours, each time using 100 grams (¼ c + 2½ tbsp) of the previous day's starter, for a total of 4 feedings.

DAYS 7 THROUGH 9

1 In a clean, high-sided storage container, combine 75 grams (½ c + 1½ tsp) of the flour and 75 grams (¾ c + 3 tbsp) of the water. Add 75 grams (¼ c + ½ tbsp) of the Day 6 starter and discard the rest. Cover and let sit at room temperature.

2 Repeat the feeding every 24 hours, each time using 75 grams (¼ c + ½ tbsp) of the previous day's starter, for a total of 3 feedings.

DAYS 10 THROUGH 20

1 In a clean, high-sided storage container, combine 75 grams (½ c + 1½ tsp) of the flour and 75 grams

(¾ c + 3 tbsp) of the water. Add 75 grams (¼ c + ½ tbsp) of the existing starter and discard the rest. Cover and let sit at room temperature.

2 Repeat the feeding every 12 hours, each time using 75 grams (¼ c + ½ tbsp) of the previous day's starter, for a total of 22 feedings.

DAY 21

1 In a clean, high-sided storage container, combine the flour and water. Add 50 grams (3 tbsp + 1 tsp) of the existing starter and discard the rest. Cover and let sit at room temperature for 6 hours.

2 At this point, it's preferable to refrigerate the starter for 60 hours before using, but it will be fine to use after 12 hours.

3 Congratulations. You now have a healthy, happy starter!

MAINTAINING YOUR STARTER

1 Once every 3 days, remove the starter from the refrigerator for 6 hours. Remove and discard all but 50 grams (3 tbsp + 1 tsp) of the existing starter, then feed the starter using the same proportions as Day 21: 150 grams (1 c + 1 tbsp) of whole wheat flour, 100 grams (¼ c + 3 tbsp) of water, and 50 grams (3 tbsp + 1 tsp) of the existing starter. Cover and let rest for 6 hours, then return to the refrigerator.

2 If you plan on being away for more than 4 to 9 days, you need to slow the growth of the starter.

Remove the starter from the refrigerator and discard all but 100 grams (¼ c + 2½ tbsp) of it. Let sit for 6 hours. Then add 750 grams (5¼ c + 2 tbsp) of medium whole wheat flour and 350 grams (1¼ c + 3½ tbsp) of water, and mix well to incorporate. Refrigerate for up to 9 days.

3 If you're going away for more than 9 days, think of your starter as you would a pet. It's a living thing that must be fed and watered. Get a friend to feed it according to the 3-day feeding schedule.

60-HOUR SOURDOUGH LOAF

This is my signature bread (in France it is usually known as a *miche*). It is the direct descendant of that first bread I learned to bake with Andres, although mine is a big round loaf and his was, for lack of a better description, shaped like a log. It is most likely the bread that much of France survived on for hundreds of years. A version created in the 1970s by Lionel Poilâne in Paris is often thought to have kicked off, or at least given a big push to, the artisan bread revival of recent decades, first in France and then around the world. If I were allowed to sell just one bread, this would be it. Don't let the 60 hours scare you away; the actual work on your part is maybe an hour, with the beneficial yeast and bacteria doing the rest all on their own. You can bake this bread after 35 hours and the results are nice, but the extra fermentation time will yield even more flavor.

STARTER

50 grams (3 tbsp + 1 tsp) Sourdough Starter (page 122)
100 grams (¼ c + 3 tbsp) water at about 60°F (15°C)
100 grams (½ c + 3½ tbsp) medium whole wheat flour

DOUGH

275 grams (1¾ c + 3½ tbsp) white flour, plus additional
    as needed for working with the dough
100 grams (½ c + 3½ tbsp) medium whole wheat flour
50 grams (¼ c + 2½ tbsp) white rye flour
50 grams (¼ c + 2½ tbsp) dark rye flour
25 grams (2 tbsp + 2¼ tsp) buckwheat flour
18 grams (1 tbsp) fine sea salt
375 grams (1½ c + 1 tbsp) water at about 60°F (15°C)

Dusting Mixture (see page 35), for the lined proofing
    basket and the shaped loaf

FOR THE STARTER

1 Put the sourdough starter in a medium storage container and add the water. Break the starter into pieces with your fingers until it's almost dissolved in the water; there will still be some small pieces. Stir in the flour until fully incorporated. Cover the container and let sit at room temperature for 10 to 14 hours. The starter will be at its peak at around 12 hours.

FOR THE DOUGH

1 Stir together the white, whole wheat, white rye, dark rye, and buckwheat flours and the salt in a medium bowl.

2 Pour about one-third of the water around the edges of the starter to release it from the sides of the container. Transfer the starter and water to an extra-large bowl along with the remaining water. Using a wooden spoon, break the starter up to distribute it in the water.

3 Add the flour mixture, reserving about one-sixth of it along the edge of the bowl (see Mixing, page 282). Continue to mix with the spoon until most of the dry ingredients have been combined with the starter mixture. Switch to a plastic bowl scraper and

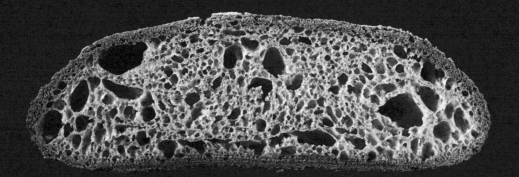

continue to mix until incorporated. At this point the dough will be sticky to the touch.

4 Push the dough to one side of the bowl. Roll and tuck the dough (see Rolling and Tucking, page 284), adding the reserved flour mixture and a small amount of additional flour to the bowl and your hands as needed. Continue rolling and tucking until the dough feels stronger and begins to resist any further rolling, about 12 times. Then, with cupped hands, tuck the sides under toward the center. Place the dough, seam-side down, in a clean bowl, cover the top of the bowl with a clean kitchen towel, and let rest at room temperature for 45 minutes.

5 For the first stretch and fold (see Stretching and Folding, page 285), lightly dust the work surface and your hands with flour. Using the plastic bowl scraper, release the dough from the bowl and set it, seam-side down, on the work surface. Gently stretch it into a roughly rectangular shape. Fold the dough in thirds from top to bottom and then from left to right. With cupped hands, tuck the sides under toward the center. Place the dough in the bowl, seam-side down, cover the bowl with the towel, and let rest for 45 minutes.

6 For the second stretch and fold, repeat the steps for the first stretch and fold, then return the dough to the bowl, cover with the towel, and let rest for 45 minutes.

7 For the third stretch and fold, once again repeat the steps for the first stretch and fold, then return the dough to the bowl, cover with the towel, and let rest for 45 minutes.

8 For the fourth and final stretch and fold, repeat the steps for the first stretch and fold, return the dough to the bowl, cover with the towel, and let rest for 30 minutes.

9 Line a 9-inch (23 cm) proofing basket or bowl with a clean kitchen towel and dust the towel fairly generously with the dusting mixture.

10 Lightly dust the work surface and your hands with flour and shape the dough into a round (see Shaping a Round Loaf, page 288). Dust the sides and top of the dough with the dusting mixture, fold the edges of the towel over the top, and let rest at room temperature for 5½ hours.

11 Transfer the bowl to the refrigerator and chill for 36 to 40 hours.

12 Position an oven rack in the lower third of the oven. Place a covered 6-quart (5.7 L), 10-inch (25 cm) round cast-iron Dutch oven on the rack. Preheat the oven to 500°F (260°C). Remove the basket of dough from the refrigerator for 20 minutes before baking. (I recommend preheating the oven for 1 hour, so take the basket out after 40 minutes.)

13 Using heavy-duty oven mitts or potholders, remove the Dutch oven, place it on a heatproof surface, and remove the lid.

14 Using the kitchen towel, lift and gently ease the dough out of the basket and onto a baking peel, seam-side down. Then carefully transfer it into the pot (the Dutch oven will be very hot). Score the top of the dough (see Scoring, page 290), cover the pot, and return it to the oven. Lower the oven temperature to 460°F (240°C) and bake for 45 minutes.

15 Rotate the Dutch oven and remove the lid. The loaf will already be a rich golden brown. Lower the oven temperature to 440°F (225°C) and bake with the lid off until the surface is a very dark brown, with a lot of spots along the score being very dark (*bien cuit*), about 15 minutes longer. (This bread is baked darker than any other loaf.)

16 Loosen the edges of the loaf with a long handled spoon and then with the help of the spoon lift out of the pot onto a cooling rack. When the bottom of the loaf is tapped, it should sound hollow. If not, return it to the oven and bake directly on the rack for 5 minutes longer.

17 Let the bread cool completely before slicing and eating, and also give it a bit of extra time for the flavors to fully develop: at least 10 hours, or up to 2 days. The acidity of the sourdough gives this bread a longer shelf life, which allows the flavors to mature even more.

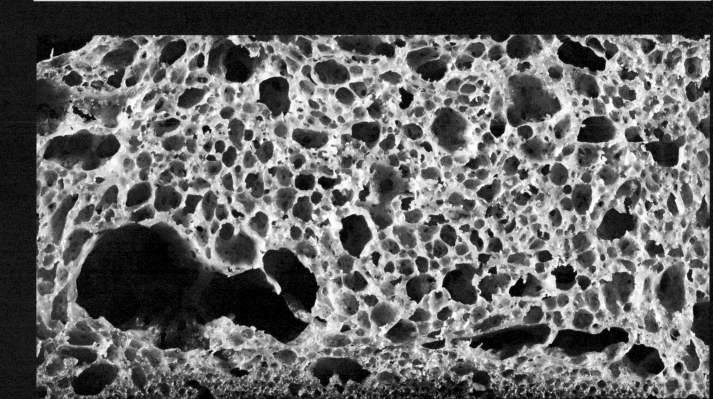

30-HOUR SOURDOUGH LOAF

Everything I said about my 60-Hour Sourdough Loaf (page 125) also applies here. Still, you may wonder if the 30-hour loaf is a lesser bread than the 60-hour loaf. Not at all; they are just different. The 60-hour loaf is extremely robust—something you want to eat all by itself or perhaps with a smear of butter. In contrast, the 30-hour loaf is not as in-your-face. Its flavor is subtler, making it a more versatile table bread to serve with other foods, such as cold cuts, pâtés, cheeses, or butter and jam. And because it is milder than the 60-hour loaf, I also use this recipe as the base dough for the two recipes which follow this one, Raisin Walnut Bread (page 132) and Olive Bread (page 134). Even so, when I say this is a bread with a subtler taste profile, I'm just speaking relatively. It is no shrinking violet. It's a hearty bread.

STARTER

50 grams (3 tbsp + 1 tsp) Sourdough Starter (page 122)
100 grams (¼ c + 3 tbsp) water at about 60°F (15°C)
100 grams (½ c + 3½ tbsp) white flour

DOUGH

300 grams (2 c + 2 tbsp) white flour, plus additional as needed for working with the dough
75 grams (½ c + 1½ tsp) medium whole wheat flour
75 grams (½ c + 2 tbsp) white rye flour
25 grams (3 tbsp + 1 tsp) dark rye flour
25 grams (2 tbsp + 2¼ tsp) buckwheat flour
15 grams (2½ tsp) fine sea salt
350 grams (1¼ c + 3½ tbsp) water at about 60°F (15°C)

Dusting Mixture (see page 35), for the lined proofing basket and shaped loaf

FOR THE STARTER

1 Put the sourdough starter in a medium storage container and add the water. Break the starter into pieces with your fingers until it's almost dissolved in the water; there will still be some small pieces. Stir in the flour until fully incorporated. Cover the container and let sit at room temperature for 10 to 14 hours. It will be at its peak at around 12 hours.

FOR THE DOUGH

1 Stir together the white, whole wheat, white rye, dark rye, and buckwheat flours and the salt in a medium bowl.

2 Pour about one-third of the water around the edges of the starter to release it from the sides of the container. Transfer the starter and water an extra-large bowl along with the remaining water. Using a wooden spoon, break the starter up to distribute it in the water.

3 Add the flour mixture, reserving about one-sixth of it along the edge of the bowl (see Mixing, page 282). Continue to mix with the spoon until most of the dry ingredients have been combined with the starter mixture. Switch to a plastic bowl scraper and

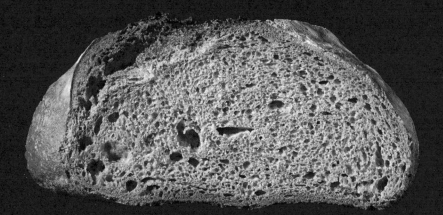

continue to mix until incorporated. At this point the dough will be sticky to the touch.

4 Push the dough to one side of the bowl. Roll and tuck the dough (see Rolling and Tucking, page 284), adding the reserved flour mixture and a small amount of additional flour to the bowl and your hands as needed. Continue rolling and tucking until the dough feels stronger and begins to resist any further rolling, about 14 times. Then, with cupped hands, tuck the sides under toward the center. Place the dough, seam-side down, in a clean bowl, cover the top of the bowl with a clean kitchen towel, and let rest at room temperature for 1 hour.

5 For the first stretch and fold (see Stretching and Folding, page 285), lightly dust the work surface and your hands with flour. Using the plastic bowl scraper, release the dough from the bowl and set it, seam-side down, on the work surface. Gently stretch it into a roughly rectangular shape. Fold the dough in thirds from top to bottom and then from left to right. With cupped hands, tuck the sides under toward the center. Place the dough in the bowl, seam-side down, cover the bowl with the towel, and let rest for 1 hour.

6 For the second stretch and fold, repeat the steps for the first stretch and fold, then return the dough to the bowl, cover with the towel, and let rest for 1 hour.

7 For the third and final stretch and fold, once again repeat the steps for the first stretch and fold, then return the dough to the bowl, cover with the towel, and let rest for 30 minutes.

8 Line a 9-inch (23 cm) proofing basket or bowl with a clean kitchen towel and dust the towel fairly generously with the dusting mixture.

9 Lightly dust the work surface and your hands with flour and shape the dough into a round (see Shaping a Round Loaf, page 288). Dust the sides and top of the dough with the dusting mixture, fold the edges of the towel over the top, and let rest at room temperature for 1½ hours.

10 Transfer the basket to the refrigerator and chill for 14 to 18 hours.

11 Position an oven rack in the lower third of the oven. Place a covered 6-quart (5.7 L), 10-inch (25 cm) round cast-iron Dutch oven on the rack. Preheat the oven to 500°F (260°C). Remove the basket of dough from the refrigerator and let it sit at room temperature while you allow the oven to preheat for about 1 hour.

12 Using heavy-duty oven mitts or potholders, remove the Dutch oven, place it on a heatproof surface, and remove the lid.

13 Using the kitchen towel, lift and gently ease the dough out of the basket and onto a baking peel, seam-side down. Then carefully transfer it into the pot (the Dutch oven will be very hot). Score the top of the dough (see Scoring, page 290), cover the pot, and return it to the oven. Lower the oven temperature to 460°F (240°C) and bake for 30 minutes.

14 Rotate the Dutch oven and remove the lid. The loaf will already be a rich golden brown. Continue baking, uncovered, until the surface is a deep, rich brown, with some spots along the score being even slightly darker (*bien cuit*), about 25 minutes longer.

15 Loosen the edges of the loaf with a long handled spoon and then with the help of the spoon lift out of the pot onto a cooling rack. When the bottom of the loaf is tapped, it should sound hollow. If not, return it to the oven and bake directly on the rack for 5 minutes longer.

16 Let the bread cool completely before slicing and eating, at least 6 hours but preferably 12 to 36 hours.

IS IT REALLY COUNTRY?

Breads like the 60-Hour Sourdough Loaf (page 125) and the 30-Hour Sourdough Loaf (page 129) are often called country breads (*pains de campagne* in French) because they are supposedly what the peasantry survived on. That sounds reasonable enough, but the problem with that romantic-sounding name is that white flour wasn't widely available to poor country folk back in the old days. I think the name country bread can be explained by the fact these loaves look so gnarly and rustic. If they make you feel like a hearty peasant, bear in mind that you don't need to spend a morning in the fields with a scythe in order to enjoy one any more than eating a ploughman's lunch requires you to till a field walking behind a horse-drawn plow.

RAISIN WALNUT BREAD

Bread and cheese is a beloved combination, but too often the bread is just a bit player, something to quiet the palate while keeping your fingers from getting cheesy. To my way of thinking, this is a discourtesy to both the cheese and the bread. When I was the baker at Le Bec-Fin, Georges Perrier was thinking along the same lines when he said to me, "Zach, I want a bread to serve with cheese that truly complements it."

Having received my assignment, I went to work. Early on I decided to try incorporating raisins and walnuts, which is a classic French combination. If you think about it, after you factor in the salt and acidity in the bread dough, raisins and walnuts give you sour, salty, umami, and bitter—in other words, all five of the basic tastes on the palate. That makes this bread ideal for underscoring the complex flavors and aromas of cheese.

The dough for the 30-Hour Sourdough Loaf (page 129), relying as it does on a long-fermented sourdough starter, balances the fattiness of cheese, cutting through it and refreshing the palate after every chew. The "stealth soloist," is the pink peppercorn: floral, with a touch of spicy heat. It truly does justice to the nuances in taste and texture that make a high-fat, long-fermented cheese, such as Fromager d'Affinois or Roquefort, such a full gastronomic experience.

Merci, Chef Georges!

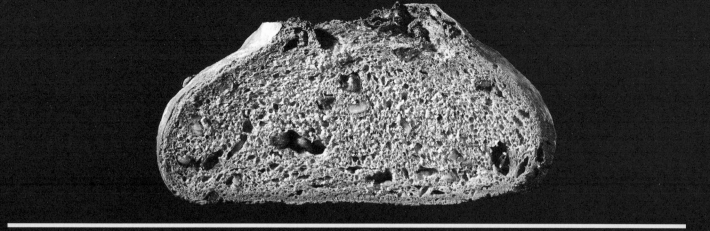

INGREDIENTS

65 grams (½ c + 1 tbsp) walnut halves

65 grams (¼ c + 3 tbsp) Thompson seedless raisins
(or any large, dark raisin)

1 gram (½ tsp) freshly ground pink peppercorns

1 recipe 30-Hour Sourdough Loaf (page 129), prepared
through to the rest after the second stretch and fold

DIRECTIONS

1 Preheat the oven to 350°F (175°C). Spread the walnuts on a small sheet pan and bake until toasted, 8 to 10 minutes. Let cool completely. Cut into ½-inch (1.5 cm) pieces. Put the walnuts in a bowl, add the raisins and pepper, and toss to combine.

2 Once the 30-hour dough has rested for 1 hour after the second stretch and fold, do the third and final stretch and fold. Gently stretch the dough into a rectangle, scatter the walnut mixture evenly over the top, then press the walnuts and raisins gently into the dough (for photos of this process, see Incorporating Add-Ins, page 292). Roll up the dough tightly from the end closest to you; at the end of the roll the dough will be seam-side down. Turn it over, seam-side up, and gently press on the seam to flatten the dough slightly. Fold in thirds from left to right and then do 1 roll and tuck sequence to incorporate the walnuts and raisins. Turn the dough seam-side down and tuck the sides under toward the center. Return the dough to the bowl, cover with the towel, and let rest for 20 minutes.

3 Follow all of the remaining steps for shaping, fermenting, baking, and cooling the 30-Hour Sourdough Loaf.

OLIVE BREAD

Olive bread wasn't on the menu when I first opened Bien Cuit, but people kept asking me for one. I'm a great believer in listening to customers, but instead of giving them exactly what they asked for, I tried to give them something even better than they imagined. I decided to use the same dough as my 30-Hour Sourdough Loaf (page 129). Could you make an olive bread with another dough? Yes, but I think the acidity of the 30-hour loaf balances the saltiness of the olives (more on that shortly), and the chew really makes the savory, briny flavor and soft texture of the olives pop.

If you've ever had a pizza covered with insipid-tasting canned black olives, you know that the wrong olive is worse than no olive. Please allow me to liberate you from some of the guesswork of choosing the right olives for this recipe. First, you want olives that are brined without vinegar. The acid fights the dough and confuses the flavor. I tried at least a dozen different olives in this bread before I settled on a firm, green, salt-brined olive. Varieties include Castelvetrano or Halkidiki (a great word, don't you think?). I like the way these olives taste when baked in the dough. Their floral fragrance infuses the crumb.

You'll notice that I bake this bread slightly longer than either the 30-Hour Sourdough Loaf or the Raisin Walnut Bread (page 132). This is a good lesson in adapting to your ingredients. As the olives bake, they add moisture to the dough, making it wetter and requiring a longer bake time. If you were to bake this exactly the same as the 30-hour loaf, the crumb would be denser and the overall rise of the loaf would be less than desired. When we make this bread, I tell my staff to bake it until it's *très bien cuit*, a truly dark mahogany.

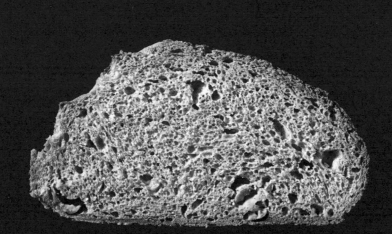

INGREDIENTS

80 grams (generous ½ c) pitted salt-brined green olives,
     cut into ½-inch (1.5 cm) slices
10 grams (1 tbsp) white flour
1 recipe 30-Hour Sourdough Loaf (page 129), prepared
     through to the rest after the second stretch and fold

DIRECTIONS

1 Pat the olives dry to remove any excess brine. In a small bowl, toss the olives with the flour until evenly coated.

2 Once the 30-hour dough has rested for 1 hour after the second stretch and fold, do the third and final stretch and fold. Gently stretch the dough into a rectangle, scatter the olives evenly over the top, then press them gently into the dough (for photos of this process, see Incorporating Add-Ins, page 292). Roll up the dough tightly from the end closest to you; at the end of the roll the dough will be seam-side down. Turn it over, seam-side up, and gently press on the seam to flatten the dough slightly. Fold in thirds from left to right and then do 1 roll and tuck sequence to incorporate the olives. Turn the dough seam-side down and tuck the sides under toward the center. Return the dough to the bowl, cover with the towel, and let rest for 20 minutes.

3 Follow all of the remaining steps for shaping and fermenting the 30-Hour Sourdough Loaf. Also bake as directed, but after removing the lid from the Dutch oven, bake for 30 minutes, not 25. Remove from the Dutch oven and cool as directed.

SOURDOUGH BUCKWHEAT BREAD

To me, this bread tastes like soba noodles crossed with a great baguette. I went through many iterations to come up with this recipe. When I hit on the right formula, it almost got me high. Don't worry; I'm not saying it's psychedelic, but the aroma and flavor will transport you. This bread has a flavor that's both earthy and delicate. Perhaps this dual personality stems from the fact that I use two starters. The first is the same starter I use for my White Pullman Loaf (page 107), Kaiser Rolls (page 221), and several doughs that are on the sweeter side. It has personality, but it's not aggressive. The second is simply buckwheat flour and water added to my standard sourdough starter. Why did I try both? Instinct: I just had the feeling that buckwheat could be the basis of a great bread, but that it needed some help to showcase its nature. I basically tried every combination of water, flours, and starter I could think of until I came up with a formula that hit the sweet spot of fermentation.

FIRST STARTER

50 grams (¼ c + 2 tbsp) white flour
5 grams (1¼ tsp) granulated sugar
1 gram (generous ¼ tsp) fine sea salt
0.2 gram (pinch) instant yeast
44 grams (2 tbsp + 2¼ tsp) cold whole milk

SECOND STARTER

50 grams (3 tbsp + 1 tsp) Sourdough Starter (page 122)
100 grams (¼ c + 3 tbsp) water at about 60°F (15°C)
100 grams (½ c + 3½ tbsp) buckwheat flour

DOUGH

350 grams (2½ c) white flour, plus additional as
    needed for working with the dough
100 grams (½ c + 3½ tbsp) buckwheat flour
50 grams (¼ c + 2 tbsp) medium whole wheat flour
15 grams (2½ tsp) fine sea salt
1 gram (generous ¼ tsp) instant yeast
350 grams (1¼ c + 3½ tbsp) water at about 60°F (15°C)

Dusting Mixture (see page 35), for the lined proofing
    basket and the shaped loaf

FOR THE FIRST STARTER

1 Stir together the flour, sugar, salt, and yeast in a medium storage container. Pour in the milk. Mix with your fingers, pressing the mixture into the sides, bottom, and corners until all of the flour is wet and fully incorporated. This starter is best if covered and left at room temperature for 6 hours, then chilled in the refrigerator for 6 hours. But if the timing is better, you can also leave it at room temperature for 2 to 3 hours and then move it to the refrigerator to chill for 9 to 12 hours.

FOR THE SECOND STARTER

1 Put the sourdough starter in a medium storage container and add the water. Break the starter into pieces with your fingers until it's almost dissolved in the water; there will still be some small pieces. Stir in the flour until fully incorporated. Cover the container and let sit at room temperature for 12 to 18 hours. The starter will be at its peak at around 15 hours.

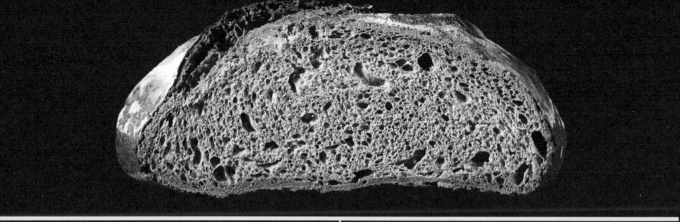

FOR THE DOUGH

1 Stir together the white, buckwheat, and whole wheat flours, salt, and yeast in a medium bowl.

2 Pour about one-third of the water around the edges of each of the starters to release them from the sides of the containers. Transfer both starters and the water to an extra-large bowl along with the remaining water. Using a wooden spoon, break the two starters up to distribute them in the water.

3 Add the flour mixture, reserving about one-sixth of it along the edge of the bowl (see Mixing, page 282). Continue to mix with the spoon until most of the dry ingredients have been combined with the starter mixture. Switch to a plastic bowl scraper and continue to mix until incorporated. At this point the dough will be sticky to the touch.

4 Push the dough to one side of the bowl. Roll and tuck the dough (see Rolling and Tucking, page 284), adding the reserved flour mixture and a small amount of additional flour to the bowl and your hands as needed. Continue rolling and tucking until the dough feels stronger and begins to resist any further rolling, about 12 times. Then, with cupped hands, tuck the sides under toward the center. Place

the dough, seam-side down, in a clean bowl, cover the top of the bowl with a clean kitchen towel, and let rest at room temperature for 45 minutes.

5 For the first stretch and fold (see Stretching and Folding, page 285), lightly dust the work surface and your hands with flour. Using the plastic bowl scraper, release the dough from the bowl and set it, seam-side down, on the work surface. Gently stretch it into a roughly rectangular shape. Fold the dough in thirds from top to bottom and then from left to right. With cupped hands, tuck the sides under toward the center. Place the dough in the bowl, seam-side down, cover the bowl with the towel, and let rest for 45 minutes.

6 For the second and final stretch and fold, repeat the steps for the first stretch and fold, then return the dough to the bowl, cover with the towel, and let rest for 30 minutes.

7 Line a 9-inch (23 cm) proofing basket or bowl with a clean kitchen towel and dust the towel fairly generously with the dusting mixture.

8 Lightly dust the work surface and your hands with flour and shape the dough into a round (see Shaping a Round Loaf, page 288). Dust the sides and top of the dough with the dusting mixture, fold the edges of the towel over the top, and transfer to the refrigerator to chill for 16 to 20 hours.

9 Position an oven rack in the lower third of the oven. Place a covered 6-quart (5.7 L), 10-inch (25 cm) round cast-iron Dutch oven on the rack. Preheat the oven to 500°F (260°C). Remove the basket of dough from the refrigerator and let it sit at room temperature while you allow the oven to preheat for about 1 hour.

10 Using heavy-duty oven mitts or potholders, remove the Dutch oven, place it on a heatproof surface, and remove the lid.

11 Using the kitchen towel, lift and gently ease the dough out of the basket and onto a baking peel, seam-side down. Then carefully transfer it into the pot (the Dutch oven will be very hot). Score the top of the dough (see Scoring, page 290), cover the pot,

and return it to the oven. Lower the oven temperature to 460°F (240°C) and bake for 30 minutes.

12 Rotate the Dutch oven and remove the lid. The loaf will already be a rich golden brown. Continue baking, uncovered, until the surface is a deep, rich brown, with some spots along the score being even slightly darker (*bien cuit*), about 20 minutes longer.

13 Loosen the edges of the loaf with a long handled spoon and then with the help of the spoon lift out of the pot onto a cooling rack. When the bottom of the loaf is tapped, it should sound hollow. If not, return it to the oven and bake directly on the rack for 5 minutes longer.

14 Before slicing and eating, let the bread cool completely, at least 4 hours but preferably 8 to 24 hours.

-BREAD QUEST-
LITHUANIAN TABLE BREAD

On a hot summer's day when Peter and I were testing bread recipes, we took a lunch break while our doughs were resting between folds. *Why not check out some new breads?* we thought. We had been on the trail of great rye bread and, up to that point, had found good but not great specimens. But just that morning, a Czech friend, Viera Karpiakova, had told us of a place in Sunset Park, a Brooklyn neighborhood not far from the bakery that services my restaurant accounts. So we hopped in the car and headed over, but no bakery was to be seen. There was, however, a store with a big red sign in Polish writing. We had no idea what it said, but on the last line was the word *baleron*, which I misread as "bakeron" and figured it sounded enough like bakery for me.

Upon entering, we were enveloped in the aromas of garlic, spices, and smoky cured meat. A big case filled with gorgeous cold cuts took center stage. There were shelves full of brined and pickled vegetables that I didn't even know you could pickle, like celery root (it turned out to be absolutely wonderful). But it was the cold cuts that grabbed my attention. "What's this?" I asked the clerk, and was answered with something unpronounceably Polish, with lots of "k" sounds. As we pointed at the cold cuts, the friendly lady, who spoke halting English, sliced this and that as we kept nodding. Just behind her, we noticed a few round dark loaves. "Lithuanian bread from Queens," she said. It was dark, but not black the way rye-heavy northern European breads can be. We added a loaf to our order, along with the celery root, chicken pâté, two cans of sardines in tomato sauce, and two tins of mackerel fillets in oil.

We headed back to the bakery. We didn't have high hopes for that store-bought loaf from a sausage emporium, but it was, in fact, quite good. I sliced the whole loaf and made twenty *tartines* (open-faced sandwiches) for my bakers, spreading the bread with mustard, topping it with the cold cuts, pâté, and fish we'd bought, and using the crunchy celery root as a finishing touch. The dense crumb and subtle, slightly sweet rye and wheat flavors provided a fitting backdrop for the meat, and, to the soundtrack of traditional Mexican *canciones rancheras* on somebody's iPod and competing Jamaican hip-hop on another, my staff made short work of the *tartines*.

Working from the ingredients listed on the bread, I baked a trial loaf. I liked the resulting bread a lot, but I sensed that something was missing. Then, weeks later a Latvian baker at our warehouse consulted his grandmother, and she said I needed to use rye malt syrup, which I could find in a recently opened Russian supermarket in Brighton Beach, where many Russians have settled in the past few decades. So on a truly lousy day, with sheets of rain riding in on a cold wind that came onshore at Coney Island, Peter and I went looking for this elusive liquid. As the windshield wipers momentarily let us peek through the cascade pouring off the elevated tracks of the D train, we spotted the Gourmanoff Market, located inside a refurbished movie theater.

Inside, it was like a Russian version of Whole Foods: an array of smoked fish 20 feet (6 m) long, sausages of every size and seasoning, hams from everywhere, dried mushrooms, fresh fruits (which get pride of place in any market whose customers remember

the fruitless fare of the Soviet Union)—but no rye malt syrup.

Feeling a bit defeated, we retreated through the continuing downpour only to find that a large truck had double-parked next to my car. As an alternative to standing in the rain, we ducked into a small food market nearby. It was very old-school. A big box of dried smoked sturgeon sat next to an open box of poppy seed pastries. I wondered whether the flavors mixed, and if they did, whether that was a good thing or a bad thing.

Then, at eye level, like a beacon cutting through the darkness of a moonless night, I saw six jars of dark syrup. The Russian label told us little, but the list of ingredients in English noted "rye malt.'" I loaded up with every bottle of the shelf. We drove back to Bien Cuit, where I mixed up a dough with the missing ingredient. It added just the right amount of color and, more importantly, a smooth sweetness with the deep and haunting characteristics found in malted rye beverages.

You don't have to go on a bread obsessive's trip to a Russian neighborhood to buy rye malt syrup, also known as rye malt extract. I later found that it's sold on Amazon, alongside other supplies for home brewers. But I enjoyed the thrill of the hunt, and the chicken breast with gravy stuffed between two potato pancakes that they served at Gourmanoff was, as they say in the Michelin guides, "worth a detour."

STARTER

20 grams (1 tbsp + 1 tsp) Sourdough Starter (page 122)
40 grams (2 tbsp + 2 tsp) water at about 60°F (15°C)
40 grams (¼ c + 1 tbsp) white flour

DOUGH

380 grams (2½ c + 3 tbsp) white flour, plus additional
    as needed for working with the dough
120 grams (1 c) white rye flour
13 grams (2¼ tsp) fine sea salt
2 grams (½ tsp) instant yeast
325 grams (1¼ c + 2 tbsp) water at about 60°F (15°C)
125 grams (⅓ c) rye malt extract

Dusting Mixture (see page 35), for the lined proofing
    basket and the shaped loaf

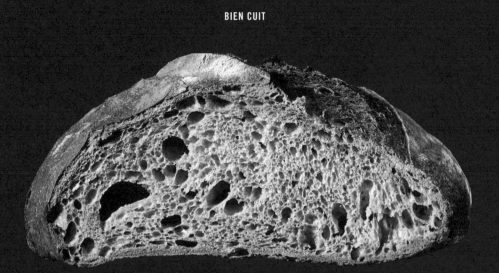

FOR THE STARTER

1 Put the sourdough starter in a medium storage container and add the water. Break the starter into pieces with your fingers until it's almost dissolved in the water; there will still be some small pieces. Stir in the flour until fully incorporated. Cover the container and let sit at room temperature for 10 to 16 hours. The starter will be at its peak at around 13 hours.

FOR THE DOUGH

1 Stir together the white and white rye flours, salt, and yeast in a medium bowl.

2 Pour about one-third of the water around the edges of the starter to release it from the sides of the container. Transfer the starter and water to an extra-large bowl along with the remaining water and the rye malt extract. Using a wooden spoon, break the starter up to distribute it in the liquid. The extract will not break up easily and will be stringy and a bit clumped together at this point.

3 Add the flour mixture, reserving about one-sixth of it along the edge of the bowl (see Mixing, page

282). Continue to mix with the spoon until most of the dry ingredients have been combined with the starter mixture. Switch to a plastic bowl scraper and continue to mix until incorporated. At this point the dough will be slightly sticky to the touch.

4 Push the dough to one side of the bowl. Roll and tuck the dough (see Rolling and Tucking, page 284), adding the reserved flour mixture and a small amount of additional flour to the bowl and your hands as needed. Continue rolling and tucking until the dough feels stronger and begins to resist any further rolling, about 10 times. Then, with cupped hands, tuck the sides under toward the center. Place the dough, seam-side down, in a clean bowl, cover the top of the bowl with a clean kitchen towel, and let rest at room temperature for 45 minutes.

5 For the first stretch and fold (see Stretching and Folding, page 285), lightly dust the work surface and your hands with flour. Using the plastic bowl scraper, release the dough from the bowl and set it, seam-side down, on the work surface. Gently stretch it into a roughly rectangular shape. Fold the dough in thirds from top to bottom and then from left to right. With cupped hands, tuck the sides under toward the center.

Place the dough in the bowl, seam-side down, cover the bowl with the towel, and let rest for 45 minutes.

6 For the second stretch and fold, repeat the steps for the first stretch and fold, then return the dough to the bowl, cover with the towel, and let rest for 45 minutes.

7 For the third and final stretch and fold, once again repeat the steps for the first stretch and fold, then return the dough to the bowl, cover with the towel, and let rest for 20 minutes.

8 Line a 9-inch (23 cm) proofing basket or bowl with a clean kitchen towel and dust the towel fairly generously with the dusting mixture.

9 Lightly dust the work surface and your hands with flour and shape the dough into a round (see Shaping a Round Loaf, page 288). Dust the sides and top of the dough with the dusting mixture, fold the edges of the towel over the top, and transfer to the refrigerator to chill for 20 to 28 hours.

10 Position an oven rack in the lower third of the oven. Place a covered 6-quart (5.7 L), 10-inch (25 cm) round cast-iron Dutch oven on the rack. Preheat the oven to 500°F (260°C). Remove the basket of dough from the refrigerator and let it sit at room temperature while you allow the oven to preheat for about 1 hour.

11 Using heavy-duty oven mitts or potholders, remove the Dutch oven, place it on a heatproof surface, and remove the lid.

12 Using the kitchen towel, lift and gently ease the dough out of the basket and onto a baking peel, seam-side down. Then carefully transfer it into the pot (the Dutch oven will be very hot). Score the top of the dough (see Scoring, page 290), cover the pot,

and return it to the oven. Lower the oven temperature to 460°F (240°C) and bake for 30 minutes.

13 Rotate the Dutch oven and remove the lid. The loaf will already be a rich golden brown. Continue baking, uncovered, until the surface is a deep, rich brown, with some spots along the score being even slightly darker (*bien cuit*), about 15 minutes longer.

14 Loosen the edges of the loaf with a long handled spoon and then with the help of the spoon lift out of the pot onto a cooling rack. When the bottom of the loaf is tapped, it should sound hollow. If not, return it to the oven and bake directly on the rack for 5 minutes longer.

15 Let the bread cool completely before slicing and eating, at least 4 hours but preferably 12 to 36 hours.

USING MALT

Malting involves sprouting grain for a few days under slightly heated conditions. The malt used for bread is usually made from the same grains utilized in the malt for beer or whiskey: barley and rye. In bread making, malt is used to accelerate the action of enzymes on the dough. Without getting too deep into the chemistry of this, the malt powder used in bread making contains the enzyme diastase so it is called diastatic. During the malting process, the diastase enzyme converts starch in the sprouted grain to produce maltose, a sugar. This explains why bread made with the malted grain flour has sweet undertones even when no additional sweetener is added.

In eastern European countries, rye has long been an important base for malt, often in the form of a syrup, which is used as a sweetener. It was especially useful in the shtetls and peasant villages of my ancestors, where cane sugar and even beet sugar might have been too costly and rye malt syrup did the job just fine.

HOW TO TASTE BREAD

Tasting bread and assessing its flavor is different than with most other foods. With a steak, a scoop of ice cream, or a ripe peach, the process is usually the same: You take a bite, your teeth come together as you begin to chew, aromas drift into your nose, and only then do you decide, *This is how this thing tastes*. You do this naturally, without even thinking about it. It's a bit of a different story with bread, which has a long finish, as wine enthusiasts might say. When you take a bite of bread, the flavor changes, deepens, and broadens as you chew, and you get echoes of flavor as you swallow.

Even though bread is made very simply from just a few ingredients, the flavor of a well-made loaf is as elegant as a dish at a great restaurant. And as with the best wine or cheese, there is enormous subtlety and nuance depending on how these few ingredients are prepared. The difference between right and almost-right preparation is crucial.

Just as Cabernet grapes will express themselves differently in a Bordeaux wine than in a Napa Valley Cabernet Sauvignon, a sourdough rye will also express itself differently in Birmingham than in Brooklyn. Much depends on the origin and quality of the grain. Then, when making dough, external factors such as humidity, altitude, temperature, and mineral content of the water affect the outcome. The makeup of the local wild yeast population comes into play as well, especially with sourdoughs.

Make a bread in two different places and you will have two different outcomes. I once did an experiment when I was working in Las Vegas in which I fermented two identical batches of dough in two different environments. I stored one in a cold room that was devoted entirely to bread dough. I placed the other in the garde-manger, where fruits and vegetables are stored. After leaving them for a day, I tested the doughs for flavor and aroma. The bread from my fermenting room tasted as I expected it to. The flavors were pure and strong. The loaf from the fruit and vegetable storeroom and compared it with the bread that had been stored as usual, it smelled a bit like a very jumbled fruit salad—confusing and not very bread-like. Moral of the story: Much depends on where you make your dough.

SUNFLOWER RYE BREAD

One of the glories of cuisine is the way that certain ingredients come together—in this case rye and sunflower seeds. Together, they exert a mystical alchemy that French bakers discovered centuries ago. To my way of thinking, the result is a perfect bread that's enjoyable on its own, without accompaniments. If you're a backpacker and you don't want to carry much with you, just throw a loaf of sunflower rye in your knapsack. It's packed with protein, carbohydrates, and, most of all, flavor.

I can't claim I've done all that much to improve upon the time-honored recipe for this bread, although I have fiddled somewhat with ratios of ingredients and flours. And because it employs acidic sourdough fermentation, it has a longer shelf life than many other sunflower rye breads. What's truly critical, however, is the seemingly minor step of toasting the sunflower seeds before incorporating them in the dough. Then, as the bread bakes, the oil from the toasted seeds seeps into the crumb, creating a deeply nutty flavor that balances the sharpness of the rye.

STARTER

50 grams (3 tbsp + 1 tsp) Sourdough Starter (page 122)
100 grams (¼ c + 3 tbsp) water at about 60°F (15°C)
100 grams (¾ c + 1½ tbsp) white rye flour

DOUGH

75 grams (½ c) sunflower seeds
300 grams (2 c + 2 tbsp) white flour, plus additional
    as needed for working with the dough
150 grams (1 c + 3½ tbsp) white rye flour
50 grams (¼ c + 2½ tbsp) dark rye flour
15 grams (2½ tsp) fine sea salt
1 gram (generous ¼ tsp) instant yeast
340 grams (1¼ c + 3 tbsp) water at about 60°F (15°C)
25 grams (1 tbsp + 1 tsp) honey

Dusting Mixture (see page 35), for the lined proofing
    basket and the shaped loaf

FOR THE STARTER

1 Put the sourdough starter in a medium storage container and add the water. Break the starter into pieces with your fingers until it's almost dissolved in the water; there will still be some small pieces. Stir in the flour until fully incorporated. Cover the container and let sit at room temperature for 10 to 14 hours. The starter will be at its peak at around 12 hours.

FOR THE DOUGH

1 Preheat the oven to 375°F (190°C). Spread the sunflower seeds on a quarter sheet pan and bake until toasted, 6 to 8 minutes. Let cool completely.

2 Stir together the white, white rye, and dark rye flours, salt, and yeast in a medium bowl.

3 Pour about one-third of the water around the edges of the starter to release it from the sides of the container. Transfer the starter and water to ex-

4 Add the flour mixture, reserving about one-sixth of it along the edge of the bowl (see Mixing, page 282). Continue to mix with the spoon until most of the dry ingredients have been combined with the starter mixture. Switch to a plastic bowl scraper and continue to mix until incorporated. At this point the dough will be sticky to the touch.

5 Push the dough to one side of the bowl. Roll and tuck the dough (see Rolling and Tucking, page 284), adding the reserved flour mixture and a small amount of additional flour to the bowl and your hands as needed. Continue rolling and tucking until the dough feels stronger and begins to resist any further rolling, about 12 times. Then, with cupped hands, tuck the sides under toward the center. Place the dough, seam-side down, in a clean bowl, cover the top of the bowl with a clean kitchen towel, and let rest at room temperature for 1 hour.

6 For the first stretch and fold (see Stretching and Folding, page 285), lightly dust the work surface and your hands with flour. Using the plastic bowl scraper, release the dough from the bowl and set it, seam-side down, on the work surface. Gently stretch it into a roughly rectangular shape. Fold the dough in thirds from top to bottom and then from left to right. With cupped hands, tuck the sides under toward the

center. Place the dough in the bowl, seam-side down, cover the bowl with the towel, and let rest for 1 hour.

7 For the second stretch and fold, repeat the steps for the first stretch and fold, then return the dough to the bowl, cover with the towel, and let rest for 1 hour.

8 For the third and final stretch and fold, gently stretch the dough into a rectangle, scatter the sunflower seeds over the top, and gently press them into the dough. (For photos of the following process, see Incorporating Add-Ins, page 292.) Roll up the dough tightly from the end closest to you; at the end of the roll the dough will be seam-side down. Turn it over, seam-side up, and gently press on the seam to flatten the dough slightly. Fold in thirds from left to right and then do 1 roll and tuck sequence to incorporate the sunflower seeds. Turn the dough seam-side down and tuck the sides under toward the center. Return the dough to the bowl, cover with the towel, and let rest for 30 minutes.

9 Line a 9-inch (23 cm) proofing basket or bowl with a clean kitchen towel and dust the towel fairly generously with the dusting mixture.

10 Lightly dust the work surface and your hands with flour and shape the dough into a round (see Shaping a Round Loaf, page 288). Dust the sides and top of the dough with the dusting mixture, fold the edges of the towel over the top, and let rest at room temperature for 1½ hours.

11 Transfer the basket to the refrigerator and chill for 24 to 28 hours.

12 Position an oven rack in the lower third of the oven. Place a covered 6-quart (5.7 L), 10-inch (25 cm) round cast-iron Dutch oven on the rack. Preheat the oven to 500°F (260°C). Remove the basket of dough from the refrigerator and let it sit at room temperature while you allow the oven to preheat for about 1 hour.

13 Using heavy-duty oven mitts or potholders, remove the Dutch oven, place it on a heatproof surface, and remove the lid.

14 Using the kitchen towel, lift and gently ease the dough out of the basket and onto a baking peel, seam-side down. Then carefully transfer it into the pot (the Dutch oven will be very hot). Score the top of the dough (see Scoring, page 290), cover the pot, and return it to the oven. Lower the oven temperature to 460°F (240°C) and bake for 30 minutes.

15 Rotate the Dutch oven and remove the lid. The loaf will already be a rich golden brown. Continue baking, uncovered, until the surface is a deep, rich brown, with some spots along the score being even slightly darker (*bien cuit*), about 15 minutes longer.

16 Loosen the edges of the loaf with a long handled spoon and then with the help of the spoon lift out of the pot onto a cooling rack. When the bottom of the loaf is tapped, it should sound hollow. If not, return it to the oven and bake directly on the rack for 5 minutes longer.

17 Let the bread cool completely before slicing and eating, at least 4 hours but preferably 12 to 36 hours.

BREAD QUEST:
SOURDOUGH RYE BREAD

No too long ago there was an era, I am told, when the bread known as Jewish rye was available in bakeries and delis all over New York City. Old-timers often refer to it as "corn bread" or "corn rye," although it contains no corn whatsoever. I think they're using the word "corn" the way it's used in the British Isles, as a synonym for grain or wheat. Whatever you call it, if you search from Staten Island to the northernmost reaches of the Bronx, you're unlikely to find a rye that measures up to the old-time version. To fulfill those expectations, it must have a chewy crust and a tangy crumb with enough acidity to cut through the fattiness of a pile of steaming pastrami. In addition, it must be dense enough to keep the mustard and coleslaw from seeping through the bread and getting all over your fingers.

Peter Shelsky is a friend who sells the most wonderful smoked salmon and pickled herring, and when he heard that I was on a bread quest for traditional sourdough rye, he gave us a seeded loaf from Orwashers, a renowned bakery on the Upper East Side. As we walked from his store, we tasted the bread, which contained lots of caraway seeds, that invariably inserted themselves between the teeth. The crumb was a bit dry and somewhat astringent. The bread was good, but not great.

Another friend recommended a bakery in Brooklyn's Borough Park neighborhood, which is home to an influx of Orthodox Jews in recent decades, but we found nothing to write home about in the rye bread department. Next, a hot tip sent us out to a bakery in Midwood, which, because of the density of Jewish grandmas, is sometimes known as Deepest Chicken Soup Land. The neighborhood looked promising. We watched a couple of rabbis stroll down the street, deep in debate, waving their hands as they as they spoke. Behind them, three ladies in bright hijabs (Arab headscarves) walked and talked in similarly animated dialogue. They paused in front of a small restaurant named Garden of Eat-In, which must have seemed like a clever name when the owners thought it up. Across the street, a Walgreens displayed the Hebrew word for drugstore, and on the corner a line formed behind the counter of a nondescript pizzeria with no pretension to modern gourmet standards. No coal-fired anything, just an old gas oven, with an even older man working meticulously behind the counter. Opera blared from a tinny speaker, while expectant customers waited like enraptured pilgrims at a religious shrine. He was so meticulous and the line so long that we waited nearly an hour for our slices. It was well worth the wait, though. Those slices could only be called miraculous.

We left that pizza shop convinced that the stars had aligned and we would now find an equally great rye. We walked past a few stores to a Russian bakery that had been recommended to us. The woman by the counter had clearly received her hospitality training in the waning days of Soviet communism; she wasn't super friendly. We chose a rye from the stack in the display case. As we left the store, I grabbed a slice and handed one to Peter. Bummer. It wasn't much of a rye bread. In fact it wasn't rye at all, just an overmixed white bread with caraway seeds. I turned and went back into the store.

"Excuse me," I said. "I may have misspoke. I wanted a rye bread."

"Is rye," said the woman, in a challenging tone of voice with a Russian accent as heavy as full-fat sour cream. "We use vite rye only."

I am sure there was no "vite" (white) rye in that bread, just lowest-common-denominator commercial white flour. But arguing was going to get us nowhere, so we left no closer to our goal.

The closest we came to our goal was an artisan rye served at Manhattan's Russ & Daughters Cafe. Though it's a little heavy on the caraway for my taste (caraway can mask the flavor of the bread), it's still an excellent loaf, and it encouraged me to try my hand at something similar. The Russ & Daughters rye bore all the hallmarks of a balanced sourdough. It confirmed my assumption that a great rye bread with a properly dense crumb requires a rye sourdough starter.

With that in mind, on a late fall afternoon, I began to mix my dough. I toasted the caraway seeds to concentrate their flavor and pump up the umami, and then I ground them to infuse the dough with caraway flavors but no dental-floss-demanding seeds. The result is this bread. Its crust has a pleasant chew, the sourdough imparts the right amount of acidity to complement pastrami or corned beef, and the crumb is dense enough that the bread holds together no matter how much deli mustard and coleslaw you heap on your sandwich.

FIRST STARTER

50 grams (3 tbsp + 1 tsp) Sourdough Starter (page 122)
100 grams (¼ c + 3 tbsp) water at about 60°F (15°C)
100 grams (¾ c + 1½ tbsp) white rye flour

SECOND STARTER

60 grams (¼ c + 2½ tbsp) white flour
0.3 gram (generous pinch) instant yeast
40 grams (2 tbsp + 2 tsp) water at about 60°F (15°C)

DOUGH

9 grams (1 tbsp) caraway seeds
350 grams (2½ c) white flour, plus additional
    as needed for working with the dough
100 grams (¾ c + 1½ tbsp) white rye flour
50 grams (¼ c + 2½ tbsp) dark rye flour
5 grams (1½ tsp) diastatic or partially diastatic
    malt powder (malted barley flour)
15 grams (2½ tsp) fine sea salt
1 gram (generous ¼ tsp) instant yeast
360 grams (1½ c) water at about 60°F (15°C)

Dusting Mixture (see page 35), for the lined proofing
    basket and the shaped loaf

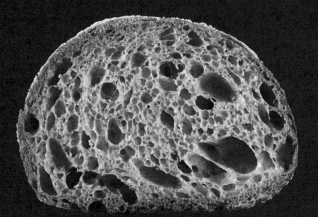

FOR THE FIRST STARTER

1 Put the sourdough starter in a medium storage container and add the water. Break the starter into pieces with your fingers until it's almost dissolved in the water; there will still be some small pieces. Stir in the flour until fully incorporated. Cover the container and let sit at room temperature for 10 to 14 hours. The starter will be at its peak at around 12 hours.

FOR THE SECOND STARTER

1 Put the flour in a medium storage container. Sprinkle the yeast into the water, stir to mix, and pour over the flour. Mix with your fingers, pressing the mixture into the sides, bottom, and corners until all of the flour is wet and fully incorporated. Cover and let sit at room temperature for 10 to 14 hours. The starter will be at its peak at around 12 hours.

FOR THE DOUGH

1 Preheat the oven to 400°F (205°C). Spread the caraway seeds on a small sheet pan and toast until aromatic, about 6 minutes. Let cool completely. Transfer to a spice grinder and process until finely ground. The caraway seeds will decrease in weight when roasted; you will need 4 grams (1½ tsp) of ground caraway seeds.

2 Stir together the white, white rye, and dark rye flours, diastatic malt powder, salt, yeast, and caraway seeds in a medium bowl.

3 Pour about one-third of the water around the edges of the starter to release it from the sides of the container. Transfer the starter and water to an extra-large bowl along with the remaining water and the honey. Using a wooden spoon, break the starter up to distribute it in the liquid.

4 Add the flour mixture, reserving about one-sixth of it along the edge of the bowl (see Mixing, page 282). Continue to mix with the spoon until most of the dry ingredients have been combined with the starter mixture. Switch to a plastic bowl scraper and continue to mix until incorporated. At this point the dough will be sticky to the touch.

5 Push the dough to one side of the bowl. Roll and tuck the dough (see Rolling and Tucking, page 284), adding the reserved flour mixture and a small amount of additional flour to the bowl and your hands as needed. Continue rolling and tucking until the dough feels stronger and begins to resist any further rolling, about 12 times. Then, with cupped hands, tuck the sides under toward the center. Place the dough, seam-side down, in a clean bowl, cover the top of the bowl with a clean kitchen towel, and let rest at room temperature for 45 minutes.

6 For the first stretch and fold (see Stretching and Folding, page 285), lightly dust the work surface and your hands with flour. Using the plastic bowl scraper, release the dough from the bowl and set it, seam-side down, on the work surface. Gently stretch it into a roughly rectangular shape. Fold the dough in thirds from top to bottom and then from left to right. With cupped hands, tuck the sides under toward the center. Place the dough in the bowl, seam-side down, cover the bowl with the towel, and let rest for 45 minutes.

7 For the second stretch and fold, repeat the steps for the first stretch and fold, then return the dough to the bowl, cover with the towel, and let rest for 45 minutes.

8 For the third and final stretch and fold, once again repeat the steps for the first stretch and fold, then return the dough to the bowl, cover with the towel, and let rest for 20 minutes.

9 Line a half sheet pan with a linen liner and dust fairly generously with the dusting mixture.

10 Lightly dust the work surface and your hands with flour. Using a bench scraper, divide the dough into 2 equal pieces. Press each piece into a 9 by 5-inch (23 by 13 cm) rectangle, then roll into a loose tube about 9 inches (23 cm) long (see Shaping a Tube or Oval Loaf, page 294). Let rest for 5 minutes. Press each piece out again and then shape into an oval loaf about 12 inches (30 cm) long. Transfer to the lined pan, seam-side up, positioning the loaves lengthwise.

Dust the top and sides of the loaves with flour. Fold the linen to create support walls on both sides of each loaf, then fold any extra length of the linen liner over the top or cover with a kitchen towel. Transfer the pan to the refrigerator and chill for 12 to 18 hours.

11 Set up the oven with a baking stone and a cast-iron skillet for steam (see Baking Stones and Steam, page 296), then preheat the oven to 500°F (260°C).

12 Using the linen liner, lift and gently flip the loaves off the pan and onto a transfer peel, seam-side down. Slide the loaves, still seam-side down, onto a dusted baking peel (see Using a Transfer Peel and Baking Peel, page 311). Score the top of each (see Scoring, page 290). Working quickly but carefully, transfer the loaves to the stone using heavy-duty oven mitts or potholders. Pull out the hot skillet, add about 3 cups of ice cubes, then slide it back in and close the oven door. Immediately lower the oven temperature to 460°F (240°C). Bake, switching the positions of the loaves about two-thirds of the way through baking, until the surface is a deep, rich brown, with some spots along the scores being very dark (*bien cuit*), about 20 minutes.

13 Using the baking peel, transfer the loaves to a cooling rack. When the bottoms of the loaves are tapped, they should sound hollow. If not, return to the stone and bake for 5 minutes longer.

14 Let the bread cool completely before slicing and eating, at least 4 hours but preferably 12 to 36 hours.

SHELSKY'S
of brooklyn
CLASSIC DELI COUNTER
NOW OPEN
OUR COWS GIVE
THE BEST
TONGUE
(AND PASTRAMI)

JUBILAT PROVISIONS

POLISH AMERICAN SPECIALITIES

PODKARPACKA WYTWORNIA WEDLIN

- BALERON
- KIELBASA
- SZYNKA
- SALCESON
- PASZTET
- KISZKA

718 768·9676

DELIVER

608

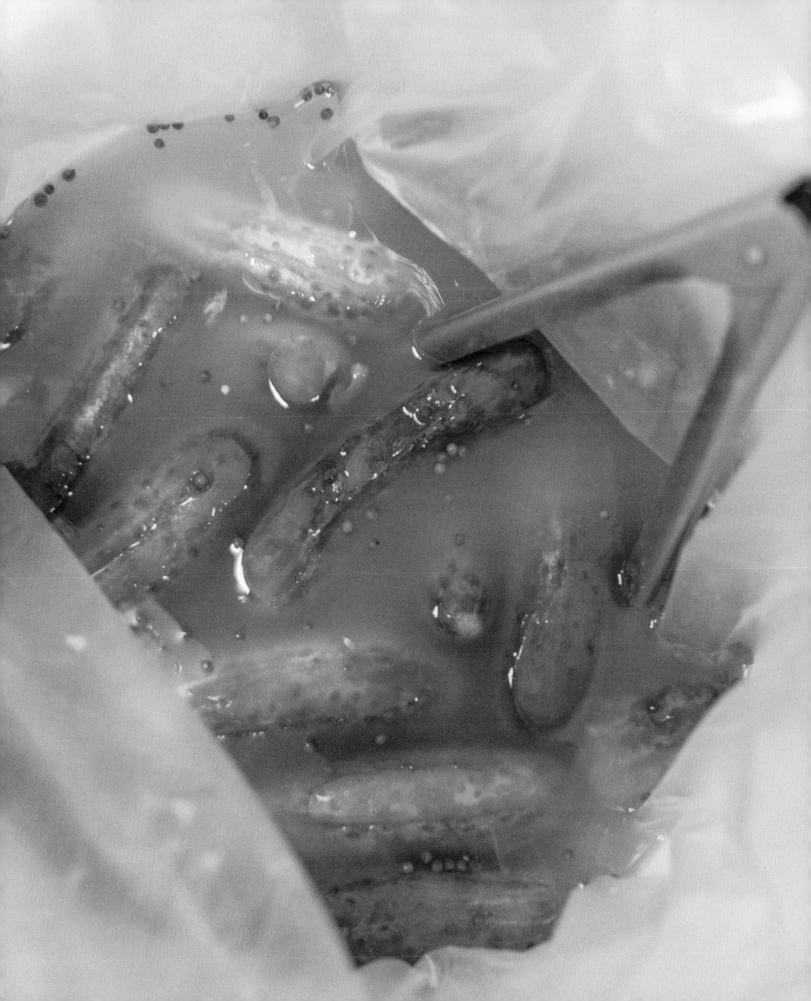

MULTIGRAIN BREAD

We've all seen our share of multigrain breads in recent years. You know the kind I mean: loaves that are on the dark side—but not *bien cuit*—and studded with all kinds of seeds and nuts. It looks like the dough was rolled in a bowl of muesli. That may sound a little judgmental, and you may wonder whether it means I'm against multigrain bread. I am not. In fact, I'm all in favor of using cracked oats and rye and fermenting them; this way you get the crunch and bite of whole grains, with the flavor boost of fermentation.

Toasting the sunflower seeds accentuates their umami and allows that toasted nutty flavor to seep into the crumb as the bread bakes. The effect of yeast on the whole grains is absolutely magical. Also, I try to make my multigrain bread with local flours, which are increasingly available at farmers' markets, including flours made from recently harvested grain. I think it's fair to say that today, home bakers have more varied grains and flours to choose from than at any time in the past. If you opt for fresh, local, and varied ingredients, they will often add up to a supremely satisfying bread.

FIRST STARTER

50 grams (3 tbsp + 1 tsp) Sourdough Starter (page 122)
100 grams (¼ c + 3 tbsp) water at about 60°F (15°C)
100 grams (½ c + 3½ tbsp) spelt flour

SECOND STARTER

35 grams (3 tbsp + 1 tsp) rye berries
35 grams (3 tbsp) oat groats
30 grams (3½ tbsp) spelt flour
25 grams (2½ tbsp) sunflower seeds
0.3 gram (generous pinch) instant yeast
125 grams (½ c + 1 tsp) water at about 80°F (25°C)

DOUGH

300 grams (2 c + 2 tbsp) white flour, plus additional
    as needed for working with the dough
100 grams (½ c + 3½ tbsp) medium whole wheat flour
100 grams (¾ c + 1½ tbsp) dark rye flour
20 grams (1 tbsp + ¼ tsp) fine sea salt
0.3 gram (generous pinch) instant yeast
350 grams (1¼ c + 3½ tbsp) water at about 60°F (15°C)

Dusting Mixture (see page 35), for the linen liner
    and shaped loaves

FOR THE FIRST STARTER

1 Put the sourdough starter in a medium storage container and add the water. Break the starter into pieces with your fingers until it's almost dissolved in the water; there will still be some small pieces. Stir in the flour until fully incorporated. Cover the container and let sit at room temperature for 10 to 14 hours. The starter will be at its peak at around 12 hours.

FOR THE SECOND STARTER

1 Stir together the rye berries, oat groats, spelt flour, and sunflower seeds in a medium storage container. Sprinkle the yeast into the water, stir to mix, and pour over the grain mixture. Mix with your fingers, pressing the mixture into the sides, bottom, and corners until all of the ingredients are wet and fully incorporated. Cover the container and let sit at room temperature for 10 to 14 hours. The starter will be at its peak at around 12 hours.

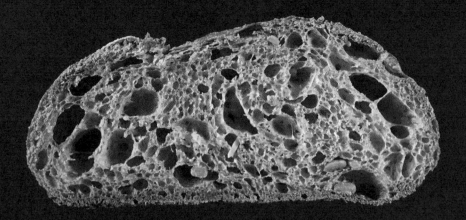

FOR THE DOUGH

1 Stir together the white, whole wheat, and dark rye flours, salt, and yeast in a medium bowl.

2 Pour about one-third of the water around the edges of the starter to release it from the sides of the container. Transfer the starter and the water to an extra-large bowl. Use a little of the remaining water to loosen the whole grain starter. Pour the whole grain starter and the remaining water into the bowl. Using a wooden spoon, break both of the starters up to distribute them in the water.

3 Add the flour mixture, reserving about one-sixth of it along the edge of the bowl (see Mixing, page 282). Continue to mix with the spoon until most of the dry ingredients have been combined with the starter mixture. Switch to a plastic bowl scraper and continue to mix until incorporated. At this point the dough will be quite sticky to the touch.

4 Push the dough to one side of the bowl. Roll and tuck the dough (see Rolling and Tucking, page 284), adding the reserved flour mixture and a small amount of additional flour to the bowl and your hands as needed. Continue rolling and tucking until the dough feels stronger and begins to resist any

further rolling, about 10 times. Then, with cupped hands, tuck the sides under toward the center. Place the dough, seam-side down, in a clean bowl, cover the top of the bowl with a clean kitchen towel, and let rest at room temperature for 45 minutes.

5 For the first stretch and fold (see Stretching and Folding, page 285), lightly dust the work surface and your hands with flour. Using the plastic bowl scraper, release the dough from the bowl and set it, seam-side down, on the work surface. Gently stretch it into a roughly rectangular shape. Fold the dough in thirds from top to bottom and then from left to right. With cupped hands, tuck the sides under toward the center. Place the dough in the bowl, seam-side down, cover the bowl with the towel, and let rest for 45 minutes.

6 For the second stretch and fold, repeat the steps for the first stretch and fold, then return the dough to the bowl, cover with the towel, and let rest for 45 minutes.

7 For the third stretch and fold, once again repeat the steps for the first stretch and fold, then return the dough to the bowl, cover with the towel, and let rest for 45 minutes.

8 For the fourth and final stretch and fold, repeat the steps for the first stretch and fold, then return the dough to the bowl, cover with a towel, and let rest for 20 minutes.

9 Line a half sheet pan with a linen liner and dust fairly generously with the dusting mixture.

10 Lightly dust the work surface and your hands with flour. Using a bench scraper, divide the dough into 2 equal pieces. Press each piece into a 9 by 5-inch (23 by 13 cm) rectangle, then roll into a loose tube about 9 inches (23 cm) long (see Shaping a Tube or Oval Loaf, page 294). Let rest for 5 minutes. Press each piece out again and then shape into an oval loaf about 12 inches (30 cm) long. Transfer to the lined pan, seam-side up, positioning the loaves lengthwise. Dust the top and sides with flour. Fold the linen to create support walls on both sides of each loaf, then fold any extra length of the linen liner over the top or cover with a kitchen towel. Transfer the pan to the refrigerator and chill for 16 to 20 hours.

11 Set up the oven with a baking stone and a cast-iron skillet for steam (see Baking Stones and Steam, page 296), then preheat the oven to 500°F (260°C).

12 Using the linen liner, lift and gently flip the loaves off the pan and onto a transfer peel, seam-side down. Slide the loaves, still seam-side down, onto a dusted baking peel (see Using a Transfer Peel and Baking Peel, page 311). Score the top of each (see Scoring, page 290). Working quickly but carefully, transfer the loaves to the stone using heavy-duty oven mitts or potholders. Pull out the hot skillet, add about 3 cups of ice cubes, then slide it back in and close the oven door. Immediately lower the oven temperature to 460°F (240°C). Bake, switching the positions of the loaves about two-thirds of the way through baking, until the surface is a warm golden brown, with some spots along the scores being darker, about 35 minutes.

13 Using the baking peel, transfer the loaves to a cooling rack. When the bottoms of the loaves are tapped, they should sound hollow. If not, return to the stone and bake for 5 minutes longer.

14 Let the bread cool completely before slicing and eating, at least 4 hours but preferably 12 to 36 hours.

GRAINS AND SEEDS BREAD

If you run a bakery in this era in which whole, natural ingredients are a big selling point, you must offer a multigrain bread. Yet at many bakeries, this is just a bread made mostly with white flour, with some seeds and whole grains mixed in. I don't care for this approach. It looks all crunchy and healthy, but in truth, the small amounts of whole ingredients don't improve the taste or nutritional value of the bread much. They are mostly "health food decoration."

There is an advantage, though, to combining grains and other ingredients to create a new flavor and texture profile, as in this recipe. It utilizes a soaker that includes amaranth, millet, and sesame seeds. Toasting them brings out nutty flavors, and soaking them adds interesting fermentation notes. Toasting also brings the oil in these ingredients to the surface, allowing it to seep more easily into the crumb of the bread while it bakes. Then, as in so many of the best recipes, the proteins and sugars combine in a fundamental chemical process called the Maillard reaction, which reveals the flavors inherent in the ingredients. I don't mean to drown you in breadspeak jargon here. This is just a complex way of saying that, once again, some simple ingredients—fermented and baked—produce beautifully complex and nuanced flavor.

FIRST STARTER

20 grams (1 tbsp + 1 tsp) Sourdough Starter (page 122)
40 grams (2 tbsp + 2 tsp) water at about 60°F (15°C)
40 grams (¼ c + 1 tbsp) white flour

SECOND STARTER

60 grams (¼ c + 1 tsp) millet
40 grams (3 tbsp) amaranth
10 grams (1 tbsp) sesame seeds, preferably black
8 grams (1 tbsp) dark rye flour
10 grams (2 tsp) Sourdough Starter (see page 122)
60 grams (¼ c) water at about 80°F (25°C)

DOUGH

370 grams (2½ c + 2½ tbsp) white flour, plus additional
    as needed for working with the dough
40 grams (¼ c + 1 tbsp) buckwheat flour
30 grams (3½ tbsp) medium whole wheat flour
30 grams (3½ tbsp) spelt flour
30 grams (¼ c) dark rye flour
16 grams (2¾ tsp) fine sea salt
1 gram (generous ¼ tsp) instant yeast
350 grams (1¼ c + 3½ tbsp) water at about 60°F (15°C)

Dusting Mixture (see page 35), for the linen
    liner and shaped loaves

FOR THE FIRST STARTER

1 Put the sourdough starter in a medium storage container and add the water. Break the starter into pieces with your fingers until it's almost dissolved in the water; there will still be some small pieces. Stir in the flour until fully incorporated. Cover the container and let sit at room temperature for 12 to 16 hours. The starter will be at its peak at around 14 hours.

FOR THE SECOND STARTER

1 Preheat the oven to 400°F (205°C). Spread the millet, amaranth, and sesame seeds on separate quarter sheet pans or in small baking pans. Bake until toasted, 6 to 8 minutes for the sesame seeds and

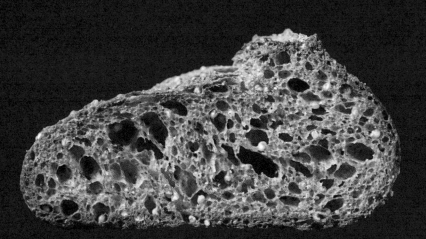

about 10 minutes for the millet and amaranth. Let cool completely. Transfer the millet, amaranth, and sesame seeds to a small bowl and stir in the flour.

2 Put the sourdough starter in a medium storage container and add the water. Break the starter into pieces with your fingers until it's almost dissolved in the water; there will still be some small pieces. Stir in the millet mixture until fully incorporated. Cover the container and let sit at room temperature for 12 to 16 hours. The starter will be at its peak at around 14 hours.

FOR THE DOUGH

1 Stir together the white, buckwheat, whole wheat, spelt, and dark rye flours, salt, and yeast in a medium bowl.

2 Pour about one-third of the water around the edges of the starter to release it from the sides of the container. Transfer the starter and the water to an extra-large bowl. Use a little of the remaining water to loosen the whole grain starter. Pour the whole grain starter and the remaining water into the bowl. Using a wooden spoon, break both of the starters up to distribute them in the water.

3 Add the flour mixture, reserving about one-sixth of it along the edge of the bowl (see Mixing, page 282). Continue to mix with the spoon until most of the dry ingredients have been combined with the starter mixture. Switch to a plastic bowl scraper and continue to mix until incorporated. At this point the dough will be slightly sticky to the touch.

4 Push the dough to one side of the bowl. Roll and tuck the dough (see Rolling and Tucking, page 284), adding the reserved flour mixture and a small amount of additional flour to the bowl and your hands as needed. Continue rolling and tucking until the dough feels stronger and begins to resist any further rolling, about 10 times. Then, with cupped hands, tuck the sides under toward the center. Place the dough, seam-side down, in a clean bowl, cover the top of the bowl with a clean kitchen towel, and let rest at room temperature for 1 hour.

5 For the first stretch and fold (see Stretching and Folding, page 285), lightly dust the work surface and your hands with flour. Using the plastic bowl scraper, release the dough from the bowl and set it, seam-side down, on the work surface. Gently stretch it into a roughly rectangular shape. Fold the dough in thirds from top to bottom and then from left to right. With cupped hands, tuck the sides under toward the center. Place the dough in the bowl, seam-side down, cover the bowl with the towel, and let rest for 1 hour.

6 For the second stretch and fold, repeat the steps for the first stretch and fold, then return the dough to the bowl, cover with the towel, and let rest for 45 minutes.

7 For the third and final stretch and fold, once again repeat the steps for the first stretch and fold, then return the dough to the bowl, cover with the towel, and let rest for 20 minutes.

8 Line a half sheet pan with a linen liner and dust fairly generously with the dusting mixture.

9 Lightly dust the work surface and your hands with flour. Using a bench scraper, divide the dough into 2 equal pieces. Press each into a 7 by 5-inch (18 by 13 cm) rectangle, then roll into a loose tube about 9 inches (23 cm) long (see Shaping a Tube or Oval Loaf, page 294). Let rest for 5 minutes. Press each piece out again and then shape into an oval about 11 inches (28 cm) long. Transfer to the lined pan, seam-side up, positioning the loaves lengthwise. Dust the top and sides of the loaves with flour. Fold the linen to create support walls on both sides of each loaf, then fold any extra length of the linen liner over the top or cover with a kitchen towel. Transfer the pan to the refrigerator and chill for 12 to 18 hours.

10 Set up the oven with a baking stone and a cast-iron skillet for steam (see Baking Stones and Steam, page 296), then preheat the oven to 480°F (250°C).

11 Using the linen liner, lift and gently flip the loaves off the pan and onto a transfer peel, seam-side down. Slide the loaves, still seam-side down, onto a dusted baking peel (see Using a Transfer Peel and Baking

Peel, page 311). Score the top of each (see Scoring, page 290). Working quickly but carefully, transfer the loaves to the stone using heavy-duty oven mitts or potholders. Pull out the hot skillet, add about 3 cups of ice cubes, then slide it back in and close the oven door. Immediately lower the oven temperature to 440°F (225°C). Bake, switching the positions of the loaves about two-thirds of the way through baking, until the surface is a warm golden brown, with some spots along the scores being darker, about 30 minutes.

12 Using the baking peel, transfer the loaves to a cooling rack. When the bottoms of the loaves are tapped, they should sound hollow. If not, return to the stone and bake for 5 minutes longer.

13 Let the bread cool completely before slicing and eating, at least 4 hours but preferably 12 to 36 hours.

ROLLS

The most obvious difference between rolls and full-sized loaves is that rolls have a much higher crust-to-crumb ratio than a slice of bread. This textural quality is very important when you eat rolls along with a soup or stew, pleasantly contrasting with the mouthfeel of these foods. And the way I look at things, anything that broadens the taste and texture experience is a plus. Rolls are also easy to break in half for that all-important task of cleaning the dish as you finish off a bowl of soup or sop up a splash of gravy.

The rolls' small size often doesn't allow for the flavor development that a full-sized loaf does. This is especially the case in the final fermentation stage, when resting shaped rolls for an extended period can lead to drier dough because they have a higher ratio of surface area for moisture to evaporate. So you have to seek other ways to add flavor. In the following recipes, I've used nuts, seeds, figs, grapes, raisins, carrots, and other ingredients to add texture, flavor, and aroma. By adding such ingredients, I've created rolls well suited to accompanying specific foods, similar to wine pairings. This can add an extra dimension of pleasure to a meal. Still, there are times when a roll is just a small version of a bread (*petit pain*) and that's fine, too.

YEMA ROLLS

I have to admit that I was unimpressed with much of the bread I encountered during the years I spent traveling through Latin America, the main exception being that miraculous bread I that was the inspiration for my Pancito Potosí (page 199). If I had to pick one other Latin American bread that interested me and was sometimes reasonably good, it would be *pan de yema*, or egg yolk bread. The method in Central America, where this bread is most popular, involves incorporating raw egg yolks into the dough. Instead I cook the yolks, shred them, and then mix them in. I use cornmeal, for both taste and texture and because corn is the most important grain in the Latin American birthplace of *pan de yema*. There's milk and honey here too, a time-honored combination (in your Bible, see the Book of Exodus).

STARTER

100 grams (½ c + 3½ tbsp) medium-grind cornmeal
0.2 gram (pinch) instant yeast
100 grams (¼ c + 2½ tbsp) cold whole milk

EGGS

7 large eggs

DOUGH

220 grams (1½ c + 1 tbsp) white flour, plus
    additional as needed for working with the dough
30 grams (¼ c) white rye flour
9 grams (1½ tsp) fine sea salt
1 gram (generous ¼ tsp) instant yeast
185 grams (½ c + 3½ tbsp) cold whole milk
30 grams (1½ tbsp) honey

Dusting Mixture (see page 35), for the linen
    liner and shaped rolls

FOR THE STARTER

1 Put the cornmeal in a medium storage container. Sprinkle the yeast into the milk, stir to mix, and pour over the flour. Mix with your fingers, pressing the mixture into the sides, bottom, and corners until all of the cornmeal is wet and fully incorporated. Cover the container and let sit at room temperature for 8 to 12 hours. The starter will be at its peak at around 10 hours.

TO COOK THE EGGS

1 Fill a medium bowl with ice water, set a large plate next to the stovetop, and bring a large saucepan of water to a boil. Using a slotted spoon, gently set the eggs in the water and boil for 7 minutes. Remove the eggs from the water and set on the plate for 2 minutes. Transfer to the ice water and let cool completely.

2 Peel the eggs and separate the yolks from the whites. Reserve the whites for another use. Using a Microplane grater or other fine grater, shred the yolks into a medium storage container. Cover and refrigerate until ready to use.

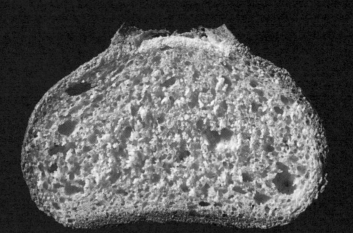

FOR THE DOUGH

1 Stir together the white and white rye flours, salt, and yeast in a small bowl.

2 Pour about one-third of the milk around the edges of the starter to release it from the sides of the container. Transfer the starter and milk to an extra-large bowl along with the remaining milk and the honey. Using a wooden spoon, break the starter up to distribute it in the liquid.

3 Add the flour mixture, reserving about one-sixth of it along the edge of the bowl (see Mixing, page 282). Continue to mix with the spoon until most of the dry ingredients have been combined with the starter mixture. Switch to a plastic bowl scraper and continue to mix. Once most of the flour has been incorporated, add 100 grams (about 1 c) of the egg yolks, and continue to mix until they are distributed throughout the dough. At this point the dough will be slightly sticky to the touch.

4 Push the dough to one side of the bowl. Roll and tuck the dough (see Rolling and Tucking, page 284), adding the reserved flour mixture and a small amount of additional flour to the bowl and your hands as needed. Continue rolling and tucking until

the dough feels stronger and begins to resist any further rolling, about 12 times. Then, with cupped hands, tuck the sides under toward the center. Place the dough, seam-side down, in a clean bowl, cover the top of the bowl with a clean kitchen towel, and let rest at room temperature for 45 minutes.

5 For the first stretch and fold (see Stretching and Folding, page 285), lightly dust the work surface and your hands with flour. Using the plastic bowl scraper, release the dough from the bowl and set it, seam-side down, on the work surface. Gently stretch it into a roughly rectangular shape. Fold the dough in thirds from top to bottom and then from left to right. With cupped hands, tuck the sides under toward the center. Place the dough in the bowl, seam-side down, cover the bowl with the towel, and let rest for 45 minutes.

6 For the second stretch and fold, repeat the steps for the first stretch and fold, then return the dough to the bowl, cover with the towel, and let rest for 45 minutes.

7 For the third and final stretch and fold, once again repeat the steps for the first stretch and fold, then return the dough to the bowl, cover with the towel, and let rest for 20 minutes.

8 Line a half sheet pan with a linen liner and dust fairly generously with the dusting mixture.

9 Lightly dust the work surface and your hands with flour. Using a bench scraper, divide the dough into 12 equal pieces (about 64 grams each). Gently roll each piece against the work surface to form a ball (see Rolling Dough into Balls, page 299). Let rest for 5 minutes.

10 Roll the balls again, adding just enough pressure to stretch them into ovals about 3 inches (8 cm) long. (These rolls are not stretched so far as to be tubes—just enough that they are a bit oblong.) Arrange the rolls, on the lined pan in three rows of four rolls each and dust well with the dusting mixture. Fold the linen to create support walls along the length of the rolls on both sides of each row (see Using a Linen Liner for Rolls, page 293). Fold any extra length of the linen liner over the top or cover with a kitchen towel. Transfer the pan to the refrigerator and chill for 12 to 16 hours.

11 Set up the oven with a cast-iron skillet for steam (see Baking Stones and Steam, page 296), then pre-heat the oven to 480°F (250°C). Line a half sheet pan with a silicone baking mat or parchment paper.

12 Using the linen liner, lift and ease each roll off the linen-lined pan and onto your hand. Set the rolls on the second pan, seam-side down, in three rows of four rolls each. Score the top of each roll with a small X (see Scoring, page 290).

13 Put the pan in the oven. Using heavy-duty oven mitts or potholders, pull out the hot skillet, add about 1½ cups of ice cubes, then slide it back in and close the oven door. Immediately lower the oven temperature to 440°F (225°C) and bake, rotating the pan about two-thirds of the way through baking, until the tops are golden brown, 12 to 16 minutes.

14 Set the sheet pan on a cooling rack. Give the rolls a few minutes to cool slightly, then place them directly on the cooling rack and let cool completely, about 1 hour. The rolls are best eaten the day they're baked, but once completely cooled they can be stored (uncut) in a paper bag or cardboard box for up to 24 hours.

TOASTED OATMEAL ROLLS

These rolls are even oatier than the Toasted Oat Bread (page 75). Basically, I deconstructed a bowl of oatmeal right down to the brown sugar, cream, and butter that I love on my warm porridge on a cold winter's day. The secret is toasting steel-cut oats and then using them in both the starter and the dough. For the starter, they're made into oatmeal. They're added to the dough in two forms: ground into a toasted oat flour, and also whole, to provide a little crunch. The heavy cream in the dough creates a soft and sweet effect, as comforting as a warm bowl of, well, oatmeal.

TOASTED OATS

165 grams (¼ c + 3 tbsp) steel-cut oats

STARTER

100 grams (¼ c + 2 tbsp) oatmeal, prepared from
    the toasted oats
33 grams (3 tbsp + 2 tsp) white flour
0.1 gram (small pinch) instant yeast
66 grams (¼ c + 1 tsp) water at about 60°F (15°C)

DOUGH

280 grams (2 c) white flour, plus additional as
    needed for working with the dough
50 grams (½ c) toasted oat flour, prepared from
    the toasted oats
33 grams (2 tbsp + 2 tsp) light brown sugar
9 grams (1½ tsp) fine sea salt
0.8 gram (¼ tsp) instant yeast
200 grams (¾ c + 2 tsp) cold whole milk
112 grams (¼ c + 3½ tbsp) cold heavy cream
65 grams (½ c + 2½ tbsp) toasted oats

Dusting Mixture (see page 35), for the linen liner
    and shaped rolls

FOR THE TOASTED OATS

1 Preheat the oven to 425°F (220°C). Spread the oats on a half sheet pan and toast for 4 minutes. Gently shake the pan, then toast for 4 minutes longer. Shake again and toast until aromatic and evenly golden brown, 2 to 4 minutes longer. Let cool completely. The oats will decrease slightly in weight when toasted (explaining why the following amounts don't quite add up to the amount prior to toasting). Set aside 35 grams (¼ c + 1½ tbsp) of the toasted oats to make the oatmeal for the starter. Measure out 50 grams (½ c) to grind into flour. Set the rest of the toasted oats aside for later use. This should be about 65 grams (½ c + 2½ tbsp).

2 Put the 50 grams (½ c) of oats to a high-powered blender or a coffee grinder and process to form a fine flour.

FOR THE STARTER

1 Combine the 35 grams (¼ c + 1½ tbsp) of the toasted oats and 135 grams (½ c + 1 tbsp) of water in a small saucepan over medium high heat. Bring to a simmer, then decrease the heat to maintain a low simmer and cook, stirring often, until the oats are softened and the water has been absorbed, about 10 minutes. You will need 100 grams (¼ c + 2 tbsp) of the prepared oatmeal for the starter.

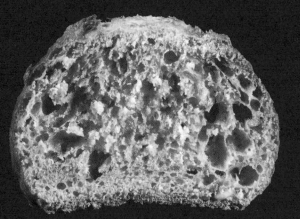

2 Stir together the 100 grams (¼ c + 2 tbsp) of pre-pared oatmeal and the white flour in a medium storage container. Sprinkle the yeast into the water, stir to mix, and pour over the oatmeal mixture. Mix with your fingers, pressing the mixture into the sides, bot-tom, and corners until all of the flour is wet and fully incorporated. Cover the container and let sit at room temperature for 10 to 15 hours. The starter will be at its peak at around 13 hours.

FOR THE DOUGH

1 Stir together the white and toasted oat flours, brown sugar, salt, and yeast in a small bowl.

2 Combine the milk and heavy cream in a measur-ing cup. Pour about one-third of the mixture around the edges of the starter to release it from the sides of the container. Transfer the starter and milk mixture to an extra-large bowl along with the remaining milk mixture. Using a wooden spoon, break the starter up to distribute it in the liquid.

3 Add the flour mixture, reserving about one-sixth of it along the edge of the bowl (see Mixing, page 282). Continue to mix with the spoon until most of the dry ingredients have been combined with the

starter mixture. Switch to a plastic bowl scraper and continue to mix until incorporated. At this point the dough will be very sticky to the touch and fairly loose.

4 Push the dough to one side of the bowl. Roll and tuck the dough (see Rolling and Tucking, page 284), adding the reserved flour mixture and a small amount of additional flour to the bowl and your hands as needed. For this dough you may need more flour, but resist the urge to add it too quickly. If the dough seems too sticky, let it rest for 5 minutes, then come back to it. Continue rolling and tucking until the dough feels stronger and begins to resist any further rolling, about 10 times. Then, with cupped hands, tuck the sides under toward the center. Place the dough, seam-side down, in a clean bowl, cover the top of the bowl with a clean kitchen towel, and let rest at room temperature for 45 minutes.

5 For the first stretch and fold (see Stretching and Folding, page 285), lightly dust the work surface and your hands with flour. Using the plastic bowl scraper, release the dough from the bowl and set it, seam-side down, on the work surface. Gently stretch it into a roughly rectangular shape. Fold the dough in thirds from top to bottom and then from left to right. With cupped hands, tuck the sides under toward the center. Place the dough in the bowl, seam-side down, cover the bowl with the towel, and let rest for 45 minutes.

6 For the second stretch and fold, repeat the steps for the first stretch and fold, then return the dough to the bowl, cover with the towel, and let rest for 45 minutes.

7 For the third and final stretch and fold, gently stretch the dough into a rectangle, scatter the toasted oats on top, and gently press them into the dough. (For photos of the following process, see Incorporating Add-Ins, page 292.) Roll up the dough tightly from the end closest to you; at the end of the roll the dough will be seam-side down. Turn it over, seam-side up, and gently press on the seam to flatten the dough slightly. Fold in thirds from left to right and then do 1 roll and tuck sequence to incorporate the oats. Turn the dough seam-side down and tuck the sides under toward the center. Return the dough to the bowl, cover with the towel, and let rest for 20 minutes.

8 Line a half sheet pan with a linen liner and dust fairly generously with the dusting mixture.

9 Lightly dust the work surface and your hands with flour. Using a bench scraper, divide the dough into 12 equal pieces (about 75 grams each). Gently roll each piece against the work surface to form a ball (see Rolling Dough into Balls, page 299). Let rest for 5 minutes.

10 Using a bowl scraper and working with one ball at a time, cut the ball almost in half, stopping just before the bottom and leaving about ⅛ inch (3 mm) uncut; keep the halves attached (see the photos on page 300). Make a second cut across the first, stopping at the same point, just before the bottom. There

will now be an X across the round. Next, using your thumb and forefinger, press two opposite sections toward the center to square off the sides. Repeat with the remaining two sides to make a square roll. Arrange the rolls, cut-side down, on the lined pan in three rows of four rolls each and dust well with the dusting mixture. Fold the linen to create support walls along the rolls on both sides of each row (see Using a Linen Liner for Rolls, page 293). Fold any extra length of the linen liner over the top or cover with a kitchen towel. Transfer the pan to the refrigerator and chill for 16 to 22 hours.

11 Set up the oven with a cast-iron skillet for steam (see Baking Stones and Steam, page 296), then preheat the oven to 500°F (260°C). Line a half sheet pan with a silicone baking mat or parchment paper.

12 Using the linen liner, lift and ease each roll off the pan and onto your hand. Set the rolls on the second pan, cut-side up, in three rows of four rolls each.

13 Put the pan in the oven. Using heavy-duty oven mitts or potholders, pull out the hot skillet, add about 1½ cups of ice cubes, then slide it back in and close the oven door. Immediately lower the oven temperature to 465°F (240°C) and bake, rotating the pan about two-thirds of the way through baking, until the tops of the rolls are golden brown, 15 to 20 minutes.

14 Set the sheet pan on a cooling rack. Give the rolls a few minutes to cool slightly, then place them directly on the cooling rack and let cool completely, about 1 hour. The rolls are best eaten the day they're baked, but once completely cooled they can be stored (uncut) in a paper bag or cardboard box for up to 24 hours.

FOUGASSE BASQUE

Traditionally, *fougasse* was baked in the ashes of a wood-fired oven as a way to assess how much—or how little—heat remained. It has a distinctive shape that's fun to see and even more fun to eat. I first tasted a version of *fougasse* that I liked at a Basque restaurant I often frequented in Seattle. Whenever the kitchen crew at that restaurant saw me coming, they tried to outdo each other preparing what was always a multicourse celebration. One night I showed up with a couple of new breads that we were working on for William Leaman, including my *fougasse*. This caused quite a stir of anticipation among the kitchen staff, and it was particularly pleasing to me when my dining partner, a three-hundred-pound chef named Jimenez, made a beeline for the fougasse. "I know this," he said. "We eat this in Basque country; the combination of olives and almonds is very Basque." And with that he went to work on one. He wore dentures, making his contest with the roll a bit of a challenge, so it was even more gratifying to see his determination to finish the whole thing and his smile of approval.

STARTER

50 grams (¼ c + 2 tbsp) buckwheat flour
0.2 gram (pinch) instant yeast
70 grams (¼ c + 2 tsp) water at about 60°F (15°C)

DOUGH

35 grams (¼ c + 2½ tbsp) sliced almonds
225 grams (1½ c + 1½ tbsp) white flour, plus additional
    as needed for working with the dough
25 grams (3 tbsp + 1 tsp) white rye flour
5 grams (¾ tsp) fine sea salt
1 gram (generous ¼ tsp) instant yeast
155 grams (½ c + 2½ tbsp) water at about 60°F (15°C)
20 grams (1 tbsp) honey
15 grams (1 tbsp + 1 tsp) extra-virgin olive oil
15 grams (1½ tbsp) minced oil-cured black olives

Dusting Mixture (see page 35), for the linen liner
    and shaped rolls

FOR THE STARTER

1 Put the flour in a medium storage container. Sprinkle the yeast into the water, stir to mix, and pour over the flour. Mix with your fingers, pressing the mixture into the sides, bottom, and corners until all of the flour is wet and fully incorporated. Cover the container and let sit at room temperature for 12 to 16 hours. The starter will be at its peak at around 14 hours.

FOR THE DOUGH

1 Preheat the oven to 400°F (205°C). Spread the almonds on a small sheet pan and bake until toasted, about 7 minutes. Let cool completely. Coarsely chop the almonds into small shards. Store in a covered container until ready to use.

2 Stir together the white and white rye flours, salt, and yeast in a small bowl.

3 Pour about one-third of the water around the edges of the starter to release it from the sides of the container. Transfer the starter and water to an

extra-large bowl along with the remaining water, the honey, and the olive oil. Using a wooden spoon, break the starter up to distribute it in the liquid.

4 Add the flour mixture, reserving about one-sixth of it along the edge of the bowl (see Mixing, page 282). Continue to mix with the spoon until most of the dry ingredients have been combined with the starter mixture. Switch to a plastic bowl scraper and continue to mix until incorporated. At this point the dough will be sticky to the touch.

5 Push the dough to one side of the bowl. Roll and tuck the dough (see Rolling and Tucking, page 284), adding the reserved flour mixture and a small amount of additional flour to the bowl and your hands as needed. Continue rolling and tucking until the dough feels stronger and begins to resist any further rolling, about 12 times. Then, with cupped hands, tuck the sides under toward the center. Place the dough, seam-side down, in a clean bowl, cover the top of the bowl with a clean kitchen towel, and let rest at room temperature for 45 minutes.

6 For the first stretch and fold (see Stretching and Folding, page 285), lightly dust the work surface and your hands with flour. Using the plastic bowl scraper, release the dough from the bowl and set it,

seam-side down, on the work surface. Gently stretch it into a roughly rectangular shape. Fold the dough in thirds from top to bottom and then from left to right. With cupped hands, tuck the sides under toward the center. Place the dough in the bowl, seam-side down, cover the bowl with the towel, and let rest for 45 minutes.

7 For the second stretch and fold, gently stretch the dough into a rectangle, scatter the almonds and olives over the top, and gently press them into the dough. (For photos of the following process, see Incorporating Add-Ins, page 292.) Roll up the dough tightly from the end closest to you; at the end of the roll the dough will be seam-side down. Turn it over, seam-side up, and gently press on the seam to flatten the dough slightly. Fold in thirds from left to right and then do 1 roll and tuck sequence to incorporate the almonds and olives. Turn the dough seam-side down and tuck the sides under toward the center. Return the bowl to the bowl, cover with the towel, and let rest for 45 minutes.

8 For the third and final stretch and fold, repeat the steps for the first stretch and fold, return the dough to the bowl, cover with the towel, and let rest for 20 minutes.

9 Line a half sheet pan with a linen liner and dust fairly generously with the dusting mixture.

10 Lightly dust the work surface and your hands with flour. Using a bench scraper, divide the dough into 12 equal pieces (about 50 grams each). Gently roll each piece against the work surface to form a ball (see Rolling Dough into Balls, page 299). Let rest for 15 minutes.

11 Flatten each ball into a disk about ½ inch (1.5 cm) thick; it should be about 2½ inches (6.5 cm) in diameter. Arrange the rolls on the lined pan in three rows of four rolls each and dust the tops well with the dusting mixture. Fold the linen to create support walls along the length of the rolls on both sides of each row. Fold any extra length of the linen liner over the top or cover with a kitchen towel. Transfer the pan to the refrigerator and chill for 20 to 26 hours.

12 Set up the oven with a cast-iron skillet for steam (see Baking Stones and Steam, page 296), then preheat the oven to 480°F (250°C). Line two half sheet pans with silicone baking mats or parchment paper.

13 These rolls will be baked in batches. Using the linen liner, lift and ease each of the rolls off the sheet pan and onto your hand. Set the rolls on one of the sheet pans lined with a silicone mat. Give each disk a slight press to make it about 3 inches (8 cm) in diameter. Using a *lame*, razor blade, or very sharp paring knife, and being careful not to cut the liner, make a slit all the way through the dough, about 1 inch (2.5 cm) in from one of the sides, slightly off of the center, leaving about ¼ inch (6 mm) on each edge. Make a second, similar cut, parallel to the first, about 1 inch (2.5 cm) in from the other side. Gently pull on the sides of the round, stretching the slits open to about

¾ inch (2 cm) across, so the roll is oval and looks like an oblong button. Repeat with the remaining rolls, arranging them on the sheet pan in two rows of three rolls each.

14 Put the pan in the oven. Using heavy-duty oven mitts or potholders, pull out the hot skillet, add about 1½ cups of ice cubes, then slide it back in and close the oven door. Immediately lower the oven temperature to 440°F (225°C) and bake, rotating the pan about two-thirds of the way through baking, until the tops are golden brown, 12 to 15 minutes. While the first 6 fougasse are baking, set the remaining six disks on the second silicone-lined sheet pan and shape them in the same way.

15 Set the first pan of baked fougasse on a cooling rack. Carefully pull out the skillet and pour out any remaining water. Set the skillet back on the rack and allow the oven temperature to return to 480°F (250°C). Then bake the second pan of fougasse in the same way, once again adding about 1½ cups of ice cubes to the skillet to create steam.

16 With both batches, give the rolls a few minutes to cool slightly on the pan, then place them directly on the cooling rack and let cool completely, about 1 hour. The rolls are best eaten the day they're baked, but once completely cooled they can be stored (uncut) in a paper bag or cardboard box for up to 24 hours.

LATE-HARVEST CARROT ROLLS

On the farm in Oregon where I first learned to make long-fermented bread, the last vegetables we pulled from the ground in winter were carrots. They were a far cry from the small, skinny, sweet early season carrots. These were big, ugly, starchy, and woody. But they had gone through a lot to get to that stage, so we figured they must be good for something, and juice was an obvious answer.

Thinking back on those days as I created new breads for this book, I considered making a starter and dough with carrot juice. The starches would turn to sugar and provide unique fermentation notes. To complement the juice, I decided to dice additional carrots, roast them until caramelized, and fold them into the dough. This recipe is the result, yielding rolls with a beautiful balance of sweetness and earthiness and an amber-orange crumb. Their rich, full flavor speaks well for the end of the harvest season. Note that for this recipe you'll need to juice about 750 grams (about 1 pound, 10 /2 oz) carrots, or 24 fluid ounces of high-quality bottled carrot juice.

STARTER

66 grams (¼ c + 3½ tbsp) white flour
0.1 gram (small pinch) instant yeast
66 grams (¼ c + ½ tbsp) carrot juice

ROASTED CARROTS

300 grams (10½ oz) large carrots
7 grams (2 tsp) light brown sugar
2 grams (¼ + ⅛ tsp) fine sea salt
15 grams (1 tbsp) unsalted butter

DOUGH

248 grams (1¾ c + 1½ tsp) white flour, plus additional
    as needed for working with the dough
60 grams (¼ c + 2½ tbsp) buckwheat flour
25 grams (2 tbsp + 2¼ tsp) medium whole wheat flour
8 grams (1¼ tsp) fine sea salt
0.8 gram (¼ tsp) instant yeast
255 grams (1 c + ½ tbsp) carrot juice
25 grams (1¾ tbsp) unsalted butter, at room temperature

Dusting Mixture (see page 35), for the linen liner
    and shaped rolls

FOR THE STARTER

1 Put the flour in a medium storage container. Sprinkle the yeast into the carrot juice, stir to mix, and pour over the flour. Mix with your fingers, pressing the mixture into the sides, bottom, and corners until all of the flour is wet and fully incorporated. Cover the container and let sit at room temperature for 10 to 14 hours. The starter will be at its peak at around 12 hours.

FOR THE CARROTS

1 Preheat the oven to 400°F (205°C). Trim and peel the carrots, then cut them into ¼-inch (6 mm) dice. Put the carrots in a medium bowl, sprinkle with the sugar and salt, then toss until evenly coated.

2 Put the butter on a half sheet pan and put the pan in the oven just long enough to melt the butter. Spread the carrots on the pan and toss to evenly coat with the butter. Spread the carrots in an even layer, then bake, stirring every 10 minutes, until tender and golden brown, about 30 minutes. Let cool completely, then refrigerate until ready to use.

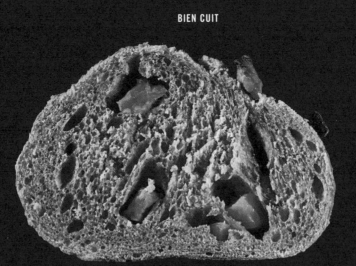

FOR THE DOUGH

1 Stir together the white, buckwheat, and whole wheat flours, salt, and yeast in a small bowl.

2 Pour about one-third of the carrot juice around the edges of the starter to release it from the sides of the container. Transfer the starter and carrot juice to an extra-large bowl along with the remaining juice. Using a wooden spoon, break the starter up to distribute it in the juice.

3 Add the flour mixture, reserving about one-sixth of it along the edge of the bowl (see Mixing, page 282). Continue to mix with the spoon until most of the dry ingredients have been combined with the starter mixture. Switch to a plastic bowl scraper and continue to mix until incorporated. At this point the dough will be sticky to the touch.

4 Push the dough to one side of the bowl. Roll and tuck the dough (see Rolling and Tucking, page 284), adding the reserved flour mixture and a small amount of additional flour to the bowl and your hands as needed. Continue rolling and tucking until the dough feels stronger and begins to resist any further rolling, about 10 times. Then, with cupped hands, tuck the sides under toward the center. Place

the dough, seam-side down, in a clean bowl, cover the top of the bowl with a clean kitchen towel, and let rest at room temperature for 45 minutes.

5 For the first stretch and fold (see Stretching and Folding, page 285), lightly dust the work surface and your hands with flour. Using the plastic bowl scraper, release the dough from the bowl and set it, seam-side down, on the work surface. Gently stretch it into a roughly rectangular shape. Fold the dough in thirds from top to bottom and then from left to right. With cupped hands, tuck the sides under toward the center. Place the dough in the bowl, seam-side down, cover the bowl with the towel, and let rest for 45 minutes.

6 For the second stretch and fold, repeat the steps for the first stretch and fold, then return the dough to the bowl, cover with the towel, and let rest for 30 minutes.

7 For the third stretch and fold, gently stretch the dough into a rectangle. Pinch the butter into pieces, distributing them over the top of the dough. Using your fingers or a spatula, spread the butter across the surface of the dough. (For photos of the following process, see Incorporating Add-Ins, page 292.) Roll up the dough tightly from the end closest to you; at the end of the roll the dough will be seam-side down. Turn it over, seam-side up, and gently press on the seam to flatten the dough slightly. Fold in thirds from left to right and then do 4 or 5 roll and tuck sequences to incorporate the butter. Turn the dough seam-side down and tuck the sides under toward the center. Return the dough to the bowl, cover with the towel, and let rest for 30 minutes.

8 For the fourth and final stretch and fold, gently stretch the dough into a rectangle, scatter the roasted carrots over the top, and gently press them into the dough. Roll up the dough tightly from the end closest to you; at the end of the roll the dough will be seam-side down. Turn it over, seam-side up, and gently press on the seam to flatten the dough slightly. Fold in thirds from left to right and then do 1 roll and tuck sequence to incorporate the carrots. Turn the dough seam-side down and tuck the sides under toward the center. Return the dough to the bowl, seam-side down, cover with the towel, and let rest for 20 minutes.

9 Line a half sheet pan with a linen liner and dust fairly generously with the dusting mixture.

10 Lightly dust the work surface and your hands with flour. Using a bench scraper, divide the dough into 12 equal pieces (about 70 grams each). Let rest for 5 minutes.

11 Tightly roll up the pieces into small tubes about 4 inches (10 cm) long (see Shaping Small Tubes, page 301). Arrange the rolls on the lined pan in three rows of four rolls each and dust well with the dusting mixture. Fold the linen to create support walls along the length of the rolls on both sides of each row (see Using a Linen Liner for Rolls, page 293). Fold any extra length of the linen liner over the top or cover

with a kitchen towel. Transfer the pan to the refrigerator and chill for 16 to 22 hours.

12 Set up the oven with a cast-iron skillet for steam (see Baking Stones and Steam, page 296), then preheat the oven to 500°F (260°C). Line a half sheet pan with a silicone baking mat or parchment paper.

13 Using the linen liner, lift and ease each roll off the pan and onto your hand. Set the rolls on the second pan with the length of the rolls running across the pan, in two rows of six rolls each. Score the top of each roll (see Scoring, page 290).

14 Put the pan in the oven. Using heavy-duty oven mitts or potholders, pull out the hot skillet, add about 1½ cups of ice cubes, then slide it back in and close the oven door. Immediately lower the oven temperature to 465°F (240°C) and bake, rotating the pan about two-thirds of the way through baking, until the tops are golden brown, 15 to 20 minutes.

15 Set the sheet pan on a cooling rack. Give the rolls a few minutes to cool slightly, then place them directly on the cooling rack and let cool completely, about 1 hour. The rolls are best eaten the day they're baked, but once completely cooled they can be stored (uncut) in a paper bag or cardboard box for up to 24 hours.

PINE NUT AND HERB ROLLS

The overall effect in these rolls is a pronounced background note of pine nuts and herbs—just enough to let you know they are there, but not so much that the flavor takes over. I include pine nuts here in two forms: soaked and then blended, as well as roasted, to capture their full flavor spectrum and highlight umami. As for the herbs, they are blended in milk, which helps preserve their freshness as the dough is prepared. I like this combination of herbs, but feel free to improvise. You may have other herbs that you prefer, or the dish you are serving the rolls with might suggest another herb (for example, sage with roast chicken). Serve these rolls with fava beans or asparagus and, if you're lucky enough to find some, fiddlehead ferns sautéed in butter. Back on the farm where I worked in Oregon, I might have served them with wild steelhead trout taken from one of the region's swift-flowing rivers. Salmon would also be a good choice.

STARTER

90 grams (½ c + 2½ tbsp) medium whole wheat flour
0.2 gram (pinch) instant yeast
110 grams (¼ c + 3½ tbsp) water at about 60°F (15°C)

PINE NUT WATER

20 grams (2½ tbsp) pine nuts
80 grams (¼ c + 1½ tbsp) warm water

DOUGH

50 grams (¼ c + 2 tbsp) pine nuts
75 grams (¼ c + 2 tsp) cold whole milk
8 grams (½ c, packed) basil leaves
7 grams (⅓ c, packed) sorrel leaves
7 grams (⅓ c, packed) parsley leaves
5 grams (¼ c, packed) chervil leaves
180 grams (1¼ c + 2 tsp) white flour, plus additional
    as needed for working with the dough
80 grams (½ c + 1 tbsp) medium whole wheat flour
8 grams (1¼ tsp) fine sea salt
1 gram (generous ¼ tsp) instant yeast
25 grams (2 tbsp) extra-virgin olive oil

Dusting Mixture (see page 35), for the linen liner and
    shaped rolls

FOR THE STARTER

1 Put the flour in a medium storage container. Sprinkle the yeast into the water, stir to mix, and pour over the flour. Mix with your fingers, pressing the mixture into the sides, bottom, and corners until all of the flour is wet and fully incorporated. Cover the container and let sit at room temperature for 12 to 16 hours. The starter will be at its peak at around 14 hours.

FOR THE PINE NUT WATER

1 Put the pine nuts in a medium heatproof storage container. Pour in the water, cover, and let sit at room temperature for 8 to 12 hours.

2 Transfer to a blender, preferably a high-powered one, and blend well.

FOR THE DOUGH

1 Preheat the oven to 375°F (190°C). Spread the pine nuts on a quarter sheet pan and toast for 4 minutes. Gently shake the pan, then toast until aromatic and evenly golden brown, about 4 minutes longer. Let cool completely.

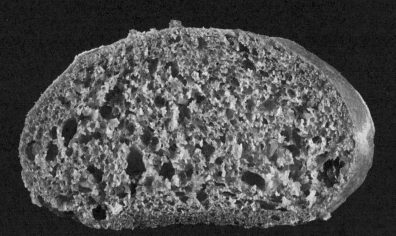

2 Transfer the toasted pine nuts to a high-powered blender or coffee grinder and process into a paste. The pine nuts will decrease in weight when toasted. You will need 30 grams (3 tbsp) for this recipe.

3 Put the milk, basil, sorrel, parsley, and chervil in a blender and blend well. There may still be some small flecks of herb.

4 Stir together the white and whole wheat flours, pine nut paste, salt, and yeast in a small bowl.

5 Pour about one-third of the herb milk around the edges of the starter to release it from the sides of the container. Transfer the starter and herb milk to an extra-large bowl along with the remaining herb milk, the pine nut water, and the olive oil. Using a wooden spoon, break the starter up to distribute it in the liquid.

6 Add the flour mixture, reserving about one-sixth of it along the edge of the bowl (see Mixing, page 282). Continue to mix with the spoon until most of the dry ingredients have been combined with the starter mixture. Switch to a plastic bowl scraper and continue to mix until incorporated. At this point the dough will be just a bit sticky and pretty stiff.

7 Push the dough to one side of the bowl. Roll and tuck the dough (see Rolling and Tucking, page 284), adding the reserved flour mixture and a small amount of additional flour to the bowl and your hands as needed. Continue rolling and tucking until the dough feels stronger and begins to resist any further rolling, about 10 times. Then, with cupped hands, tuck the sides under toward the center. Place the dough, seam-side down, in a clean bowl, cover the top of the bowl with a clean kitchen towel, and let rest at room temperature for 30 minutes.

8 For the first stretch and fold (see Stretching and Folding, page 285), lightly dust the work surface and your hands with flour. Using the plastic bowl scraper, release the dough from the bowl and set it, seam-side down, on the work surface. Gently stretch it into a roughly rectangular shape. Fold the dough in thirds from top to bottom and then from left to right. With cupped hands, tuck the sides under toward the center. Place the dough in the bowl, seam-side down, cover the bowl with the towel, and let rest for 30 minutes.

9 For the second stretch and fold, repeat the steps for the first stretch and fold, then return the dough to the bowl, cover with the towel, and let rest for 30 minutes.

10 For the third and final stretch and fold, once again repeat the steps for the first stretch and fold, then return the dough to the bowl, cover with the towel, and let rest for 30 minutes.

11 Line a half sheet pan with a linen liner and dust fairly generously with the dusting mixture.

12 Lightly dust the work surface and your hands with flour. Using a bench scraper, divide the dough into 12 equal pieces (about 56 grams each). Let rest for 5 minutes.

13 Tightly roll up the pieces into small tubes about 4 inches (10 cm) long (see Shaping Small Tubes, page 301). Arrange the rolls on the lined pan in three rows of four rolls each and dust well with the dusting mixture. Fold the linen to create support walls along the lengths of the rolls on both sides of each row (see Using a Linen Liner for Rolls, page 293). Fold any extra length of the linen liner over the top or cover with a kitchen towel. Transfer the pan to the refrigerator and chill for 18 to 26 hours.

14 Set up the oven with a cast-iron skillet for steam (see Baking Stones and Steam, page 296), then pre-heat the oven to 480°F (250°C). Line a half sheet pan with a silicone baking mat or parchment paper.

15 Using the linen liner, lift and ease each roll off the pan and onto your hand. Set the rolls on the second pan with the length of the rolls running across the pan, in two rows of six rolls each. Score the top of each roll (see Scoring, page 290).

16 Put the pan in the oven. Using heavy-duty oven mitts or potholders, pull out the hot skillet, add about 1½ cups of ice cubes, then slide it back in and close the oven door. Immediately lower the oven temperature to 440°F (225°C) and bake, rotating the pan about two-thirds of the way through baking, until the tops are only very lightly browned, 12 to 17 minutes.

17 Set the sheet pan on a cooling rack. Give the rolls a few minutes to cool slightly, then place them directly on the cooling rack and let cool completely, about 1 hour. The rolls are best eaten the day they're baked, but once completely cooled they can be stored (uncut) in a paper bag or cardboard box for up to 24 hours.

PANCITO POTOSÍ

This roll is meant as a "Thank you" by way of gratitude toward a woman whose name I never knew but whose image, even after so many years, is as clear as any I can recall. I was walking the pre-dawn streets of Potosí, Bolivia, when I smelled bread—good bread! This was astonishing because in two years of travels in South America I hadn't encountered even one good bread. Most of the bread usually looked and tasted like the lovechild of a hamburger bun and a bad English muffin. Maybe all that has changed as the food revolution has swept the world, but back then there wasn't much bread to get excited about, except . . .

To my surprise, I smelled good bread in the oven somewhere in Potosí. I let my nose guide me down back alleys, across ancient courtyards, and past shuttered stores. I just kept sniffing and sniffing until I found where it was coming from. It's kind of amazing that I did find it, because it was just a little hole in a wall—a round, barred window measuring perhaps a foot and a half by a foot. I peered inside, where I saw a small woman in traditional garb, a cloud of fabric wrapped around her. Beneath the billowing, brightly colored cloth, her skin looked old as the earth. She worked by the light of a fire in the hearth and a few candles. In front of her lay a row of miniature bâtards (oval loaves), perfectly fermented and perfectly scored. By the looks of her bread, I could have been peering through the window of a French boulangerie. And after purchasing a loaf, I found that the taste, too, was one I remembered from childhood trips to France. I felt like I was having a beautiful dream and then awakening to discover it was real. This petit pain is my homage to that Inca woman from long ago.

STARTER

90 grams (½ c + 2½ tbsp) white flour
0.2 gram (pinch) instant yeast
90 grams (¼ c + 2 tbsp) water at about 60°F (15°C)

DOUGH

225 grams (1½ c + 1½ tbsp) white flour, plus additional
     as needed for working with the dough
25 grams (3 tbsp + 1 tsp) dark rye flour
9 grams (1½ tsp) fine sea salt
0.2 gram (pinch) instant yeast
110 grams (¼ c + 3½ tbsp) water at about 60°F (15°C)

Dusting Mixture (see page 35), for the linen liner and
     shaped rolls

FOR THE STARTER

1 Put the flour in a medium storage container. Sprinkle the yeast into the water, stir to mix, and pour over the flour. Mix with your fingers, pressing the mixture into the sides, bottom, and corners until all of the flour is wet and fully incorporated. Cover the container and let sit at room temperature for 8 to 14 hours. The starter will be at its peak at around 11 hours.

FOR THE DOUGH

1 Stir together the white and dark rye flours, salt, and yeast in a small bowl.

2 Pour about one-third of the water around the edges of the starter to release it from the sides of the

container. Transfer the starter and water to an extra-large bowl along with the remaining water. Using a wooden spoon, break the starter up to distribute it in the water.

3 Add the flour mixture, reserving about one-sixth of it along the edge of the bowl (see Mixing, page 282). Continue to mix with the spoon until most of the dry ingredients have been combined with the starter mixture. Switch to a plastic bowl scraper and continue to mix until incorporated. At this point the dough will be sticky to the touch and pretty stiff.

4 Push the dough to one side of the bowl. Roll and tuck the dough (see Rolling and Tucking, page 284), adding the reserved flour mixture and a small amount of additional flour to the bowl and your hands as needed. Continue rolling and tucking until the dough feels stronger and begins to resist any further rolling, about 10 times. Then, with cupped hands, tuck the sides under toward the center. Place the dough, seam-side down, in a clean bowl, cover the top of the bowl with a clean kitchen towel, and let rest at room temperature for 45 minutes.

5 For the first stretch and fold (see Stretching and Folding, page 285), lightly dust the work surface

and your hands with flour. Using the plastic bowl scraper, release the dough from the bowl and set it, seam-side down, on the work surface. Gently stretch it into a roughly rectangular shape. Fold the dough in thirds from top to bottom and then from left to right. With cupped hands, tuck the sides under toward the center. Place the dough in the bowl, seam-side down, cover the bowl with the towel, and let rest for 45 minutes.

6 For the second stretch and fold, repeat the steps for the first stretch and fold, then return the dough to the bowl, cover with the towel, and let rest for 45 minutes.

7 For the third and final stretch and fold, once again repeat the steps for the first stretch and fold, then return the dough to the bowl, cover with the towel, and let rest for 20 minutes.

8 Line a half sheet pan with a linen liner and dust fairly generously with the dusting mixture.

9 Lightly dust the work surface and your hands with flour. Using a bench scraper, divide the dough into 12 equal pieces (about 45 grams each). Gently roll each piece against the work surface to form a ball (see Rolling Dough into Balls, page 299). Let rest for 5 minutes.

10 Press each ball into a disk about 3 inches (8 cm) in diameter. (For photos of the following process, see Shaping Small Ovals, page 302.) Fold the top edge of the disk over to meet the bottom edge, press against the seam, and roll until seam-side down. Applying gentle pressure, roll until 3½ to 4 inches (10 cm) long, using a bit more pressure on the ends to taper them. Arrange the rolls, seam-side up, on the lined pan in three rows of four rolls each and dust well with the dusting mixture. Fold the linen to create support walls along the length of the rolls on both sides of each row (see Using a Linen Liner for Rolls, page 293). Fold any extra length of the linen liner over the top or cover with a kitchen towel. Transfer the pan to the refrigerator and chill for 12 to 16 hours.

11 Set up the oven with a cast-iron skillet for steam (see Baking Stones and Steam, page 296), then preheat the oven to 480°F (250°C). Line a half sheet pan with a silicone baking mat or parchment paper.

12 Using the linen liner, lift and ease each roll off the pan and onto your hand. Set the rolls on the second pan, seam-side down, with the length of the rolls running across the pan, in two rows of six rolls each. Score the top of each roll (see Scoring, page 290).

13 Put the pan in the oven. Using heavy-duty oven mitts or potholders, pull out the hot skillet, add about 1½ cups of ice cubes, then slide it back in and close the oven door. Immediately lower the oven temperature to 440°F (225°C) and bake, rotating the pan about two-thirds of the way through baking, until the tops are only very lightly browned, about 14 minutes. (These rolls can be baked a couple minutes longer to be darker, but in that case they will dry out more quickly and should be eaten within the next 3 hours.)

14 Set the sheet pan on a cooling rack. Give the rolls a few minutes to cool slightly, then place them directly on the cooling rack and let cool completely, about 1 hour. The rolls are best eaten the day they're baked, but once completely cooled they can be stored (uncut) in a paper bag or cardboard box for up to 24 hours.

PORT AND FIG ROLLS

Port and figs have been a happy combination for at least as long as I've been around good restaurants. In developing this roll, I felt as though there were generations of pastry chefs speaking to my psyche and urging me to include chopped figs in a dinner roll—or perhaps it would be better to say an after-dinner roll. I had an instinct that using milk in the starter and dough, reinforced with cream for a velvety mouthfeel, would produce a rich and slightly sweet dough that could stand up to blue cheese or Roquefort, two cheeses that make no bones about needing huge flavors in any foods that accompany them. The marriage of port and figs also works well with soft, super-creamy cheeses, such as Camembert, Brie, or Fromager d'Affinois. Bottom line: These rolls are great with cheese.

STARTER

25 grams (2 tbsp + 2¼ tsp) white flour
0.2 gram (pinch) instant yeast
25 grams (1 tbsp + 1¾ tsp) cold whole milk

DOUGH

250 grams (1¾ c + 1 tbsp) white flour, plus
    additional as needed for working with the dough
25 grams (2 tbsp) granulated sugar
8 grams (⅛ tsp) fine sea salt
0.5 gram (⅛ tsp) instant yeast
75 grams (¼ c + 2 tsp) cold whole milk
75 grams (¼ c + 1 tbsp) cold heavy cream
80 grams (¼ c + 2 tbsp) port wine
75 grams (¼ c + 3½ tbsp) dried Mission figs,
    cut into ¼-inch (6 mm) dice

Dusting Mixture (see page 35), for the linen liner
    and shaped rolls

FOR THE STARTER

1 Put the flour in a medium storage container. Sprinkle the yeast into the milk, stir to mix, and pour over the flour. Mix with your fingers, pressing the mixture into the sides, bottom, and corners until all of the flour is wet and fully incorporated. Cover the container and let sit at room temperature for 10 to 14 hours. The starter will be at its peak at around 12 hours.

FOR THE DOUGH

1 Stir together the white flour, sugar, salt, and yeast in a small bowl.

2 Pour about one-third of the milk around the edges of the starter to release it from the sides of the container. Transfer the starter and milk to an extra-large bowl along with the remaining milk, the cream, and the port. Using a wooden spoon, break the starter up to distribute it in the liquid.

3 Add the flour mixture, reserving about one-sixth of it along the edge of the bowl (see Mixing, page 282). Continue to mix with the spoon until most of the dry ingredients have been combined with the starter mixture. Switch to a plastic bowl scraper and continue to mix until incorporated. At this point the dough will be just slightly sticky to the touch.

4 Push the dough to one side of the bowl. Roll and tuck the dough (see Rolling and Tucking, page 284), adding the reserved flour mixture and a small amount of additional flour to the bowl and your hands as needed. Continue rolling and tucking until the dough feels stronger and begins to resist any further rolling, about 10 times. Then, with cupped hands, tuck the sides under toward the center. Place the dough, seam-side down, in a clean bowl, cover the top of the bowl with a clean kitchen towel, and let rest at room temperature for 45 minutes.

5 For the first stretch and fold (see Stretching and Folding, page 285), lightly dust the work surface and your hands with flour. Using the plastic bowl scraper, release the dough from the bowl and set it, seam-side down, on the work surface. Gently stretch it into a roughly rectangular shape. Fold the dough in thirds from top to bottom and then from left to right. With cupped hands, tuck the sides under toward the center. Place the dough in the bowl, seam-side down, cover the bowl with the towel, and let rest for 45 minutes.

6 For the second stretch and fold, repeat the steps for the first stretch and fold, then return the dough to the bowl, cover with the towel, and let rest for 45 minutes.

7 For the third and final stretch and fold, gently stretch the dough into a rectangle, scatter the chopped figs over the top, and gently press them into the dough. (For photos of the following process, see Incorporating Add-Ins, page 292.) Roll up the dough tightly from the end closest to you; at the end of the roll the dough will be seam-side down. Turn it over, seam-side up, and gently press on the seam to flatten the dough slightly. Fold in thirds from left to right and then do 1 roll and tuck sequence to incorporate the figs. Turn the dough seam-side down and tuck the sides under toward the center. Return the dough to the bowl, cover with the towel, and let rest for 20 minutes.

8 Line a half sheet pan with a linen liner and dust fairly generously with the dusting mixture.

9 Lightly dust the work surface and your hands with flour. Using a bench scraper, divide the dough into 12 equal pieces (about 55 grams each). Gently roll each piece against the work surface to form a ball (see Rolling Dough into Balls, page 299). Let rest for 5 minutes.

10 Press each ball into a disk about 3 inches (8 cm) in diameter. (For photos of the following process, see Shaping Small Ovals, page 302.) Fold the top edge of the disk over to meet the bottom edge, press against the seam, and roll until seam-side down. Applying gentle pressure, roll until 3½ to 4 inches (9 to 10 cm) long, using a bit more pressure on the ends to taper them. Arrange the rolls, seam-side up, on the sheet in three rows of four rolls each and dust well with the dusting mixture. Fold the linen to create support walls along the lengths of the rolls on both sides of each row (see Using a Linen Liner for Rolls, page 293). Fold any extra length of the linen liner over the top or cover with a kitchen towel. Transfer the pan to the refrigerator and chill for 16 to 20 hours.

11 Set up the oven with a cast-iron skillet for steam (see Baking Stones and Steam, page 296), then pre-heat the oven to 480°F (250°C). Line a half sheet pan with a silicone baking mat or parchment paper.

12 Using the linen liner, lift and ease each roll off the pan and onto your hand. Set the rolls on the second pan, seam-side down, with the length of the rolls running across the pan, in two rows of six rolls each. Score the top of each roll (see Scoring, page 290).

13 Put the pan in the oven. Using heavy-duty oven mitts or potholders, pull out the hot skillet, add about 1½ cups of ice cubes, then slide it back in and close the oven door. Immediately lower the oven temperature to 440°F (225°C) and bake, rotating the pan about two-thirds of the way through baking, until the tops are only very lightly browned, 14 to 18 minutes.

14 Set the sheet pan on a cooling rack. Give the rolls a few minutes to cool slightly, then place them directly on the cooling rack and let cool completely, about 1 hour. The rolls are best eaten the day they're baked, but once completely cooled they can be stored (uncut) in a paper bag or cardboard box for up to 24 hours.

RAISIN WATER ROLLS

If you've made my sourdough starter (page 122), you know that it uses pureed grapes mixed with rye flour. After a few days, the mixture has a pleasant wine-like aroma. I've also made starters with raisins, which are, after all, simply dried grapes with concentrated sweetness. I often try to think of ways to use dried fruits in the winter months, when their summer flavors are sorely missed. For these rolls, I decided to plump raisins in hot water, then blend them and use the resulting puree in the dough to showcase the raisins in a subtle way, rather than using them as pinpoints of intense sweetness. The final rolls capture much of the flavor profile of grapes, and the sugars in the raisins also feed the yeast to create distinctive fermented notes.

RAISIN WATER

60 grams (¼ c + 2½ tbsp) Thompson seedless raisins
   (or any large, dark raisin)
135 grams (½ c + 1 tbsp) warm water

STARTER

60 grams (¼ c + 2½ tbsp) buckwheat flour
0.1 gram (small pinch) instant yeast
86 grams (¼ c + 2 tbsp) water at about 60°F (15°C)

DOUGH

280 grams (2 c) white flour, plus additional as needed for
   working with the dough
50 grams (¼ c + 2 tbsp) medium whole wheat flour
9 grams (1½ tsp) fine sea salt
0.8 gram (¼ tsp) instant yeast
66 grams (¼ c) cold whole milk
33 grams (2¼ tbsp) unsalted butter, at room temperature

Dusting Mixture (see page 35), for the linen liner and
   shaped rolls

FOR THE RAISIN WATER

1 Put the raisins in a medium heatproof storage container. Pour in the water, cover, and let sit at room temperature for 8 to 12 hours.

FOR THE STARTER

1 Put the flour in a medium storage container. Sprinkle the yeast into the water, stir to mix, and pour over the flour. Mix with your fingers, pressing the mixture into the sides, bottom, and corners until all of the flour is wet and fully incorporated. Cover the container and let sit at room temperature for 8 to 13 hours. The starter will be at its peak at around 9 hours.

FOR THE DOUGH

1 Transfer the raisins and their soaking water to a blender, preferably a high-powered one, and blend well.

2 Stir together the white and whole wheat flours, salt, and yeast in a small bowl.

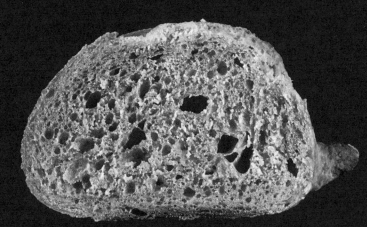

water. Using a wooden spoon, break the starter up to distribute it in the liquid.

4 Add the flour mixture, reserving about one-sixth of it along the edge of the bowl (see Mixing, page 282). Continue to mix with the spoon until most of the dry ingredients have been combined with the starter mixture. Switch to a plastic bowl scraper and continue to mix until incorporated. At this point the dough will be slightly sticky but silky to the touch.

5 Push the dough to one side of the bowl. Roll and tuck the dough (see Rolling and Tucking, page 284), adding the reserved flour mixture and a small amount of additional flour to the bowl and your hands as needed. Continue rolling and tucking until the dough feels stronger and begins to resist any further rolling, about 10 times. Then, with cupped hands, tuck the sides under toward the center. Place the dough, seam-side down, in a clean bowl, cover the top of the bowl with a clean kitchen towel, and let rest at room temperature for 45 minutes.

6 For the first stretch and fold (see Stretching and Folding, page 285), lightly dust the work surface and your hands with flour. Using the plastic bowl scraper, release the dough from the bowl and set it, seam-side down, on the work surface. Gently stretch

it into a roughly rectangular shape. Fold the dough in thirds from top to bottom and then from left to right. With cupped hands, tuck the sides under toward the center. Place the dough in the bowl, seam-side down, cover the bowl with the towel, and let rest for 45 minutes.

7 For the second stretch and fold, repeat the steps for the first stretch and fold, then return the dough to the bowl, cover with the towel, and let rest for 30 minutes.

8 For the third stretch and fold, gently stretch the dough into a rectangle. Pinch the butter into pieces, distributing them over the top of the dough. Using your fingers or a spatula, spread the butter across the surface of the dough. (For photos of the following process, see Incorporating Add-Ins, page 292.) Roll up the dough tightly from the end closest to you; at the end of the roll the dough will be seam-side down. Turn it over, seam-side up, and gently press on the seam to flatten the dough slightly. Fold in thirds from left to right and then do 4 or 5 roll and tuck sequences to incorporate the butter. Turn the dough seam-side down and tuck the sides under toward the center. Return the dough to the bowl, cover with the towel, and let rest for 30 minutes.

9 For the fourth and final stretch and fold, repeat the steps for the first stretch and fold, then return the dough to the bowl, cover with the towel, and let rest for 20 minutes.

10 Line a half sheet pan with a linen liner and dust fairly generously with the dusting mixture.

11 Lightly dust the work surface and your hands with flour. Using a bench scraper, divide the dough into 12 equal pieces (about 65 grams each). Gently roll each piece against the work surface to form a ball (see Rolling Dough into Balls, page 299). Let rest for 5 minutes.

12 Press each ball into a disk about 3 inches (8 cm) in diameter. (For photos of the following process, see Shaping Small Ovals, page 302.) Fold the top edge of the disk over to meet the bottom edge, press against the seam, and roll until seam-side down. Applying gentle pressure, roll until 3½ to 4 inches (9 to 10 cm) long, using a bit more pressure on the ends to taper them. Arrange the rolls, seam-side up, on the lined pan in three rows of four rolls each and dust well with the dusting mixture. Fold the linen to create support walls along the lengths of the rolls on both sides of each row (see Using a Linen Liner for Rolls, page 293). Fold any extra length of the linen liner over the top or cover with a kitchen towel. Transfer the pan to the refrigerator and chill for 16 to 22 hours.

13 Set up the oven with a cast-iron skillet for steam (see Baking Stones and Steam, page 296), then preheat the oven to 500°F (260°C). Line a half sheet pan with a silicone baking mat or parchment paper.

14 Using the linen liner, lift and ease each roll off the pan and onto your hand. Set the rolls on the sec-ond pan, seam-side down, with the length of the rolls running across the pan, in two rows of six rolls each. Score the top of each roll with a double slash on the diagonal (see Scoring, page 290).

15 Put the pan in the oven. Using heavy-duty oven mitts or potholders, pull out the hot skillet, add about 1½ cups of ice cubes, then slide it back in and close the oven door. Immediately lower the oven temperature to 465°F (240°C) and bake, rotating the pan about two-thirds of the way through baking, until the tops are golden brown, 15 to 20 minutes.

16 Set the sheet pan on a cooling rack. Give the rolls a few minutes to cool slightly, then place them directly on the cooling rack and let cool completely, about 1 hour. The rolls are best eaten the day they're baked, but once completely cooled they can be stored (uncut) in a paper bag or cardboard box for up to 24 hours.

SUN-DRIED TOMATO MINI BAGUETTES

The idea for these rolls flows from the same inspiration as the Raisin Water in the preceding recipe. Soaking sun-dried tomatoes—in which the sugars and fruitiness of ripe tomatoes are highly concentrated—creates a liquid that suffuses dough with all the nuances of fresh tomato flavor, but not their pungency or acidity. So these rolls are nothing like pizza. Instead, they have a beautiful, lightly rose-colored crumb with a pleasant tomato bouquet that mixes well with the heartier notes of buckwheat. These rolls are great with any white-fleshed fish. I've also served them with gazpacho where they complement the garden-fresh flavors of the vegetables. Or, for a very simple presentation, serve them sliced open and topped with fresh tomatoes cut into quarters. To my pleasant surprise, this recipe is a kid-pleaser as well: When Amy Vogler tested this recipe, her young daughter, Aurora, devoured them and we all know how picky kids can be.

SUN-DRIED TOMATO WATER

35 grams (¾ c + 2 tbsp) sun-dried tomatoes

105 grams (¼ c + 3 tbsp) warm water

STARTER

50 grams (¼ c + 2 tbsp) buckwheat flour

0.2 gram (pinch) instant yeast

65 grams (¼ c + 1 tsp) water at about 60°F (15°C)

DOUGH

210 grams (1½ c) white flour, plus additional as needed for working with the dough

40 grams (¼ c + 1 tbsp) medium whole wheat flour

7 grams (1⅛ tsp) fine sea salt

0.2 gram (pinch) instant yeast

85 grams (¼ c + 1½ tbsp) cold whole milk

25 grams (1¾ tbsp) unsalted butter, at room temperature

Dusting Mixture (see page 35), for the linen liner and shaped rolls

FOR THE SUN-DRIED TOMATO WATER

1 Put the sun-dried tomatoes in a medium heatproof storage container. Pour in the water, cover, and let sit at room temperature for 8 to 12 hours.

FOR THE STARTER

1 Put the flour in a medium storage container. Sprinkle the yeast into the water, stir to mix, and pour over the flour. Mix with your fingers, pressing the mixture into the sides, bottom, and corners until all of the flour is wet and fully incorporated. Cover the container and let sit at room temperature for 12 to 16 hours. The starter will be at its peak at around 14 hours.

FOR THE DOUGH

1 Transfer the tomatoes and their soaking water to a blender, preferably a high-powered one, and process until the texture is similar to thin marinara sauce.

2 Stir together the white and whole wheat flours,

3 Pour about one-third of the milk around the edges of the starter to release it from the sides of the container. Transfer the starter and milk to an extra-large bowl along with the remaining milk and the sun-dried tomato water. Using a wooden spoon, break the starter up to distribute it in the liquid.

4 Add the flour mixture, reserving about one-sixth of it along the edge of the bowl (see Mixing, page 282). Continue to mix with the spoon until most of the dry ingredients have been combined with the starter mixture. Switch to a plastic bowl scraper and continue to mix until incorporated. At this point the dough will be slightly sticky but silky to the touch.

5 Push the dough to one side of the bowl. Roll and tuck the dough (see Rolling and Tucking, page 284), adding the reserved flour mixture and a small amount of additional flour to the bowl and your hands as needed. Continue rolling and tucking until the dough feels stronger and begins to resist any further rolling, about 10 times. Then, with cupped hands, tuck the sides under toward the center. Place the dough, seam-side down, in a clean bowl, cover the top of the bowl with a clean kitchen towel, and let rest at room temperature for 45 minutes.

6 For the first stretch and fold (see Stretching and Folding, page 285), lightly dust the work surface and your hands with flour. Using the plastic bowl scraper, release the dough from the bowl and set it, seam-side down, on the work surface. Gently stretch it into a roughly rectangular shape. Fold the dough in thirds from top to bottom and then from left to right. With cupped hands, tuck the sides under toward the center. Place the dough in the bowl, seam-side down, cover the bowl with the towel, and let rest for 45 minutes.

7 For the second stretch and fold, repeat the steps for the first stretch and fold, then return the dough to the bowl, cover with the towel, and let rest for 30 minutes.

8 For the third stretch and fold, gently stretch the dough into a rectangle. Pinch the butter into pieces, distributing them over the top of the dough. Using your fingers or a spatula, spread the butter across the surface of the dough. (For photos of the following process, see Incorporating Add-Ins, page 292.) Roll up the dough tightly from the end closest to you; at the end of the roll the dough will be seam-side down. Turn it over, seam-side up, and gently press on the seam to flatten the dough slightly.

Fold in thirds from left to right and then do 4 or 5 roll and tuck sequences to incorporate the butter. Turn the dough seam-side down and tuck the sides under toward the center. Return the dough to the bowl, cover with the towel, and let rest for 30 minutes.

9 For the fourth and final stretch and fold, repeat the steps for the first stretch and fold, then return the dough to the bowl, cover with the towel, and let rest for 20 minutes.

10 Line a half sheet pan with a linen liner and dust fairly generously with the dusting mixture.

11 Lightly dust the work surface and your hands with flour. Using a bench scraper, divide the dough into 12 equal pieces (about 65 grams each). Let rest for 5 minutes.

12 Tightly roll up the pieces into small tubes about 3 inches (8 cm) long. Let rest for 5 minutes. (For photos of the following process, see Shaping Small Baguettes, page 303.) Gently roll each tube until it is about 6 inches (15 cm) long, using a bit more pressure on the ends to taper them. Arrange the baguettes on the lined pan, placing them across the width in one row, and dust well with the dusting mixture. Fold the linen to create support walls along the lengths of the rolls on both sides of each. Fold any extra length of the linen liner over the top or cover with a kitchen towel. Transfer the pan to the refrigerator and chill for 16 to 22 hours.

13 Set up the oven with a cast-iron skillet for steam (see Baking Stones and Steam, page 296), then pre-heat the oven to 480°F (250°C). Line two half sheet pans with silicone baking mats or parchment paper.

14 These rolls will be baked in batches. Using the linen liner, lift and ease each of the rolls off the pan and onto your hand. Set six of them on each of the sheet pans lined with a silicone mat, with the length of the rolls running across the pan. Score the top of each roll with a single, straight score or a triple slash on the diagonal (see Scoring, page 290).

15 Put one pan of rolls in the oven. Using heavy-duty oven mitts or potholders, pull out the hot skillet, add about 1½ cups of ice cubes, then slide it back in and close the oven door. Immediately lower the oven temperature to 440°F (225°C) and bake, rotating the pan about two-thirds of the way through baking, until the tops are a light golden brown (best seen along the edges where the roll was scored), 12 to 16 minutes.

16 Set the first pan of rolls on a cooling rack. Carefully pull out the skillet and pour out any remaining water. Set the skillet back on the rack and allow the oven temperature to return to 480°F (250°C). Then bake the second pan of rolls in the same way, once again adding about 1½ cups of ice cubes to the skillet to create steam.

17 With both batches, give the rolls a few minutes to cool slightly, then place them directly on the cooling rack and let cool completely, about 1 hour. The rolls are best eaten the day they're baked, but once completely cooled they can be stored (uncut) in a paper bag or cardboard box for up to 24 hours.

SUN-DRIED PEAR AND TOASTED POPPY SEED MINI BAGUETTES

The overall effect of enhancing a sourdough roll with pears and poppy seeds is a roll that's sweet, nutty, and slightly crunchy all at once. These rolls are especially well suited to harder alpine cheeses from grass-fed cows, such as Gruyère or Mimolette, or even a great domestic cow's milk cheese such as Cabot Clothbound Cheddar. I think one reason we usually reach for red wine with cheese is that the cheese is often served after the meat course, so you find yourself with some red wine in your glass at that point. Do yourself a favor and try a white wine, especially a Chardonnay. It lightens and brightens the cheese course and will echo the flavor notes of the dried pears in these rolls. At the end of a heavy meal, lighter is often better.

FIRST STARTER

10 grams (2 tsp) Sourdough Starter (page 122)
20 grams (1 tbsp + 1 tsp) water at about 60°F (15°C)
20 grams (2 tbsp + ¾ tsp) medium whole wheat flour

SECOND STARTER

100 grams (½ c + 3½ tbsp) white flour
0.2 gram (pinch) instant yeast
100 grams (¼ c + 3 tbsp) water at about 60°F (15°C)

DOUGH

10 grams (1 tbsp + ¾ tsp) poppy seeds
225 grams (1½ c + 1½ tbsp) white flour, plus additional
    as needed for working with the dough
25 grams (3 tbsp + 1 tsp) white rye flour
8 grams (1¼ tsp) fine sea salt
1 gram (generous ¼ tsp) instant yeast
175 grams (¾ c) water at about 60°F (15°C)
50 grams (generous ¼ c) dried pears, cut into ¼-inch
    (6 mm) dice

Dusting Mixture (see page 35), for the linen liner
    and shaped rolls

FOR THE FIRST STARTER

1 Put the sourdough starter in a medium storage container and add the water. Break the starter into pieces with your fingers until it's almost dissolved in the water; there will still be some small pieces. Stir in the flour until fully incorporated. Cover the container and let sit at room temperature for 10 to 14 hours. The starter will be at its peak at around 12 hours.

FOR THE SECOND STARTER

1 Put the flour in a medium storage container. Sprinkle the yeast into the water, stir to mix, and pour over the flour. Mix with your fingers, pressing the mixture into the sides, bottom, and corners until all of the flour is wet and fully incorporated. Cover the container and let sit at room temperature for 10 to 14 hours. The starter will be at its peak at around 12 hours.

FOR THE DOUGH

1 Preheat the oven to 400°F (205°C). Spread the poppy seeds on a small sheet pan and bake, shaking occasionally, until toasted, about 7 minutes. Let

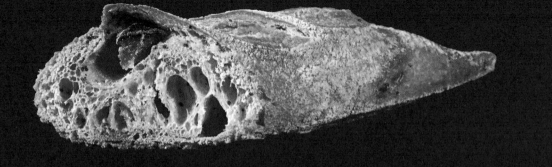

2 Stir together the white and white rye flours, salt, and yeast in a small bowl.

3 Pour about one-third of the water around the edges of each of the starters to release them from the sides of their containers. Transfer the starters and water to an extra-large bowl along with the remaining water. Using a wooden spoon, break the starters up to distribute them in the water.

4 Add the flour mixture, reserving about one-sixth of it along the edge of the bowl (see Mixing, page 282). Continue to mix with the spoon until most of the dry ingredients have been combined with the starter mixture. Switch to a plastic bowl scraper and continue to mix until incorporated. At this point the dough will be sticky to the touch.

5 Push the dough to one side of the bowl. Roll and tuck the dough (see Rolling and Tucking, page 284), adding the reserved flour mixture and a small amount of additional flour to the bowl and your hands as needed. Continue rolling and tucking until the dough feels stronger and begins to resist any further rolling, about 12 times. Then, with cupped hands, tuck the sides under toward the center. Place the dough, seam-side down, in a clean bowl, cover

the top of the bowl with a clean kitchen towel, and let rest at room temperature for 45 minutes.

6 For the first stretch and fold (see Stretching and Folding, page 285), lightly dust the work surface and your hands with flour. Using the plastic bowl scraper, release the dough from the bowl and set it, seam-side down, on the work surface. Gently stretch it into a roughly rectangular shape. Fold the dough in thirds from top to bottom and then from left to right. With cupped hands, tuck the sides under toward the center. Place the dough in the bowl, seam-side down, cover the bowl with the towel, and let rest for 45 minutes.

7 For the second stretch and fold, repeat the steps for the first stretch and fold, then return the dough to the bowl, cover with the towel, and let rest for 30 minutes.

8 For the third stretch and fold, gently stretch the dough into a rectangle, scatter the poppy seeds and pear over the top, and gently press them into the dough. (For photos of this process, see Incorporating Add-Ins, page 292.) Roll up the dough tightly from the end closest to you; at the end of the roll the dough will be seam-side down. Turn it over, seam-side up, and gently press on the seam to flatten the dough slightly. Fold in thirds from left to right and then do 1 roll and tuck sequence to incorporate the poppy seeds and pear. Turn the dough seam-side down and tuck the sides under toward the center. Return the dough to the bowl, cover with the towel, and let rest for 20 minutes.

9 For the fourth and final stretch and fold, repeat the steps for the first stretch and fold, then return the dough to the bowl, cover with the towel, and let rest for 10 minutes.

10 Line a half sheet pan with a linen liner and dust fairly generously with the dusting mixture.

11 Lightly dust the work surface and your hands with flour. Using a bench scraper, divide the dough into 12 equal pieces (about 60 grams each). Let rest for 5 minutes.

12 Tightly roll up the pieces into small tubes about 3 inches (8 cm) long. Let rest for 5 minutes. (For photos of the following process, see Shaping Small Baguettes, page 303.) Gently roll each tube until it is about 6 inches (15 cm) long, using a bit more pressure on the ends to taper them. Arrange the baguettes on the lined pan, placing them across the width in one row, and dust well with the dusting mixture. Fold the linen to create support walls along the lengths of the rolls on both sides of each. Fold any extra length of the linen liner over the top or cover with a kitchen towel. Transfer the pan to the refrigerator and chill for 12 to 16 hours.

13 Set up the oven with a cast-iron skillet for steam (see Baking Stones and Steam, page 296), then preheat the oven to 480°F (250°C). Line two half sheet pans with silicone baking mats or parchment paper.

14 These rolls will be baked in batches. Using the linen liner, lift and ease each of the rolls off the pan and onto your hand. Set six of them on each of the sheet pans lined with a silicone mat, with the length of the rolls running across the pan. Score the top of each roll with a single, straight score or a triple slash on the diagonal (see Scoring, page 290).

15 Put one pan of rolls in the oven. Using heavy-duty oven mitts or potholders, pull out the hot skillet, add about 1½ cups of ice cubes, then slide it back in and close the oven door. Immediately lower the oven temperature to 440°F (225°C) and bake, rotating the pan about two-thirds of the way through baking, until the tops are a light golden brown (best seen along the edges where the roll was scored), 12 to 15 minutes.

16 Set the first pan of rolls on a cooling rack. Carefully pull out the skillet and pour out any remaining water. Set the skillet back on the rack and allow the oven temperature to return to 480°F (250°C). Then bake the second pan of rolls in the same way, once again adding about 1½ cups of ice cubes to the skillet to create steam.

17 With both batches, give the rolls a few minutes to cool slightly, then place them directly on the cooling rack and let cool completely, about 1 hour. The rolls are best eaten the day they're baked, but once completely cooled they can be stored (uncut) in a paper bag or cardboard box for up to 24 hours.

BREAD QUEST:
KAISER ROLLS

There is an old Yiddish tale about the virtuous but hapless Bontche Schweig, who dies and is rewarded with a place in heaven. God tells him he can have anything he wants, to which he replies, "I'd like a roll and butter."

I have always pictured a Kaiser roll as the roll that humble Bontche requested, but it would have been a far different roll than the crusty hamburger bun with a funny shape that passes for a Kaiser roll these days. This is another one of those "Why can't they make 'em like they used to?" breads. In different parts of the country, what passes for a Kaiser roll might be called a Vienna or bulky roll, and up in Buffalo and the Niagara Frontier it's known as a weck or kummelweck, or simply a hard roll. It was one of the first breads I thought about trying to resurrect when I started to develop new breads for this book.

I had tried my hand at Kaiser rolls when I was at Pearl Bakery in Portland, in that case achieving the classic five-lobed shape by tying the dough in a knot. But they were impractical to make in an artisanal way while still selling for a profit. Then I forgot about them until Peter reminisced about the rolls his grandma used to make for him, topped with a fried egg, in the back of her little grocery store in Kearny, New Jersey, at the edge of the Meadowlands. My goal was to create a good roll for sandwiches, something with a more substantial crust than the classic Kaiser roll and with plenty of flavor in the crumb, but not so much that it would compete with the ingredients of sandwich fixings or other toppings.

I began with a simple starter of yeast, white flour, and water. The result was okay, but not really special. Then I thought to enrich the dough with an additional starter, this one made with yeast and milk, like the one in my White Pullman Loaf (page 107). I also added white rye flour to the dough for even more sweet nuance and acidity. Finally, to create a thin, crispy crust, I opted not to cover the shaped rolls during the final dehydration. This allows a skin to form. The result, after a few iterations, was very gratifying. And then, for the ultimate test drive, I tried one with mortadella (aka bologna), a slice of tomato, and mustard. Bingo!

Why is it called a Kaiser roll? According to legend, it was invented, like so many breads, by the ingenious bakers of Vienna. The way the rolls are folded calls to mind a five-pointed crown, so in honor of Kaiser Franz Josef I of Austria, it was called a Kaiser roll.

If you are wondering where the poppy seeds are on my roll, I didn't forget to include them. I felt my crust had plenty of texture and flavor without complicating it with another element. If you are inconsolable about the absence of poppy seeds, brush some egg white on the top of the rolls and sprinkle with poppy seeds before baking.

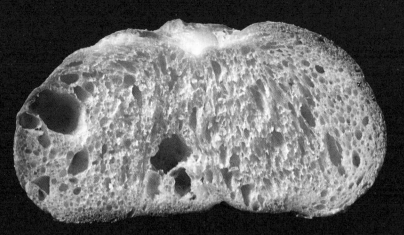

FIRST STARTER

50 grams (¼ c + 2 tbsp) white flour
5 grams (1¼ tsp) granulated sugar
1 gram (generous ⅛ tsp) fine sea salt
0.2 gram (pinch) instant yeast
44 grams (2 tbsp + 2¼ tsp) cold whole milk

SECOND STARTER

25 grams (2 tbsp + 2¼ tsp) white flour
0.1 gram (small pinch) instant yeast
25 grams (1 tbsp + 2 tsp) water at about 60°F (15°C)

DOUGH

460 grams (3¼ c +1 tsp) white flour, plus additional
    as needed for working with the dough
40 grams (⅓ c) white rye flour
15 grams (2½ tsp) fine sea salt
3 grams (¾ tsp) instant yeast
340 grams (1¼ c + 2 tbsp) cold whole milk
35 grams (1 tbsp + 2 tsp) honey

FOR THE FIRST STARTER

1 Stir together the flour, sugar, salt, and yeast in a medium storage container. Pour in the milk. Mix with your fingers, pressing the mixture into the sides, bottom, and corners until all of the flour is wet and fully incorporated. This starter is best if covered and left at room temperature for 6 hours, then chilled in the refrigerator for 6 hours. But if the timing is better, you can leave it at room temperature for 2 to 3 hours and then move it to the refrigerator to chill for 9 to 12 hours.

FOR THE SECOND STARTER

1 Put the flour in a medium storage container. Sprinkle the yeast into the water, stir to mix, and pour over the flour. Mix with your fingers, pressing the mixture into the sides, bottom, and corners until all of the flour is wet and fully incorporated. Cover the container and let sit at room temperature for 10 to 14 hours. The starter will be at its peak at around 12 hours.

FOR THE DOUGH

1 Stir together the white and white rye flours, salt, and yeast in a small bowl.

2 Pour about one-third of the milk around the edges of the starters to release them from the sides of their containers. Transfer the starters and milk to an extra-large bowl along with the remaining milk and the honey. Using a wooden spoon, break the starters up to distribute them in the liquid.

3 Add the flour mixture, reserving about one-sixth of it along the edge of the bowl (see Mixing, page 282). Continue to mix with the spoon until most of the dry ingredients have been combined with the starter mixture. Switch to a plastic bowl scraper and continue to mix until incorporated. At this point the dough will be slightly sticky to the touch.

4 Push the dough to one side of the bowl. Roll and tuck the dough (see Rolling and Tucking, page 284), adding the reserved flour mixture and a small amount of additional flour to the bowl and your hands as needed. Continue rolling and tucking until the dough feels stronger and begins to resist any further rolling, about 12 times. Then, with cupped hands, tuck the sides under toward the center. Place the dough, seam-side down, in a clean bowl, cover the top of the bowl with a clean kitchen towel, and let rest at room temperature for 45 minutes.

5 For the first stretch and fold (see Stretching and Folding, page 285), lightly dust the work surface and your hands with flour. Using the plastic bowl scraper, release the dough from the bowl and set it, seam-side down, on the work surface. Gently stretch it into a roughly rectangular shape. Fold the dough in thirds from top to bottom and then from left to right. With cupped hands, tuck the sides under toward the center. Place the dough in the bowl, seam-side down, cover the bowl with the towel, and let rest for 45 minutes.

6 For the second stretch and fold, repeat the steps for the first stretch and fold, then return the dough to the bowl, cover with the towel, and let rest for 45 minutes.

7 For the third and final stretch and fold, once again repeat the steps for the first stretch and fold, then return the dough to the bowl, cover with the towel, and let rest for 20 minutes.

8 Line a half sheet pan with a silicone baking mat or parchment paper.

9 Lightly dust the work surface and your hands with flour. Using a bench scraper, divide the dough into 12 equal pieces (about 85 grams each). Roll out into a tube (see Shaping a Tube, page 294). Let rest for 5 minutes. (For photos of the following process, see Shaping Kaiser Rolls, page 304.) Gently roll each piece into a strand about 10 inches (25 cm). Working with one strand at a time, loop the strand over itself, leaving one tail that's about 2 inches (5 cm) long and one that's about 5 inches (13 cm) long. Tuck the long tail through the loop to make a knot. Wind that same tail back around the strand and through the loop a second time. Pinch the tails together and bring them to the center. Set the completed rolls on the lined pan in two rows of six rolls each. Transfer the pan to the refrigerator and chill, uncovered, for 4 to 6 hours.

10 Cover the rolls with a clean kitchen towel and chill for 6 to 8 hours longer.

11 Set up the oven with a cast-iron skillet for steam (see Baking Stones and Steam, page 296), then pre-heat the oven to 480°F (250°C).

12 Put the pan in the oven. Using heavy-duty oven mitts or potholders, pull out the hot skillet, add about 1½ cups of ice cubes, then slide it back in and close the oven door. Immediately lower the oven temperature to 460°F (240°C) and bake, rotating the pan about two-thirds of the way through baking, until the tops are a light golden brown, about 12 minutes.

13 Set the sheet pan on a cooling rack. Give the rolls a few minutes to cool slightly, then place them directly on the cooling rack and let cool completely, about 1½ hours. The rolls are best eaten the day they're baked, but once completely cooled they can be stored (uncut) in a paper bag or cardboard box for up to 24 hours.

MASH AND MUST ROLLS

Every year, Danny Meyer—perhaps New York's most renowned restaurateur—puts on the Autumn Harvest Dinner, a culinary blowout and fundraiser to fight childhood hunger. Michael Anthony, the chef at Gramercy Tavern (one of Danny's restaurants), is renowned for his passion for peak-season local ingredients, and I've been baking bread for him since Bien Cuit's early days. One year, just after Labor Day, he called and asked if I could create a roll for the Harvest Dinner. Given Mike's reputation for serving whatever is in the market on any given day, I knew I had to come up with something that reflected the season. I wanted to evoke the flavor of corn and the brandy-like aroma of fermenting grapes that hits you on a visit to a winery during the crush. The roll that was born of this impulse was a big hit, as was the dinner. I even had the opportunity to taste a shmear of foie gras on one of these rolls when I delivered the order, and I have to say: If you have a tin of foie gras that you've been saving for a special occasion, now's the time to have at it.

Grape must is the mixture of grape skins, flesh, seeds, and juice that you get when you crush grapes in the wine-making process. Syrup is simply the reduced liquid of the must.

STARTER

100 grams (½ c + 3½ tbsp) white flour

13 grams (1 tbsp) granulated sugar

2 grams (¼ + ⅛ tsp) fine sea salt

0.3 gram (generous pinch) instant yeast

65 grams (¼ c) cold whole milk

MASH STARTER

60 grams (¼ c + 2 tbsp) medium-grind cornmeal

30 grams (3½ tbsp) white flour

10 grams (2 tsp) Sourdough Starter (page 122)

90 grams (¼ c + 2 tbsp) water at about 80°F (25°C)

DOUGH

240 grams (1½ c + 3½ tbsp) white flour, plus
    additional as needed for working with the dough

45 grams (¼ c) medium-grind cornmeal

15 grams (2 tbsp) white rye flour

8 grams (1¼ tsp) fine sea salt

1 gram (generous ¼ tsp) instant yeast

1 gram (⅛ tsp) diastatic or partially diastatic malt
    powder (malted barley flour)

120 grams (½ c) water at about 60°F (15°C)

40 grams (2 tbsp) grape must syrup, plus additional
    (about 20 grams, 1 tbsp) for brushing on the finished rolls

30 grams (2 tbsp) unsalted butter, at room temperature

Dusting Mixture (see page 35), for the linen liner and
    shaped rolls

FOR THE STARTER

1 Stir together the flour, sugar, salt, and yeast in a medium storage container. Pour in the milk. Mix with your fingers, pressing the mixture into the sides, bottom, and corners until all of the flour is wet and fully incorporated. This starter is best if covered and left at room temperature for 6 hours, then chilled in the refrigerator for 6 hours.

FOR THE MASH STARTER

1 Combine the cornmeal and flour in a small bowl. Put the sourdough starter in a medium storage container and add the water. Break the starter into pieces with your fingers until it's almost dissolved in the

water; there will still be some small pieces. Stir in the flour and cornmeal until fully incorporated. Cover the container and let sit at room temperature for 8 to 12 hours. The starter will be at its peak at around 10 hours.

FOR THE DOUGH

1 Stir together the white flour, cornmeal, white rye flour, salt, yeast, and malt powder in a small bowl.

2 Pour about one-third of the water around the edges of each of the starters to release them from the sides of their containers. Transfer the starters and water to an extra-large bowl along with the remaining water and the grape must syrup. Using a wooden spoon, break the starters up to distribute them in the liquid.

3 Add the flour mixture, reserving about one-sixth of it along the edge of the bowl (see Mixing, page 282). Continue to mix with the spoon until most of the dry ingredients have been combined with the starter mixture. Switch to a plastic bowl scraper and continue to mix until incorporated. At this point the dough will be sticky to the touch.

4 Push the dough to one side of the bowl. Roll and tuck the dough (see Rolling and Tucking, page 284), adding the reserved flour mixture and a small amount of additional flour to the bowl and your hands as needed. Continue rolling and tucking until the dough feels stronger and begins to resist any further rolling, about 12 times. Then, with cupped hands, tuck the sides under toward the center. Place the dough, seam-side down, in a clean bowl, cover the top of the bowl with a clean kitchen towel, and let rest at room temperature for 45 minutes.

5 For the first stretch and fold (see Stretching and Folding, page 285), lightly dust the work surface and your hands with flour. Using the plastic bowl scraper, release the dough from the bowl and set it, seam-side down, on the work surface. Gently stretch it into a roughly rectangular shape. Fold the dough in thirds from top to bottom and then from left to right. With cupped hands, tuck the sides under toward the center. Place the dough in the bowl, seam-side down, cover the bowl with the towel, and let rest for 45 minutes.

6 For the second stretch and fold, repeat the steps for the first stretch and fold, then return the dough to the bowl, cover with the towel, and let rest for 45 minutes.

7 For the third and final stretch and fold, gently stretch the dough into a rectangle. Pinch the butter into pieces, distributing them over the top of the dough. Using your fingers or a spatula, spread the butter across the surface of the dough. (For photos of the following process, see Incorporating Add-Ins, page 292.) Roll up the dough tightly from the end closest to you; at the end of the roll the dough will be seam-side down. Turn it over, seam-side up, and gently press on the seam to flatten the dough slightly. Fold in thirds from left to right and then do 4 or 5 roll and tuck sequences to incorporate the butter. Turn the dough seam-side down and tuck the sides under toward the center. Return the dough to the bowl, cover with the towel, and transfer to the refrigerator to chill for 1 hour so the dough will stiffen up a bit.

8 Line a half sheet pan with a linen liner and dust fairly generously with the dusting mixture.

9 Lightly dust the work surface and your hands with flour. Using a bench scraper, divide the dough into 12 equal pieces (about 72 grams each). Gently roll each piece against the work surface to form a ball (see Rolling Dough into Balls, page 299). Let rest for 5 minutes.

10 Press each ball into a disk about 3 inches (8 cm) in diameter. (For photos of the following process, see Shaping Small Ovals, page 302.) Fold the top edge of the disk over to meet the bottom edge, press against the seam, and roll until seam-side down. Applying gentle pressure, roll until 3½ to 4 inches (9 to 10 cm) long, using a bit of pressure on the ends to taper them. Arrange the rolls, seam-side up, on the

lined pan in three rows of four rolls each and dust well with the dusting mixture. Fold the linen to create support walls along the lengths of the rolls on both sides of each row (see Using a Linen Liner for Rolls, page 293). Fold any extra length of the linen liner over the top or cover with a kitchen towel. Transfer the pan to the refrigerator and chill for 10 to 14 hours.

11 Set up the oven with a cast-iron skillet for steam (see Baking Stones and Steam, page 296), then preheat the oven to 480°F (250°C). Line a half sheet pan with a silicone baking mat or parchment paper.

12 Using the linen liner, lift and ease each roll off the pan and onto your hand. Set the rolls on the second pan, seam-side down, with the length of the rolls running across the pan, in two rows of six rolls each. (These rolls are not scored).

13 Put the pan in the oven. Using heavy-duty oven mitts or potholders, pull out the hot skillet, add about 1½ cups of ice cubes, then slide it back in and close the oven door. Bake for 3 minutes.

14 Lower the oven temperature to 425°F (220°C) and bake for 6 minutes, then rotate the pan and bake until the tops are a light golden brown, not dark, about 6 minutes longer.

15 Set the sheet pan on a cooling rack and immediately brush the tops of the rolls with additional grape must syrup. Give the rolls a few minutes to cool slightly, then place them directly on the cooling rack and let cool completely, about 1 hour. The rolls are best eaten the day they're baked, but once completely cooled they can be stored (uncut) in a paper bag or cardboard box for up to 24 hours.

BREAD QUEST:
REAL BAGELS

In our quest for a great bagel, we first tried some local stores that sold such questionable combos such as the BBLT—bacon, bagel, lettuce, and tomato. What they lacked in quality (a lot) they attempted to make up for in variety. Sometimes when I see the flavors of bagels on offer—pumpkin raisin, chocolate chip, pesto, jalapeño-cheese, and so on—I don't know if I'm at a Ben & Jerry's or a Taco Bell, but I do know that I'm certainly not in an old-fashioned Jewish New York deli with its dried apricots, pickled herring, and a world-class knife handler who can carve lox so thin that you could read the *Times* through it. The old-time bagels sold in those bakeries were all that a bagel should be: chewy, crusty, dense, wheaty, and ever so slightly sweet. They were a far cry from what passes for a bagel these days, which is usually a roll so swollen that the hole in the middle is almost nonexistent.

Our first stop was Black Seed, on Elizabeth Street in SoHo. There, Noah Bernamoff has taken on the bagel quest in much the same way that his Mile End deli has revived and advanced the tradition of pastrami, chopped liver, and other delicatessen standbys. His bagels are quite good, but they are made in the Montreal style—smaller and more cakey than what we were looking for. In addition, the dough is unsalted, and the bagels are boiled with honey—a faithful and flavorful representation of the Montreal style, but not a classic New York bagel.

We put in a call to Ed Levine, who as a journalist and the guiding force behind the website seriouseats. com, has done much to promote honest traditional food across the United States. Ed has been everywhere and

eaten everything. He suggested that we meet for lunch at Russ & Daughters Cafe, a dressed-up table-service offshoot of the famous smoked fish store on the Lower East Side.

When you think of bagels on the Lower East Side, it conjures up images of pushcarts, pudgy grandmas in babushkas and sensible shoes. That was then; this is now. Russ & Daughters Cafe is stylish, light, and airy. The crowd (and the servers) are, for the most part, svelte and young. A waitress put a bread basket in front of us. The bagels were toasted. We asked for untoasted. A great bagel doesn't need to be toasted, but somehow that has become the modern default. Ed, who has written at length about bagels for the *New York Times*, said he thinks the memory of food is sometimes better than the food really was, and that he suspected this was true of bagels. Peter wasn't so sure. He maintained that over the years bagels' holes have got smaller, and the bagels themselves have gotten bigger and squishier. I just ate and listened to these old-school bagel connoisseurs discuss their bagel philosophies.

Ed reprised the history of the modern bagel: that it was considered an ethnic food until the 1960s, when a few chains went national and quality started to go downhill. The same thing happened with pizza, he said, and on that note, he made the logical leap—at least for him—to discussion of pizza. There is no such thing as a single-topic conversation with Ed. He said he was crazy for Chris Bianco's pizza, at Pizzeria Bianco in Phoenix. "It may be the best in the country," he said.

"Next time, I'm in Phoenix, I'll try it," I promised, wondering why nobody ever talks about the

second best pizza in the country. After all, it has to be pretty decent.

"Um, Ed, about bagels, ya know?" Peter asked, trying to steer the conversation back to our current quest.

In midsentence—and midbite—Ed said, "Right now, I think the best bagels I know of are being done by the chef Mark Strausman. He bakes them on a cedar plank."

I made a mental note. "Good idea."

On Ed's recommendation, we headed up to Strausman's restaurant, Fred's, which is located in Barneys—a famous department store on Fifty-Ninth Street and Madison Avenue. That part of town is definitely a high-rent neighborhood and a far cry from the Fiddler on the Roof villages of eastern Europe where the bagel was born. So on a perfect summer day, I packed my daughter, Alex, in the car, along with my wife, Kate, and Peter, and braved the Manhattan traffic.

We strode into Fred's, sat down, and proceeded to order two baskets of bagels, some coffee, and a bowl of Estelle's Chicken Soup (Estelle being Mark Strausman's grandma)—the cheapest items on the menu. When we said we were excited about the bagels, which we'd heard were the best in town, they proudly presented us with two baskets filled with plain bagels, everything bagels, and bialys. They were so good that two-year-old Alex was content to chew on her bagel in silence—a sure sign, I have learned, that she likes a particular bread.

Strausman's bagels are smaller in diameter than the puff balls you find these days, so the crust-to-crumb relationship was more balanced. To eat one, you work your way through a firm, slightly cracking crust, which is balanced correctly with the soft (but not white bread soft) interior. There was a hint of sweetness, but I was pretty sure it wasn't from sugar, and just enough salt to make the other flavors pop. I couldn't taste a lot of fermentation. I left a note thanking the chef for opening my eyes to something exceedingly simple, done exceedingly well. By the way, the chicken soup was worthy of a grandma.

STARTER

20 grams (1 tbsp + 1 tsp) Sourdough Starter (page 122)
40 grams (2 tbsp + 2 tsp) water at about 60°F (15°C)
40 grams (¼ c + 1 tbsp) white flour

DOUGH

500 grams (3½ c + 1 tbsp) white flour, plus additional
    as needed for working with the dough
15 grams (2½ tsp) fine sea salt
275 grams (1 c + 2½ tbsp) water at about 60°F (15°C)
40 grams (2 tbsp) rye malt extract

I believed I was ready to make a Bien Cuit bagel. I thought I had figured it out, but it took more trial and error than any other recipe in this book to get it right. I tried to track down recipes that New York bagel makers used in the old days, but I couldn't find any. This seemed odd at first, but in the course of my research I learned that bagel bakers had their own union and guarded their recipes jealously. So all I could refer to was Peter's taste memory and a few recipes written by longtime bagel bakers. What they shared in common was using a lot of commercial yeast, the goal being to produce bagels without long fermentation. This went against my mantra that long, cold fermentation is always essential for developing flavor, and the bagels I attempted with the over-yeasted method confirmed my misgivings.

It occurred to me that before the widespread use of commercial yeast in the latter half of the nineteenth century, bakers who wanted to make bagels had no choice but to use a sourdough starter. And to sweeten the dough, the most readily available and economic sweetener would have been rye malt extract. So I incorporated both into my recipe. The resulting bagels were better, but still not great. Then I realized that traditional bagel making methods didn't involve fermenting shaped bagels for a long time; they used bulk fermentation, with an entire batch of dough being fermented for a longer time in cold conditions. It wasn't apparent to me why that would produce a better bagel, but I figured it was worth a try. So on my twenty-fourth attempt at a bagel recipe, I baked a bunch of bulk-fermented bagels alongside an identical batch that had first been shaped and then cold fermented. Voila! The sourdough-based, malt-sweetened, bulk-fermented bagel won hands down.

By the way, I eventually found evidence vindicating Mark Strausman's cedar plank method. As it turns out, old-time bagel bakers baked their bagels on blocks of wood that had been soaked in water so a crust wouldn't form on the underside too quickly during baking. Steam from the wood gently heats the bagel, leaving the surface supple until it's removed from the wood and baked a bit longer, crisping up in the process. Instead of using oak blocks, I use cedar grilling planks, the kind you can find in fish stores, cooking supply stores, or online.

FOR THE STARTER

1 Put the sourdough starter in a medium storage container and add the water. Break the starter into pieces with your fingers until it's almost dissolved in the water; there will still be some small pieces. Stir in the flour until fully incorporated. Cover the container and let sit at room temperature for 10 to 14 hours. The starter will be at its peak at around 12 hours.

FOR THE DOUGH

1 Stir together the flour and salt in a medium bowl.

2 Pour about one-third of the water around the edges of the starter to release it from the sides of the container. Transfer the starter and water to an extra-large bowl along with the remaining water and the rye malt extract. Using a wooden spoon, break the starter up to distribute it in the liquid. The extract will not break up easily and will be stringy and a bit clumped together at this point.

3 Add the flour mixture, reserving about one-sixth of it along the edge of the bowl (see Mixing, page 282). Continue to mix with the spoon until most of the dry ingredients have been combined with the starter mixture. Switch to a plastic bowl scraper and continue to mix until incorporated. At this point the dough will be a little sticky to the touch and pretty stiff.

4 Push the dough to one side of the bowl. Roll and tuck the dough (see Rolling and Tucking, page 284), adding the reserved flour mixture and a small amount of additional flour to the bowl and your hands as needed. Continue rolling and tucking 10 times. It is important to do 10 full roll and tuck sequences on this dough even if it begins to feel quite stiff and resistant. Then, with cupped hands, tuck the sides under toward the center. Place the dough, seam-side down, in a clean bowl, cover the top of the bowl with a clean kitchen towel, and let rest at room temperature for 45 minutes.

5 For the first stretch and fold (see Stretching and Folding, page 285), lightly dust the work surface and your hands with flour. Using the plastic bowl scraper, release the dough from the bowl and set it, seam-side down, on the work surface. Gently stretch it into a roughly rectangular shape. Fold the dough in thirds from top to bottom and then from left to right. With cupped hands, tuck the sides under toward the center. Place the dough in the bowl, seam-side down, cover the bowl with the towel, and let rest for 45 minutes.

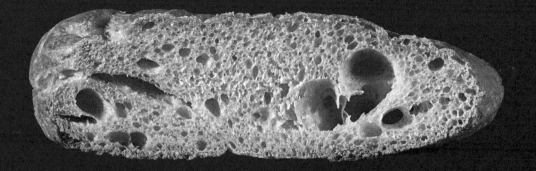

6 For the second stretch and fold, repeat the steps for the first stretch and fold, then return the dough to the bowl, cover with the towel, and let rest for 45 minutes.

7 For the third and final stretch and fold, once again repeat the steps for the first stretch and fold, then return the dough to the bowl, cover with the towel, and transfer to the refrigerator to chill for 12 to 18 hours.

8 Soak four 5½ by 11-inch (14 by 28 cm) cedar grilling planks in water while shaping the bagels.

9 Generously flour a large board or half sheet pan. (The shaped bagels will undergo a final fermentation and then be transferred directly to a pot of boiling water; this will be easier if they are on a surface that can be moved closer to the stovetop.)

10 Lightly dust the work surface and your hands with flour. Using the plastic bowl scraper, turn the dough out onto a lightly floured work surface and press the dough into a round about 1½ inches (4 cm) thick and 6 inches (15 cm) in diameter. (For photos of the following process, see Shaping Bagels, page 306.) Using a bench scraper, make a 1½-inch (4 cm) cut into the round from the outside. (For the rest of the process of cutting of the dough, think of cutting the round of dough as being cut to make an unraveling spiral.) Then, using the bench scraper and the initial 1½-inch (4 cm) cut as the starting point, cut along the circle, uncoiling the dough as you do so, to create one long tube strip of dough about 24 inches (61 cm) long. After cutting, the tube dough may have some rough spots on the surface. Roll the tube dough against the work surface to smooth them out and form a tube.

11 Starting at one end of the tube, put the end of the dough against the center of your palm. Bring the dough across your palm, around the back of your hand, and then back across your palm, slightly overlapping the end you started with. Pinch the dough to tear and separate the remainder of the dough from the ring you just made around your hand. Roll the overlapping ends of the ring between the work surface and your palm to smooth it and even it out with the rest of the ring. Place it on the floured board.

12 Repeat the process, wrapping, portioning, and sealing the rings until you've used all of the dough. Depending on the size of your hand, you'll end up with 10 to 12 shaped bagels. Let them rest for 5 minutes. Then, stretch the rings so that the hole in the center is about 2 inches (5 cm) in diameter. Cover with a plastic tub or a damp kitchen towel.

13 Set up the oven with a baking stone on the center rack (see Baking Stones and Steam, page 296), then preheat the oven to 500°F (260°C).

14 The dough will be ready to bake when an impression remains for 2 to 3 seconds after you gently press it with your fingertip and then slowly begins to fill back in; that will take 45 minutes or perhaps longer depending on the temperature of the room, but begin checking after 30 minutes if the room is 72°F (22°C) or higher.

15 Put 6 inches (15 cm) of water in a stockpot and bring to a boil. Put a half sheet pan near the stockpot, propping up one end a bit. The bagels will be transferred from the boiling water to the sheet pan, so it should have enough of a tilt that the water runs down the pan and away from the bagels.

16 Remove the grilling planks from the water and set them on a half sheet pan. Fill a large bowl with ice water.

17 Using a bench scraper, gently transfer one of the bagels into the boiling water. It may initially sink, but after a few seconds it should float to the top. If it sinks all the way to the bottom, it's okay to give it a small nudge, but don't disrupt it too much. (If the bagel doesn't rise to the top after a few seconds, the dough hasn't fermented enough. Let the bagels proof for about 15 minutes longer and then try again.) Boil the bagel for about 45 seconds, turning it one or two times so it cooks evenly. Transfer to the ice bath for about 20 seconds, then transfer to the tilted half sheet pan. Working in batches, boil the remaining bagels three or four at a time.

18 Determine how many planks will fit comfortably on your baking stone, then arrange the bagels on the cedar planks. They can be close, but they shouldn't be touching. (I bake 3 per plank). If the bagel has a smoother-looking side, place that side down. Place the planks on the baking stone. You can bake as many planks of bagels at once as your baking stone will accommodate. Bake for 8 minutes. At this point, the bagels will still be pale in color.

19 Using heavy-duty oven mitts, one at a time, lift the planks, flip the bagels over onto the baking stone, and remove the planks; now the smoother side will be up. Bake until the crust is a rich golden brown, about 14 minutes longer.

20 Using a baking peel or a large spatula, transfer the bagels to a cooling rack. Let cool completely, about 1 hour. The bagels are best eaten the day they're baked, but once completely cooled they can be stored (uncut) in a paper bag or cardboard box for up to 24 hours.

BIALYS

In New York, any place that sells lox and bagels is sure to have bialys. Softer than a bagel, with a well in the center filled with caramelized onions, it is the bagel's overlooked sibling. Legend has it that it was invented in the town of Bialystok in eastern Poland. That could be true, but *bialy* also means "pale" in Polish, and it is a pale roll when compared to a golden bagel. I like to believe that both stories are true. The thing I've noticed about bialys is that no one ever goes into a bakery and orders just bialys. Usually, it's "Give me a half dozen bagels and a couple bialys." Yet bialys have their own undeniable virtues. For example, I find that pickled herring in cream sauce, smoked sturgeon, and whitefish are all better suited to the bialy than the bagel, perhaps because the bialy's pale color suggests serving it with a white-fleshed fish.

Properly caramelized onions are critical to a proper bialy. They add kokumi, a newly identified flavor discovered by Japanese scientists. It's prominent in shallots, garlic, and onions. Kokumi is said to increase mouthfeel and amplify flavor. Taste a bialy without onions and you will agree: It's incomplete.

It took me a while to hit on the right recipe for bialys, and I don't claim that you'll find crème fraîche used in the Polish original, but it has a marvelous flavor, and its texture further boosts the mouthfeel.

STARTER

15 grams (1 tbsp) Sourdough Starter (page 122)
30 grams (2 tbsp) water at about 60°F (15°C)
30 grams (3½ tbsp) white flour

DOUGH

375 grams (2½ c + 3 tbsp) white flour, plus additional
    as needed for working with the dough
12 grams (2 tsp) fine sea salt
206 grams (1 c + 2 tbsp) water at about 60°F (15°C)
22 grams (1 tbsp) rye malt extract
8 grams (1⅛ tsp) honey
30 grams (2 tbsp) unsalted butter, at room temperature
96 grams (¼ c + 3 tbsp) crème fraîche
144 grams (¾ c) Caramelized Onions (page 72)

FOR THE STARTER

1 Put the sourdough starter in a medium storage container and add the water. Break the starter into pieces with your fingers until it's almost dissolved in the water; there will still be some small pieces. Stir in the flour until fully incorporated. Cover the container and let sit at room temperature for 10 to 14 hours. The starter will be at its peak at around 12 hours.

FOR THE DOUGH

1 Stir together the flour and salt in a medium bowl.

2 Pour about one-third of the water around the edges of the starter to release it from the sides of the container. Transfer the starter and water to an extra-large bowl along with the remaining water, the rye malt extract, and the honey. Using a wooden spoon, break the starter up to distribute it in the liquid. The extract will not break up easily and will be stringy and a bit clumped together at this point.

3 Add the flour mixture, reserving about one-sixth of it along the edge of the bowl (see Mixing, page 282). Continue to mix with the spoon until most of the dry ingredients have been combined with the starter mixture. Switch to a plastic bowl scraper and continue to mix until incorporated. At this point the dough will be a little sticky to the touch and pretty stiff.

4 Push the dough to one side of the bowl. Roll and tuck the dough (see Rolling and Tucking, page 284), adding the reserved flour mixture and a small amount of additional flour to the bowl and your hands as needed. Continue rolling and tucking 12 times. It is important to do 12 full roll and tuck sequences on this dough even if it begins to feel quite stiff and resistant. Then, with cupped hands, tuck the sides under toward the center. Place the dough, seam-side down, in a clean bowl, cover the top of the bowl with a clean kitchen towel, and let rest at room temperature for 45 minutes.

5 For the first stretch and fold (see Stretching and Folding, page 285), lightly dust the work surface and your hands with flour. Using the plastic bowl scraper, release the dough from the bowl and set it, seam-side down, on the work surface. Gently stretch it into a roughly rectangular shape. Fold the dough in thirds from top to bottom and then from left to right. With cupped hands, tuck the sides under toward the center. Place the dough in the bowl, seam-side down, cover the bowl with the towel, and let rest for 45 minutes.

6 For the second stretch and fold, repeat the steps for the first stretch and fold, then return the dough to the bowl, cover with the towel, and let rest for 45 minutes.

7 For the third and final stretch and fold, gently stretch the dough into a rectangle. Pinch the butter into pieces, distributing them over the top of the dough. Using your fingers or a spatula, spread the butter across the surface of the dough. (For photos of the following process, see Incorporating Add-Ins, page 292.) Roll up the dough tightly from the end closest to you; at the end of the roll the dough will be seam-side down. Turn it over, seam-side up, and gently press on the seam to flatten the dough slightly. Fold in thirds from left to right and then do 5 roll and tuck sequences to incorporate the butter. Return the dough to the bowl, cover with the towel, and let rest at room temperature for 45 minutes. Transfer to the refrigerator to chill 10 to 16 hours.

8 Set up the oven with a cast-iron skillet for steam (see Baking Stones and Steam, page 296), then preheat the oven to 475°F (245°C). Shaping the bialys will take about 30 minutes, so I recommend preheating the oven for 30 minutes and then starting to shape.

9 Line two half sheet pans with silicone baking mats or parchment paper. Lightly dust the work surface and your hands with flour. Using the plastic bowl scraper, turn the dough out onto the work surface. Using a bench scraper, divide the dough into 12 equal pieces (about 60 grams each). Gently roll each piece against the work surface to form a ball (see Rolling Dough into Balls, page 299). Let rest for 5 minutes.

10 Press each ball into a disk about 2½ inches (6.5 cm) in diameter. (For photos of the following process, see Shaping Bialys, page 295.) Working

with one disk at a time, flour both sides, then use two fingers to make a depression in the center. The dough in the center should be about ⅛ inch (3 mm) thick. Using your thumb and the first two fingers of both hands, pick up the disk and carefully rotate and stretch the dough until the thinner center area is 2½ to 3 inches (6.5 to 8 cm) in diameter. Set the dough back on the floured work surface, stretching it a bit more as you do so. The disk should look a bit like a mini pizza, with a thinner center and a rim that's about a ½ inch (1.5 cm) wide. Use your fingertips to press the center to flatten it a bit more. Repeat with the remaining disks and let rest for 5 minutes.

11 After resting, the center of the disks will have shrunk. Lift the disks and stretch them until the centers are about 2 inches (5 cm) in diameter, then transfer to the prepared sheet pans, putting six on each pan, in two rows of three bialys each. Cover the second sheet pan with a clean kitchen towel.

TO TOP AND BAKE THE BIALYS

1 The bialys will be baked in batches. Fill the bialys on the first pan, using a small offset spatula or the back of a spoon to spread 8 grams (2 tsp) of the crème fraîche in the center of each bialy. Top each with 12 grams (1 tbsp) of the onions.

2 Put the pan in the oven. Using heavy-duty oven mitts or potholders, pull out the hot skillet, add about 1½ cups of ice cubes, then slide it back in and close the oven door. Bake, rotating the pan about two-thirds of the way through baking, until the crust is a rich golden brown, 10 to 12 minutes. Some of the onions will be dark.

3 Set the first pan of bialys a cooling rack. Carefully pull out the skillet and pour out any remaining water. Set the skillet back on the rack and allow the oven temperature to return to 475°F (245°C). Meanwhile, top the second pan of bialys with crème fraîche and the onions. Then bake them in the same way, once again adding about 1½ cups of ice cubes to the skillet to create steam.

4 With both batches, give the bialys a few minutes to cook slightly on the pan, then place them directly on the cooling rack and let cool completely, about 1 hour. The bialys are best eaten the day they're baked, but once completely cooled they can be stored (uncut) in a paper bag or cardboard box for up to 24 hours.

QUICK BREADS

Biscuits and scones are considered quick breads, meaning you mix and bake immediately. There's no waiting for dough to ferment or rise, and they aren't leavened with yeast.

BISCUITS

When most of us think of the taste and texture of the ideal biscuit, we picture something golden, buttery, and flaky, leavened with baking powder or baking soda (although you can make biscuits with sourdough as well).

Biscuits were the classic American bread for much of US history, more so than leavened loaves, in part because they're easier and quicker to make. Biscuit recipes often call for buttermilk, which is slightly tart and lends bright acidity to the flavor. Still, buttermilk isn't a very common ingredient these days, and for years I wondered why it was so central to biscuit making. Then, as a result of a recent foray into making my own cultured butter and crème fraîche, a possible answer came to me. Butter is made from cream, which is poured off from the milk and churned. The liquid that remains after churning is traditional buttermilk. (The commercial buttermilk sold these days is quite different, being made by culturing nonfat or low-fat milk with lactic acid bacteria.) In the past, dairy farmers who made their own butter always had traditional buttermilk on hand. If you were to take 1 quart (1 L) of old-fashioned (not homogenized) whole milk, pour off the cream, and churn it, you would end up with almost exactly the same proportions of milk, butter, and buttermilk called for in classic biscuit recipes. If you look at it that way, it could be a recipe that almost invented itself.

As for my biscuit-making technique, my grandmother Georgia Coy definitely got me started. Her way with butter and flour was masterful. She always used very cold butter and also chilled her flour. She would cut the butter into cubes, then pinch it by hand into the cold flour. Whew! Glad I got that in there. No self-respecting chef or baker would ever write a cookbook without a shout-out to Grandma.

BASIC BUTTERMILK BISCUITS

Thank you, Jane Gibson, originally from Arkansas by way of Seattle. When I met Jane, she had already made her way from a short order cook in Arkansas to a truly elite pastry chef in Seattle. At her home, she was a damn fine Southern cook. Flash-forward a few years to my time Las Vegas, during which I was tasked with coming up with a good biscuit for the M Resort, so I called up Jane. She was tickled that out of all the things I could have asked—and she's a font of knowledge when it comes to French pastry—the one thing I wanted was a biscuit. She took great pains to describe how to make the dough and how it should feel, but somehow the right words eluded her. She said it was important to develop the gluten, but not too much—which didn't throw a whole lot of light on the subject. Finally, she tossed in the towel on trying to explain it with delicacy and said, "I don't know a better way to describe than to tell you the dough is right when it feels like a nice ass." Not your usual baking descriptor...but very apt.

INGREDIENTS

300 grams (2 c + 2 tbsp) white flour, plus additional
   for the work surface

20 grams (1 tbsp + 1 tsp) baking powder

7 grams (1⅛ tsp) fine sea salt

120 grams (8½ tbsp) cold unsalted butter,
   cut into ¼-inch (6 mm) pieces

125 grams (½ c) cold whole milk

125 grams (½ c) cold buttermilk, plus additional
   for brushing the top of the biscuits)

DIRECTIONS

1 Position a rack in the upper third of the oven, then preheat the oven to 400°F (205°C). Line a half sheet pan with a silicone baking mat or parchment paper. Dust a work surface with flour.

2 Stir together the flour, baking powder, and salt in a large bowl. Add the butter, tossing the pieces to coat them in the flour mixture. Working quickly and using just your fingertips, squeeze the pieces of butter until flattened while continuing to toss them in the flour, then break the pieces up a bit more. Pour in the milk and buttermilk. Using a plastic bowl scraper, fold the flour mixture over the milk a few times to combine, just until the mixture has almost come together; the dough might be slightly shaggy at this point.

3 Using the plastic bowl scraper, turn the dough out onto the work surface. Bring together then flatten with a plastic bowl scraper. Gently pat the dough out until about 1 inch (2.5 cm) thick. Using the scraper and your hands, fold the dough into thirds. Repeat the folding until the dough is firm, but not tough.

4 Press the dough into a 4 by 12-inch (10 by 30 cm) rectangle about 1 inch (2.5 cm) thick. Using a bench scraper, cut the dough into eight equal squares (two

rows of four). Using a spatula, transfer the biscuits to the lined pan and brush with buttermilk.

5 Bake, rotating the pan about two-thirds of the way through baking, until golden brown, about 18 minutes.

6 The biscuits are best if eaten within 1 hour of baking, but once completely cooled they can be stored (uncut) in a paper bag or cardboard box for up to 24 hours.

CHEROKEE BISCUITS

Baker Jane Gibson, who generously shared her biscuit recipe with me (see Basic Buttermilk Biscuits, page 252) has a bit of Cherokee blood in her. Come to think of it, a lot of people in the South, where I spent a decade of my formative years, proudly claim some Cherokee ancestry. That Native American influence comes to the fore in this hearty biscuit recipe, which, instead of using butter, relies on schmutz (in this case, pan drippings) and crispy bits that stick to the bottom of the skillet when you cook bacon. In the waste-not-want-not culture of many Native Americans, this has long been a delicious and nutritious way to utilize bacon. The smoky flavor is quite enticing, and surprisingly, the texture isn't overly dense. Topped with jam, these biscuits make for a satisfying breakfast, and served with scrambled eggs, they'll hold you until lunch. If you use them to swab up sausage gravy, you will feel like a bonafide child of the South. To have enough bacon fat for this recipe, you'll need to save the drippings from a few batches of bacon, or you can start from scratch by cooking about 2 pounds (900 g) of bacon.

INGREDIENTS

300 grams (2 c + 2 tbsp) white flour,
    plus additional for the work surface

20 grams (1 tbsp + 1 tsp) baking powder

7 grams (1⅛ tsp) fine sea salt

120 grams (½ c + 1 tbsp) cold bacon fat with
    browned bits cut into ¼-inch (6 mm) pieces

125 grams (½ c) cold whole milk

125 grams (½ c) cold buttermilk, plus additional
    for brushing the top of the biscuits

DIRECTIONS

1 Position a rack in the upper third of the oven, then preheat the oven to 400°F (205°C). Line a half sheet pan with a silicone baking mat or parchment paper. Dust a work surface with flour.

2 Stir together the flour, baking powder, and salt in a large bowl. Add the bacon fat and toss the pieces to coat them in the flour mixture. Working quickly and using just your fingertips, squeeze the pieces of bacon fat until flattened while continuing to toss them in the flour, then break the pieces up a bit more. Pour in the milk and buttermilk. Using a plastic bowl scraper, fold the flour mixture over the milk a few times to combine, just until the mixture has almost come together; the dough might be slightly shaggy at this point.

3 Using the plastic bowl scraper, turn the dough out onto the work surface. Bring together then flatten with a plastic bowl scraper. Gently pat the dough out until about 1 inch (2.5 cm) thick. Using the scraper and your hands, fold the dough into thirds. Repeat the folding until the dough is firm, but not tough.

4 Press the dough into a 4 by 12-inch (10 by 30 cm) rectangle about 1 inch (2.5 cm) thick. Using a bench scraper, cut the dough into eight equal squares (two rows of four). Using a spatula, transfer the biscuits to the lined pan and brush with buttermilk.

5 Bake, rotating the pan about two-thirds of the way through baking, until golden brown, about 18 minutes.

6 The biscuits are best if eaten within 1 hour of baking, but once completely cooled they can be stored (uncut) in a paper bag or cardboard box for up to 24 hours.

TEXAS Q BISCUITS

In Austin, I worked alongside the talented David Quintanilla at Asti Trattoria, a posh Italian restaurant. David is one of those rare people who are natural chefs. Give him any ingredient, and he can just intuit how it wants to be prepared. If I were more mystical, I would say he's found a spiritual path to communicating with ingredients. He makes the best beef chili and barbecue brisket I've ever eaten, and I just had to invent a biscuit to go with them, for two reasons: first, because David's food deserves it and second, because he's a self-described "master bastard," and I fear he might do me bodily harm if I were to write an entire book without inventing a recipe for him.

When developing these biscuits, I thought about the flavors of the southwest, and Texas in particular. Like a melody you can't get out of your head, the words "Cheddar," "jalapeño," and "corn" took hold of me. It has to be good Cheddar though, well-aged and smoked. Also, it's important to cook the jalapeños before incorporating them into the dough, both for a smoky flavor and to tame their heat a little bit. Are we cool, Q?

INGREDIENTS

2 large jalapeño chiles

5 grams (1 tsp) vegetable oil or other cooking oil

7 grams (1⅛ tsp) fine sea salt, plus a pinch
    for cooking the jalapeños

190 grams (1¼ c + 2 tbsp) white flour, plus additional
    for the work surface

106 grams (½ c + 2 tbsp) medium-grind cornmeal

17 grams (1 tbsp + ½ tsp) baking powder

120 grams (8½ tbsp) cold unsalted butter,
    cut into ¼-inch (6 mm) pieces

40 grams (3 tbsp) crème fraîche

80 grams (¼ c + 1 tbsp) cold whole milk

118 grams (¼ c + 3½ tbsp) cold buttermilk,
    plus additional for brushing the top of the biscuits

80 grams (½ c) grated smoked Cheddar cheese

DIRECTIONS

1 Wearing rubber gloves, stem the jalapeños, cut them in half, and scoop out and discard the seeds. Cut the jalapeños into ¼-inch (6 mm) dice. You will need 20 grams (2 tbsp + 1 tsp) for this recipe.

2 Turn on the ventilation fan over the stove and, if possible, open some windows. Heat a small skillet over high heat and add the oil and a pinch of salt. When the oil just begins to smoke, add the jalapeños and cook, stirring often, until they begin to blacken, about 3 minutes. Remove from the heat and let cool completely.

3 Position a rack in the upper third of the oven, then preheat the oven to 400°F (205°C). Line a half sheet pan with a silicone baking mat or parchment paper. Dust a work surface with flour.

4 Stir together the flour, cornmeal, baking powder, and salt in a large bowl. Add the butter, tossing the pieces to coat them in the flour mixture. Working quickly and using just your fingertips, squeeze the pieces of butter until flattened while continuing to

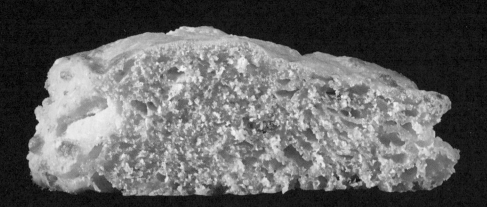

toss them in the flour, then break the pieces up a bit more. Pour in the crème fraîche, milk, and buttermilk. Using a plastic bowl scraper, fold the flour mixture over the milk a few times to combine. When the mixture has almost come together, add the jalapeños and Cheddar and give the mixture another fold or two; the dough might be slightly shaggy at this point.

5 Using the plastic bowl scraper, turn the dough out onto the work surface. Bring together then flatten with a plastic bowl scraper. Gently pat the dough out until about 1 inch (2.5 cm) thick. Using the scraper and your hands, fold the dough into thirds. Repeat the folding until the dough is firm, but not tough.

6 Press the dough into a 4 by 12-inch (10 by 30 cm) rectangle about 1 inch (2.5 cm) thick. Using a bench scraper, cut the dough into eight equal squares (two rows of four). Using a spatula, transfer the biscuits to the lined pan and brush with buttermilk.

7 Bake, rotating the pan about two-thirds of the way through baking, until golden brown, about 18 minutes.

8 The biscuits are best if eaten within 1 hour of baking, but once completely cooled they can be stored (uncut) in a paper bag or cardboard box for up to 24 hours.

SCONES

When I was ten years old, my family moved from Portland, Oregon, to England for a year. As an American kid on his first trip abroad, I guess the two-word description for my reaction would be "culture shock": cars on the wrong side of the road, candy bars with funny names, red double-decker buses, and a variety of strange accents. The one thing I knew (or thought I knew) about England was English muffins, so I was surprised that I never came across an English muffin in England—crumpets, yes, tea biscuits, yes, but no English muffins. I particularly remember liking the scones. To this day, most scones on this side of the Atlantic still leave me unmoved. All too often they have the texture I imagine you'd get with a baked hockey puck: dense, dry, and over-sweetened (when they aren't undersweetened). Most English scones, on the other hand, are a type of tender, unyeasted bread, and they're slightly sweet but not overly so. Breakfast scones and tea scones tend to be sweet, while with savory scones, which are nice at lunch, the sweetness is dialed back a bit. Finally, if you don't eat a well-made scone over a plate or napkin, you're definitely going to get crumbs on your shirt or the table. Good scones are crumbly; that's part of what makes them so crisp yet tender.

CANDIED LEMON AND BLACKBERRY SCONES

This is a fruity, bright, and sweet scone that evokes summer, with the flavors of a glass of lemon-ade and a bowl of perfectly ripe berries. The recipe was a lucky accident that followed an unlucky grocery order. One of my sous chefs at the bakery thought it would be a great idea to order a whole case of candied lemon peel. What a waste! It would take forever and a day to use that much. (Plus, store-bought candied lemon peel often has a bitter taste from the white pith inside the rind. That's why I recommend that you make your own.) As for the blackberries, if you freeze them when freshly picked, their summer flavor will last through the winter. My little trick is to cut or slice berries after freezing them, which prevents getting blackberry juice on everything—a baker's trick that every apprentice learns in the interest of wardrobe preservation.

INGREDIENTS

50 grams (1.8 oz) blackberries (about 9 berries), preferably fresh
120 grams (¾ c + 2 tbsp) white flour, plus additional
    for the work surface
7 grams (1½ tsp) baking powder
1 gram (generous ⅛ tsp) fine sea salt
50 grams (¼ c) granulated sugar
35 grams (2½ tbsp) cold unsalted butter,
    cut into ¼-inch (6 mm) pieces
30 grams (2 tbsp) cold crème fraîche
70 grams (¼ c + 2 tsp) cold buttermilk,
    plus additional for brushing the top of the scones
12 grams (1 tbsp) finely chopped Candied
    Lemon Peel (recipe follows)

DIRECTIONS

1 Line a quarter sheet pan with plastic wrap. Spread the berries on the pan and carefully place the pan in the freezer, being careful that the berries aren't touching. Freeze until firm, about 2 hours, or until ready to use.

2 Position a rack in the upper third of the oven, then preheat the oven to 400°F (205°C). Line a half sheet pan with a silicone baking mat or parchment paper. Dust the work surface with flour.

3 Stir together the flour, baking powder, and salt in a small bowl.

4 Put the sugar in a large bowl, add the butter, and toss to coat. Using the rounded edge of a plastic bowl scraper, chop the butter into smaller pieces while continuing to coat the pieces in the sugar. Add the flour mixture and, still using a chopping motion, mix until the ingredients are evenly distributed but the texture is still fairly chunky.

5 Pour in the crème fraîche and buttermilk and, still using a chopping motion, mix until almost completely incorporated.

6 Remove the berries from the freezer and, working quickly, cut them into ¼-inch (6 mm) pieces (about three slices per berry). Add them to the dough, along with the candied lemon peel, and use the scraper to gently fold them in just until evenly distributed. Avoid overmixing, or the berries will bleed into the dough and give it a muddy appearance. This may seem like a small amount of dough, but it's enough.

7 Empty the scone batter onto a floured surface. Bring together then flatten with a plastic scraper. Cut the dough in half and place one half on top of the other. Next, cut one-third of the dough and place it on the top of the remaining dough, in the middle. Cut the remaining third and place it on top of the two layers. Flatten the dough and repeat two more times. The last time, press the dough into a 3 by 8-inch (8 by 20 cm) rectangle about 1 inch (2.5 cm) thick.

8 Using a bench scraper, cut the dough into six equal rectangles. Turn each rectangle on its side so that what was a cut surface is now the top, and gently press each just enough to create an oval shape.

Transfer the scones to the lined pan, with the long dimension running the length of the pan and checkerboarding them in two rows of two and two rows of single pieces. Brush the tops with buttermilk.

9 Bake, rotating the pan about two-thirds of the way through baking, until golden brown, about 13 minutes.

10 The scones are best if eaten within 1 hour of baking, but once completely cooled, they can be stored (uncut) in a paper bag or cardboard box for up to 24 hours.

CANDIED LEMON PEEL

MAKES ABOUT 55 GRAMS (1.9 OZ)

Candying lemon peel is a four-day process, but it keeps for a long time, and you'll find other uses for it—I promise. Try it in cakes, sorbets, ice cream, and salads.

DIRECTIONS:

1 Using a vegetable peeler, peel the zest off the lemons in lengthwise strips. (Store the lemon flesh in the refrigerator for another use.) With a paring knife, scrape off any white pith from inside the strips of lemon peel.

2 Prepare a medium bowl of ice water. Bring 120 grams (½ c) of the water and the salt to a boil in a small saucepan. Add the lemon peel and cook until tender enough that you can puncture the outside of the peel with a fingernail, about 5 minutes. Using a slotted spoon, transfer the lemon peel to the ice bath and let cool completely. Drain well, then transfer the lemon peel to a small, heatproof storage container.

3 In a clean small saucepan, combine the remaining 50 grams (3 tbsp + 1 tsp) water and 50 grams (¼ c) of the sugar, and bring to a simmer, stirring to dissolve the sugar. Pour the syrup over the lemon peel, cover, and let sit at room temperature for 24 hours.

4 Strain the liquid into a clean small saucepan, add 20 grams (1 tbsp + 2 tsp) of the sugar, and bring to a simmer, stirring to dissolve the sugar. Pour the syrup over the lemon peel, cover, and let sit at room temperature for 24 hours.

5 Repeat the previous step two more times.

INGREDIENTS

3 lemons, preferably Meyer lemons
170 grams (½ c + 3 ½ tbsp) water
10 grams (1 ½ tsp) fine sea salt
110 grams (½ c + 2 ½ tsp) granulated sugar
20 grams (1 tbsp) honey or glucose syrup, optional

6 The candied lemon peels can be refrigerated for up to 2 months or frozen for up to 1 year. If you think you'll be storing some of the candied peels for more than a few days, add the honey or glucose syrup when adding the final 20 grams (1 tbsp + 2 tsp) of sugar to the syrup, to prevent crystallization.

MISSION FIG, ROSEMARY, ANISE, AND PISTACHIO SCONES

———

I was playing around with a few ideas for scone flavor combinations one afternoon when Peter suggested rosemary and dried fig: a pungent, savory herb matched with a sweetly strong fruit. When it came time for me to show my cards, I said I thought anise, though savory, has a real affinity for sweetness and that pistachios would add a toasty, buttery crunch. We were pretty much sold on the combination before we even tried it; some recipes just sound right in the conceptual stage. You need to be careful with rosemary, though, because it wants to take over. So in this recipe, I use it in the form of an infused butter. This technique allows you to control how much presence an herb has in the final flavor. I find this to be a nice scone for winter since the ingredients are all readily available. It has just enough sweetness to qualify as a scone and therefore is perfect for times when you're looking for something more savory for breakfast or tea.

ROSEMARY-INFUSED BUTTER

65 grams (4 tbsp + 2 tsp) unsalted butter

3 grams (1½ tbsp) fresh rosemary leaves

DOUGH

60 grams (¼ c + 2 tbsp) unsalted shelled pistachios

120 grams (¾ c + 2 tbsp) white flour,
    plus additional for the work surface

7 grams (1½ tsp) baking powder

1 gram (generous ⅛ tsp) fine sea salt

1 gram (½ tsp) ground anise seeds

35 grams (3 tbsp) granulated sugar

25 grams (2 tbsp) light brown sugar

95 grams (¼ c + 2½ tbsp) cold buttermilk,
    plus additional for brushing the top of the scones

45 grams (¼ c + ½ tbsp) dried Mission figs,
    cut into ¼-inch (6 mm) rounds

FOR THE ROSEMARY-INFUSED BUTTER

1 Set a small fine-mesh strainer over a small storage container. Melt the butter in a small saucepan over medium-low heat until the solids and the fat separate but the butter isn't bubbling yet; the ideal temperature is about 150°F (65°C). Decrease the heat to low. Stir in the rosemary, submerging it in the butter, and cook, stirring continuously, for 90 seconds. Strain the butter, pressing on the leaves to extract as much butter and flavor as possible. Cover the container and refrigerate for 10 minutes.

2 Stir the butter with a fork, bringing the solids and the fat back together if they've separated, then return to the refrigerator. Repeat this process, stirring and refrigerating the butter two more times, then chill until the butter is solidified, about 1 hour longer.

3 Cut the butter into ¼-inch (6 mm) pieces, then put the pieces in the container and refrigerate until firm again. You will need 35 grams (2½ tbsp) of the infused butter for this recipe; reserve the remainder for another use.

FOR THE DOUGH

1 Position a rack in the upper third of the oven, then preheat the oven to 400°F (205°C). Spread the pistachios on a quarter sheet pan and toast until fragrant and golden, about 5 minutes. Let cool completely, then coarsely chop. Leave the oven on.

2 Line a half sheet pan with a silicone baking mat or parchment paper. Dust the work surface with flour.

3 Stir together the flour, baking powder, salt, and anise in a small bowl.

4 Combine the granulated and brown sugars in a large bowl. Add the 35 grams (2½ tbsp) of infused butter and toss to coat. Using the rounded edge of a plastic bowl scraper, chop the butter into smaller pieces while continuing to coat the pieces in the sugar. Add the flour mixture and, still using a chopping motion, mix until the ingredients are evenly distributed but the texture is still fairly chunky.

5 Pour in the buttermilk and, still using a chopping motion, mix until almost completely incorporated. Fold in the figs and pistachios. This may seem like a small amount of dough, but it's enough.

6 Empty the scone batter onto a floured surface. Bring together then flatten with a plastic scraper. Cut the dough in half and place one half on top of the other. Next, cut one-third of the dough and place it on the top of the remaining dough, in the middle. Cut the remaining third and place it on top of the two layers. Flatten the dough and repeat two more times. The last time, press the dough into a 3 by 8-inch (8 by 20 cm) rectangle about 1 inch (2.5 cm) thick.

7 Using a bench scraper, cut the dough into six equal rectangles. Turn each rectangle on its side so that what was a cut surface is now the top, and gently press each just enough to create an oval shape. Transfer the scones to the lined pan, with the long dimension running the length of the pan and checkerboarding them in two rows of two and two rows of single pieces. Brush the tops with buttermilk.

8 Bake, rotating the pan about two-thirds of the way through baking, until golden brown, about 13 minutes.

9 The scones are best if eaten within 1 hour of baking, but once completely cooled, they can be stored (uncut) in a paper bag or cardboard box for up to 24 hours.

ALSATIAN SCONES

To envision this recipe, think *tarte Alsacienne* (a pastry-based appetizer topped with cheese, bacon, and onions) crossing the English Channel and showing up promptly at teatime. These scones also provide an opportunity to use some of the caramelized onions you spent so much time making for the Caramelized Onion Bread (page 69). Like a good croissant, these scones have just a hint of sweetness, with bits of bacon added to amp up the flavor even more. Also, make sure you use a good Gruyère cheese, not generic "Swiss." This flavor combination of bacon, onions, and Gruyère has worked for centuries. Why mess with it?

INGREDIENTS

120 grams (¾ c + 2 tbsp) white flour, plus
  additional for the work surface

7 grams (1½ tsp) baking powder

1 gram (generous ⅛ tsp) fine sea salt

30 grams (2½ tbsp) granulated sugar

30 grams (2 tbsp) cold unsalted butter,
  cut into ¼-inch (6 mm) pieces

30 grams (2 tbsp) cold crème fraîche

65 grams (¼ c + 1 tsp) cold buttermilk,
  plus additional for brushing the top of the scones

20 grams (1½ tbsp) Caramelized Onions (page 72)

20 grams (2 tbsp) shredded Gruyère cheese

15 grams (2 tbsp) cooked bacon, cut into ¼-inch (6 mm) pieces

DIRECTIONS

1 Position a rack in the upper third of the oven, then preheat the oven to 400°F (205°C). Line a half sheet pan with a silicone baking mat or parchment paper. Dust the work surface with flour.

2 Stir together the flour, baking powder, and salt in a small bowl.

3 Put the sugar in a large bowl, add the butter, and toss to coat. Using the rounded edge of a plastic bowl scraper, chop the butter into smaller pieces while continuing to coat the pieces in the sugar. Add the flour mixture and, still using a chopping motion, mix until the ingredients are evenly distributed but the texture is still fairly chunky.

4 Pour in the crème fraîche and buttermilk and, still using a chopping motion, mix until almost completely incorporated. Fold in the onions, Gruyère, and bacon. This may seem like a small amount of dough, but it's enough.

5 Empty the scone batter onto a floured surface. Bring together then flatten with a plastic scraper. Cut the dough in half and place one half on top of the other. Next, cut one-third of the dough and place it on the top of the remaining dough, in the middle. Cut the remaining third and place it on top of the two

layers. Flatten the dough and repeat two more times. The last time, press the dough into a 3 by 8-inch (8 by 20 cm) rectangle about 1 inch (2.5 cm) thick.

6 Using a bench scraper, cut the dough into six equal rectangles. Turn each rectangle on its side so that what was a cut surface is now the top, and gently press each just enough to create an oval shape. Transfer the scones to the lined pan, with the long dimension running the length of the pan and check-erboarding them in two rows of two and two rows of single pieces. Brush the tops with buttermilk.

7 Bake, rotating the pan about two-thirds of the way through baking, until golden brown, about 13 minutes.

8 The scones are best if eaten within 1 hour of bak-ing, but once completely cooled, they can be stored (uncut) in a paper bag or cardboard box for up to 24 hours.

MARGHERITA SCONES

These scones feature basil and tomatoes: the same ingredients that serve as a topping for the most basic—and to me, the most wonderful—pizza. Although slightly sweet, this is a savory scone, akin to the Alsatian Scones (page 271) and the Mission Fig, Rosemary, Anise, and Pistachio Scones (page 267). The step that elevates these scones is an herb-infused butter. It allows the floral notes of fresh, young basil to suffuse the crumb. I often make a nice light lunch of these scones. They are delightful with fried eggs, especially when you swoosh them in a runny yolk.

BASIL-INFUSED BUTTER

65 grams (4 tbsp + 2 tsp) unsalted butter

50 grams (4 c, loosely packed, from about 1 large bunch) fresh basil leaves

DOUGH

120 grams (¾ c + 2 tbsp) white flour, plus additional for the work surface

7 grams (1½ tsp) baking powder

1 gram (generous ⅛ tsp) fine sea salt

30 grams (2½ tbsp) granulated sugar

45 grams (3½ tbsp) cold crème fraîche

80 grams (¼ c + 1½ tbsp) cold heavy cream, plus additional for brushing the top of the scones

35 grams (¾ c + 2 tbsp) sun-dried tomatoes, preferably not oil packed, cut into ¼-inch (6 mm) strips

15 grams (1½ tbsp) grated Parmigiano-Reggiano cheese

FOR THE BASIL-INFUSED BUTTER

1 Set a small fine mesh strainer over a small storage container. Melt the butter in a small saucepan over medium-low heat until the solids and the fat separate but the butter isn't bubbling yet; the ideal temperature is about 150°F (65°C). Decrease the heat to low. Stir in the basil, pushing it down to submerge it in the butter, and cook, stirring continuously, for about 45 seconds, until the basil turns dark green. Strain the butter, pressing on the leaves to extract as much butter and flavor from them as possible. Cover the container and refrigerate for 10 minutes.

2 Stir the butter with a fork, bringing the solids and the fat back together if they've separated, then return to the refrigerator. Repeat this process, stirring and refrigerating the butter two more times, then chill until the butter is solidified, about 1 hour longer.

3 Cut the butter into ¼-inch (6 mm) pieces, then put the pieces in the container and refrigerate until firm again. You will need 35 grams (2½ tbsp) of the infused butter for this recipe; reserve the remainder for another use.

FOR THE DOUGH

1 Position a rack in the upper third of the oven, then preheat the oven to 400°F (205°C). Line a half sheet

275

pan with a silicone baking mat or parchment paper. Dust the work surface with flour.

2 Stir together the flour, baking powder, and salt in a small bowl.

3 Put the sugar in a large bowl, add the 35 grams (2½ tbsp) of infused butter, and toss to coat. Using the rounded edge of a plastic bowl scraper, chop the butter into smaller pieces while continuing to coat the pieces in the sugar. Add the flour mixture and, still using a chopping motion, mix until the ingredients are evenly distributed but the texture is still fairly chunky.

4 Pour in the crème fraîche and heavy cream and, still using a chopping motion, mix until almost completely incorporated. Fold in the sun-dried tomatoes and Parmigiano-Reggiano. This may seem like a small amount of dough, but it's enough.

5 Empty the scone batter onto a floured surface. Bring together then flatten with a plastic scraper. Cut the dough in half and place one half on top of the other. Next, cut one-third of the dough and place it on the top of the remaining dough, in the middle. Cut the remaining third and place it on top of the two

layers. Flatten the dough and repeat two more times. The last time, press the dough into a 3 by 8-inch (8 by 20 cm) rectangle about 1 inch (2.5 cm) thick.

6 Using a bench scraper, cut the dough into six equal rectangles. Turn each rectangle on its side so that what was a cut surface is now the top, and gently press each just enough to create an oval shape. Transfer the scones to the lined pan, with the long dimension running the length of the pan and checkerboarding them in two rows of two and two rows of single pieces. Brush the tops with buttermilk.

7 Bake, rotating the pan about two-thirds of the way through baking, until golden brown, about 13 minutes.

8 The scones are best if eaten within 1 hour of baking, but once completely cooled, they can be stored (uncut) in a paper bag or cardboard box for up to 24 hours.

TECHNIQUE & PROCESS

PREPPING A SOURDOUGH STARTER TO MAKE A LOAF

A

B

C

D

E

F

G

H

Gather all your ingredients and tools (A).

Measure your sourdough starter and water (B).

Pour your water over the starter (C) and break up the starter with your fingers (D).

Using a wooden spoon, combine the starter and water (E). Then, add the flour and mix with the wooden spoon until the mixture is thoroughly combined (F-I).

Transfer the mixture to an airtight container (J-K). Let ferment at room temperature according to the recipe's directions (L).

MIXING

A

B

C

D

Pour some of your pre-measured water into the storage container to help release the starter (A-B).

In a large bowl, use a wooden spoon to combine your starter with the remaining water (C).

Add salt, yeast, and flour and combine, reserving about a sixth of your flour on one side of the bowl (D–E).

You'll incorporate this flour bit by bit to keep the dough from sticking as you proceed to tuck and fold.

As the dough stiffens from mixing with the spoon, exchange the spoon for a bowl scraper (F–G) and begin rolling and tucking the dough (see following pages) (H).

E   F
G   H

TIMING

A part from dealing with a hungry infant or pulling all-night guard duty in the military, there is no occupation with such a demanding schedule as bread baking. Of course, I'm not asking you to keep the hours we do at the bakery, where we bake in the middle of the night so our customers can have fresh bread each morning. Still, from start to finish, making bread is a long process. The good news is, in terms of the actual time spent making the starter, mixing the dough, shaping loaves, and finally baking the bread, it adds up to only about 1 hour of time. The rest of the work is done by your five billion little helpers, otherwise known as yeast.

The real trick to all of this timing is to make it work with your own daily schedule. For many breads, if you make the starter in the morning, you can return to the process in the evening and, over the course of a few hours, mix, roll and tuck, stretch and fold, and then shape. Then you can store the loaf in the refrigerator for its final fermentation and bake it the following afternoon or evening. Alternatively, it may be better for you if you make the starter in the evening, then do the next stages in the morning. With this approach, you'll put it in the refrigerator by early afternoon and can bake the following morning. Either way, the soonest you'll be baking is about 24 hours after you mix the starter. But again, 98 percent of the work—and much of the time—is expended by the yeast, along with bacteria and enzymes.

ROLLING AND TUCKING

A

C

B

D

Note: As you continue the rolling and tucking started on the previous pages, you will find that it is more effective to begin to work with the dough by hand, but you may find it easier to start with a bowl scraper. Remember to incorporate the reserved flour bit by bit when the dough sticks to your hands or the work surface.

Start by coaxing the dough into a somewhat rectangular shape, with a short end facing you. Slide your fingers (or scraper) under the first 3 inches (8 cm) of the part of the dough and lift it up (A).

Roll it towards you, then push down lightly with the side of your hand, tucking the folded end into the mass of dough (B–D). Repeat several times until the dough is all rolled up, giving a slight push down on the last roll to leave the rolled dough seam-side down. Rotate the dough 90 degrees so the short side is once again facing you. Flip it over seam-side up, and press gently on the seam with your palm hand (or the flat side of a scraper) to create a roughly rectangular shape measuring about 4 by 10 inches (10 by 25 cm).

Repeat the process as before, ending with the dough seam-side down. At this point, you will have completed one full roll and tuck. You can now rotate the dough 90 degrees and begin the next roll and tuck.

Note: Experienced bakers may be able to accomplish four rolls while working down the length of the dough; those who are less experienced may manage only three rolls. Don't worry about it. If the dough is quite sticky at first, have patience; it will strengthen and become more manageable with each roll and tuck. When the dough strengthens, you'll notice that it begins to resist further rolling. A general rule of thumb is that when the dough becomes difficult to fold and begins to tear, it's time to stop.

Transfer the dough, seam-side down, to a clean bowl at least 12 inches (30 cm) in diameter. Cover it with a clean kitchen towel and let it rest.

STRETCHING AND FOLDING

Remove the dough from the bowl and place on a lightly floured surface. Pulling from the middle of the dough outwards, gently stretch it to a rectangle about 10 by 12 inches (25 cm x 30 cm) (A–D).

Roll the front third of the dough toward the center (E). Roll the back third over the dough you have just folded (F). You will now have 3 layers of dough (G).

Repeat the process as shown, starting by folding left to right (H–I). When completed, you will now have 9 layers. This completes the process of one stretch and fold (J).

Gently shape the folded dough into a round (K–N) and return to a lightly floured bowl (O–Q). Cover and rest as called for by recipe.

STRETCHING AND FOLDING

G

H

I

J

K

L

M

N

O

P

Q

SHAPING A ROUND LOAF

A

B

C

D

For round loaves (French bakers call it a *boule*), begin by lining a proofing basket or bowl with a clean kitchen towel, and then flour the towel fairly generously (see Dusting Mixture, page 35) (A).

Working on a lightly floured surface, slightly flatten and stretch the dough (B).

Fold the dough in half (C) and, with the folded side facing up, tuck in the sides and the corners to form a ball (D).

With cupped hands, shape the loaf by pulling the dough toward you and slightly to the right or left, allowing friction against the table to help tighten the round (E–G). You may need to repeat this process a few times until the dough is tight enough. The surface will be smooth and firm enough to hold its shape (H).

Place the dough in a bowl and fold the corners of the towel over gently (I).

SCORING

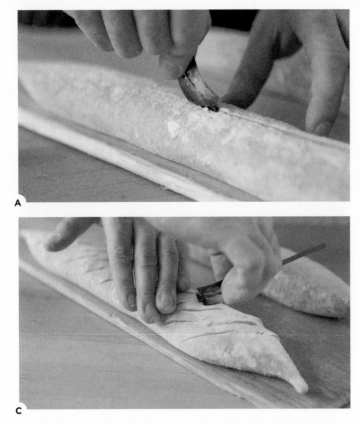

A

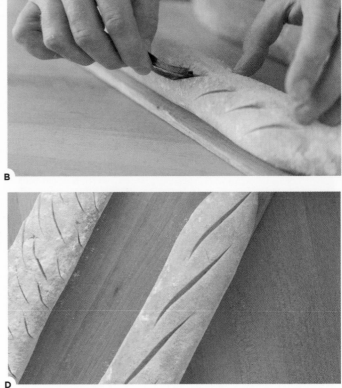

B

C

D

Scoring the surface of the dough will guide its natural tendency to expand. A score can be straightforward or more ornate. For most of the loaves in this book, I use a single straight score (A).

Working quickly, insert the tip of a single-edge razor blade (see Equipment, page 24) into the center of one end of the dough on an angle. Run it across the surface loaf. Make a single straight cut, about ¼ inch deep.

As you get more proficient you may want to try other decorative scores (B–D).

BAKING IN A DUTCH OVEN

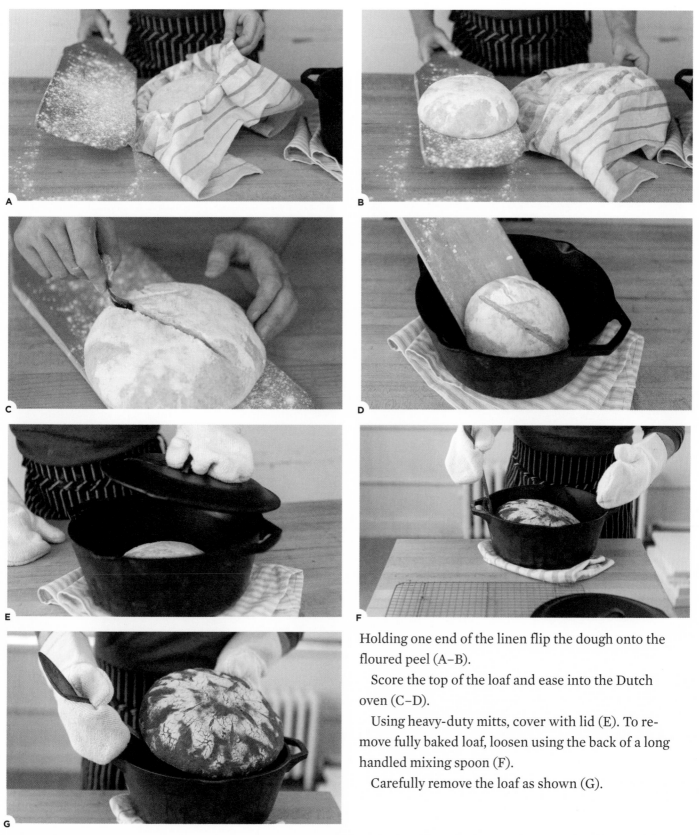

Holding one end of the linen flip the dough onto the floured peel (A–B).

Score the top of the loaf and ease into the Dutch oven (C–D).

Using heavy-duty mitts, cover with lid (E). To remove fully baked loaf, loosen using the back of a long handled mixing spoon (F).

Carefully remove the loaf as shown (G).

INCORPORATING ADD-INS

A

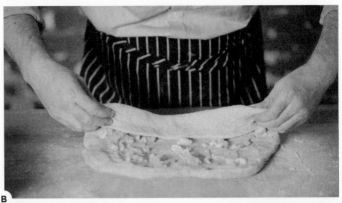

B

C

D

E

F

For doughs that call for added ingredients such as potatoes, olives, or nuts, incorporate them after the dough has had some time to develop.

Gently stretch the dough into a roughly rectangular shape measuring about 6 by 10 inches (15 by 25 cm). Scatter the add-ins over the top, then gently press them into the dough (A). Tightly roll the dough around the ingredients (B–D). Turn seam-side up and gently press to seal. Fold the dough in thirds from right to left (E–F), and then roll and tuck. Tuck the sides under toward the center and return the dough to the bowl.

When adding a fat like butter or lard in this way, 4 or 5 roll and tuck sequences will be required to ensure that the fat is evenly incorporated.

USING A LINEN LINER

A

B

Place a linen liner or dishtowel on a sheet pan or large cutting board. Dust generously with flour. Gather the linen into a fold between each row of loaves or rolls (A–B). Cover with the remaining cloth, or, if needed, a new cloth.

SHAPING A TUBE OR OVAL LOAF

A

B

C

D

E

F

To begin, gently press the dough into a rectangle or square, as indicated in the recipe. Then, starting at the top, position your thumbs, touching each other, up against and parallel to the edge of the dough (A).

Roll it toward you and then push down slightly, tucking the fold under the roll (B–D). Repeat this rolling and pressing motion 3 to 4 times down the length of the dough.

When all the dough is rolled up, pinch the seam to complete the shape (E).

Roll the ends of each loaf to achieve tapered ends (F).

SHAPING BIALYS

A

B

C

D

E

F

Press each ball of dough into a disk about 2½ inches (6.5 cm) in diameter. Working with one disk at a time, flour both sides, and then use two fingers to make a depression in the center (A–B).

Using your thumb and the first two fingers of both hands, pick up a disk and carefully rotate the dough, stretching it in the same way you stretch a pizza dough until the indentation or well in the center is 2½ to 3 inches (6.5 to 8 cm) in diameter (C–E). Repeat with the remaining dough.

Place the disks back on the floured work surface,

stretching them slightly as they are lain down. Use your fingertips to press the centers slightly. Let the disks rest for 5 minutes.

Lift each disk up and stretch it so the center is about 2 inches (5 cm) in diameter (F). Place them on two sheet pans lined with silicone baking mats or parchment paper, placing them in two rows of three bialys each.

BAKING STONES AND STEAM

A B C D E F

Slide the loaves onto the pre-heated stone (A).

Use transfer peel to make sure loaves do not touch (B). Once your loaves are fully loaded, very carefully drop ice into cast-iron skillet (C–E). Carefully, push the skillet back in and quickly shut the door (F).

SHAPING AN OVAL

A

B

C

D

E

Once you have made a roll (see 299), allow it to rest for one minute, then roll back and forth with open palm as shown.

SCORING BOURBON BREAD

Using a bench scraper, make 3 to 5 cuts on the diagonal down the loaf (A). Then make 3 to 5 cuts in the opposite direction, crossing the first set of cuts, to make diamonds (B).

Using a bench scraper, gently flip the loaf onto a floured linen (C–D).

ROLLING DOUGH INTO BALLS

A

B

C

D

E

Gently roll each piece of dough into a ball (A-B).

Cup your fingers around the ball and shape it by pulling it towards you and slightly to the right or left, allowing friction against the table to help tighten the surface of the dough (C).

It will be smooth and firm enough to hold its shape (D). Transfer the balls to the baking sheet (E).

SCORING OATMEAL ROLLS

Using a bowl scraper, cut the dough ball almost in half, stopping just before the bottom, leaving about ⅛ inch (3 mm) uncut; keep the halves attached (A). Make a second cut across the first, also stopping just before the bottom (B). Using your thumb and forefinger, press two opposite sections toward the center to square off the sides (C). Repeat with the remaining two sides to make a square roll (D).

SHAPING SMALL TUBES

A

B

C

Divide your dough into rectangular pieces of the same size (A). Let rest for 5 minutes.

Tightly roll up the pieces of dough (B) and pinch them to form a seam (C).

SHAPING SMALL OVAL TUBES

After the dough has been shaped into a ball and rested for about 5 minutes, press into disks about 3 inches (8 cm) in diameter (A–B). Fold the top edge over to meet the bottom edge (C), press against the seam, and roll to be seam-side down (D). Gently roll the ovals until 3 to 4 inches (9 to 10 cm) long, adding a bit of pressure to taper the ends (E–F).

SHAPING SMALL BAGUETTES

Using a pre-shaped tube (page 301), gently roll the dough with an open palm, pushing out as you do (A–D). Add a bit of pressure to taper the ends (E–F).

SHAPING KAISER ROLLS

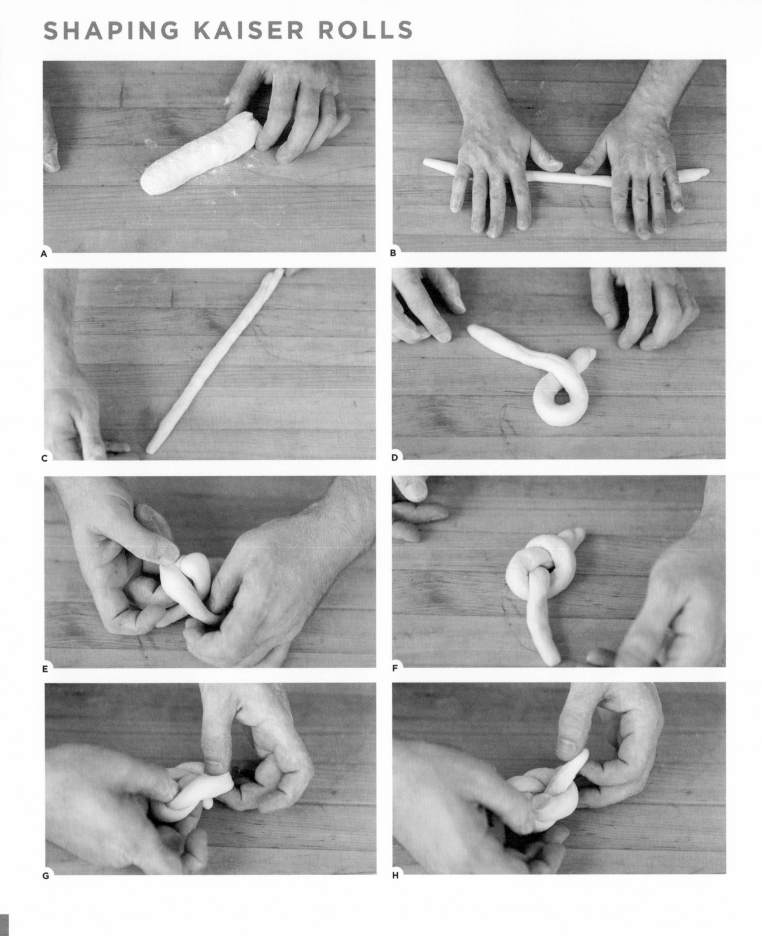

Roll out your preshaped tube (page 301) into a 10-inch strand (A-C). Let rest for 5 minutes. Roll one end over the other allowing for a 1-inch (2.5 cm) hole (D). Pull the long end under and through the hole (E–F). Pull the same end under and through the hole again (G–I). Pinch both ends together over the center of the roll (J–K). Flip over as shown (L–M).

SHAPING BAGELS

Press the dough on a floured surface and sprinkle the top with flour (A). Shape into a round about 1½ inches (4 cm) thick and 6 inches (15 cm) in diameter (B). It should be pretty uniform in thickness. Using a bench scraper, and starting from the outside, make a 1½-inch cut into the round (C).

Continue cutting along the round, uncoiling the dough as you go, until it is one long tube about 24 inches (61 cm) long (D–E). Roll the tube against the work surface to smooth it out (F–H).

Starting at one end of the tube, place the end of the dough against the center of your palm. Lay the dough across your palm, around the back of your hand and then back across your palm, slightly overlapping the end you started with (I–J). Pinch off the dough, giving it a tear with your other hand if needed (K).

Roll the overlapping ends against the work surface and your palm to smooth it out and even it out with the rest of the dough to form an even ring (L). You may need to give the ring a stretch to keep it open (M).

SHAPING SCONES

A

B

C

D

E

F

G

H

Empty the scone dough onto a floured surface. Bring together then flatten with a plastic scraper (A-B).

Cut the dough in half and place one half on top of the other (C-E).

Next, cut one-third of the dough and place it on the top of the remaining dough, in the middle, as shown (F-G).

Cut the remaining third and place it on top of the two layers (H-I).

Flatten (J) and repeat two more times.

Cut into six even pieces (K). Turn each piece on its side and flatten slightly to create an oval (L)."

SHAPING BISCUITS

Using the plastic bowl scraper, turn the dough out onto the work surface. Bring together then flatten with a plastic scraper (A-B).

Gently pat the dough out until about 1 inch (2.5 cm) thick (C).

Using the scraper and your hands, fold the dough into thirds (D-E). Repeat the folding until the dough is firm, but not tough.

Press the dough into a 4 by 12-inch (10 by 30 cm) rectangle about 1 inch (2.5 cm) thick. Using a bench scraper, cut the dough into eight equal squares (two rows of four) (F-G).

USING A TRANSFER PEEL AND BAKING PEEL

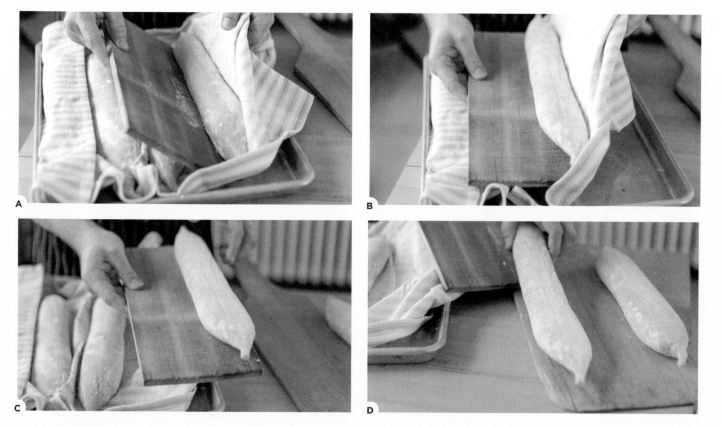

Holding the linen in one hand, lift and gently flip the loaves off of the pan and onto the transfer peel seam-side down (A-B).

Slide the dough, still seam-side down, onto the dusted baking peel (C-D).

RESOURCES

BAKING REQUIRES A LOT LESS IN THE WAY OF SPECIAL INGREDIENTS THAN GENERAL COOKERY. HOWEVER, IF YOU DO FIND THAT SOME INGREDIENTS ARE HARD TO TRACK DOWN, THE FOLLOWING SUPPLIERS HAVE THEM.

Amazon

amazon.com

Colatura di Alici di Cetara anchovy juice, chestnut puree and peeled whole chestnuts, Briess liquid rye malt extract, and Maldon sea salt flakes

Bob's Red Mill

bobsredmill.com

Specialty grains and flours (some organic), including medium-grind cornmeal, steel-cut oats, whole oat groats, rye berries, hulled millet, whole amaranth, farro, hazelnut flour or meal, and spelt flour

Central Milling

centralmilling.com

Organic flours, including white (Artisan Bakers Craft Flour), Whole Wheat Hi-Pro Medium, Medum Rye, 100% Whole Dark Rye, and Buckwheat

King Arthur Flour

kingarthurflour.com

Diastatic malt powder

L'Epicerie

lepicerie.com

Pearl sugar

THANK YOU

Our deepest gratitude to Amy Vogler, who tested every recipe in this book. Her care, close reading, and writing made her a true partner in this book, not to mention the countless hours discussing pretty much everything.

As Paul McCartney once said, "Without which, whom." Thank you, thank you to Judith Regan, Lucas Wittmann, Richard Ljoenes, Lynne Ciccaglione and Nick Fauchald for all that they have done, most of all for their warm support.

Kate Wheatcroft

David Black

Lisa Queen

Sarah Smith

Mario Batali

Mark Strausman of Fred's at Barneys

Peter Shelsky of Shelsky's Smoked Fish

Mark Kelly and Lodge Manufacturing

Stephen Hosey and Vitamix

Viera Karpiakova

Donna Lennard of Il Buco

Cesare Casella

LeeAnn Golper

Tom Golper

David Wheatcroft and Eve Granick

Alexandra Golper

Ed Levine of seriouseats.com

Caitlin Schnack

Marion Nestle

Harold McGee

Sam Fromarz

Dick and Barbara Moore

Patsy Taylor

Melinda Kaminsky

Justin Binnie

June Russel

Thor Oechsner

Robert Beauchemin

Sophie Beauchemin

Kevin Richardson

Kurt Andrews

Michael Szczerban

Steve Attardo

Jasmine Starr

And, of course, the entire staff at Bien Cuit

INDEX

Maldon, 119–21

malt, using, 148

maple syrup, 59–61, 115–117

Margherita Scones, 275–76

Mash and Must Rolls, 229–31

measuring, 20–21

    digital scales, 24

    metric measurements, 20, 24

Mediterranean Mariner Bread, 119–221

metric measurements, 20, 24

Meyer, Danny, 229

Mission Fig, Rosemary, Anise, and Pistachio Scones,
    267–68

mixing, 28, 282–83

mixing bowls, 24

M Resort, 9–10

Multigrain Bread, 169–71

N

nuts

    Chestnut Holiday Bread, 115–17

    Fougasse Basque, 187–89

    Hazelnut Bread, 111–13

    Mission Fig, Rosemary, Anise, and Pistachio Scones,
        267–68

    Pine Nut and Herb Rolls, 195–97

    Raisin Walnut Bread, 132–33

O

oatmeal rolls, scoring, 300

oats and oatmeal, 18

    oat groats, 169–71

    Toasted Oat Bread, 75–77

    Toasted Oatmeal Rolls, 183–85

Olive Bread, 134–35

olives, 134–35

onions, 69–73

oval loaves, shaping, 294

ovals, shaping, 297

oval tubes, shaping small, 302

oven gloves, 26

ovens

    Dutch ovens, 21, 26, 291

    getting to know, 21

P

Pancito Potosí, 199–201

Pane Dolce, 101–5

Pane Francese, 83–85

Pan Pugliese, 37–39

Parmigiano-Reggiano cheese

    Lard Bread, 87–95

    Margherita Scones, 275–76

parsley, 195–97

parsnips, 41–43

pears

    Sun-Dried Pear and Toasted Poppy Seed Mini
        Baguettes, 215–17

peels, using, 311–12

Perrier, Georges, 10–11, 59, 69, 72, 132

Pine Nut and Herb Rolls, 195–97

pistachios, 267–68

plastic bowl scrapers, 24

poppy seeds, 215–17

port, 203–5

Port and Fig Rolls, 203–5

Portuguese Corn Bread, 49–53

potatoes, 37–39

process, 278–311

proofing baskets, 26

proofing bowls, 26

prosciutto bread, 87–93

pumpkin seeds, 45–47

Q

quick breads, 248–59

Quintanilla, David, 257

R

raisins

    Raisin Walnut Bread, 132–33

    Raisin Water Rolls, 207–9